1969

University of St. Francis
GEN   921 E583m
Mayer
Friedrich Engels

3 0301 00038366 7

W9-DFF-716

This book may b‑

FRIEDRICH ENGELS

Translated from the German for the first time by
GILBERT AND HELEN HIGHET

The translation edited by
R. H. S. CROSSMAN

ᔓ

GUSTAV MAYER

FRIEDRICH ENGELS

A BIOGRAPHY

~

New York · HOWARD FERTIG · 1969

LIBRARY
College of St. Francis
JOLIET, ILL.

First published in English in 1936

Copyright 1936 by Alfred A. Knopf, Inc.
Renewal copyright © 1964 by Alfred A. Knopf, Inc.

HOWARD FERTIG, INC. EDITION 1969
Published by arrangement with Alfred A. Knopf, Inc.

All rights reserved.

Library of Congress Catalog Card Number: 68-9596

PRINTED IN THE UNITED STATES OF AMERICA
BY NOBLE OFFSET PRINTERS, INC.

921
E583m

FRIEDRICH ENGELS

CONTENTS

49787

ILLUSTRATIONS

FRIEDRICH ENGELS

CHAPTER 1

FAMILY AND EARLY LIFE

At first sight there is little in the origins and environment of Friedrich Engels to suggest his future career; and this applies to him more than to any other man who influenced and directed the German working-class movement. He did not belong to one of the depressed classes, as Marx and Lassalle did. His family can be traced in Wuppertal as early as the end of the sixteenth century. His ancestors seem to have been farmers in a small way. Agriculture brought them no great wealth; so, as the custom of the country was, they rented their fields as bleaching-grounds to yarn-workers. They were naturally enterprising, and the next step was to engage in the textile trade themselves. It was the great-grandfather of our Friedrich Engels who, in the second half of the eighteenth century, laid the foundations of the family's future prosperity. His good qualities were long remembered in Barmen, " the Manchester of Germany." When Gustav Kühne visited the town in 1846, he wrote a eulogy of him — not without an implied disparagement of his degenerate descendant. Kühne says that old Engels first conceived the idea of settling the homeless mob of factory-hands who wandered about the country without houses or property of their own, and of giving them homes and strips of ground in proportion to their diligence and good conduct. To this end he deducted a certain amount from their wages every week as part payment on the property.

His sons and grandsons maintained and increased, by steady and prudent industry, the prosperity which the old man had bequeathed them. We hear that in 1796 his son Johann Caspar built a school for the children of his workers, and that in the famine of 1816 he was at the head of the Corn Union, whose purpose it was to give cheap food to the destitute masses of Barmen.

After Johann Caspar's death the business descended to his three sons. They disagreed and resolved to choose by lot which of them was to continue the business. The lot fell against Friedrich Engels senior. He then left the firm (which gradually declined) and, with two brothers named Ermen, founded cotton-mills — at Manchester in 1837 and at Barmen and Engelskirchen in 1841. Despite great difficulties he contrived to furnish his German business with the superior English machines, which were not then used by his competitors.

On the 28th of November 1820, when Friedrich Engels senior was twenty-four, his wife (then twenty-three) gave birth to his eldest son. This was Friedrich Engels the communist. He inherited from his father not only a lively and capable mind, full of sharp critical sense, but also the gay and amiable temperament which always distinguished him. Elise Engels, his mother, was a woman of quick perceptions and strong imagination, and her sense of humour was so pronounced that even in old age she would sometimes laugh till the tears ran down her cheeks. She belonged to a scholarly family, who had little of this world's goods, but who realized the importance of spiritual wealth far more than the merchants of Barmen.

In Barmen at that time the emotional preaching of the Pietists was more highly esteemed than anywhere else in Germany; and Pietism had reached excesses at which Friedrich's healthy nature soon rebelled, with what was at first an unconscious aversion. He was far less attracted by the gloomy heresy-hunting of Barmen than by the gay folk-life of the working classes which he saw on his short excursions on the Rhine. In his parents' house there was a strongly religious atmosphere, inherited from elder generations; but with it was mingled a sound business-like common sense. The spirit of healthy industry, which was deeply rooted in the family character and encouraged by their religion, could leave no place for excessive emotionalism or introspection. The father was a man of strictly orthodox beliefs, and brought his children up to regard the Bible as verbally inspired. Still, his frequent journeys to England and elsewhere gave him a critical outlook and kept him free from illiberal prejudice.

We have scanty information about the childhood of Friedrich Engels. He was the eldest of a family of eight. Family records emphasize the fact that his kind and charitable nature showed itself early — he often gave all his little savings to the poor. Until he was fourteen he attended the primary school in Barmen. He then transferred to the high school of Elberfeld, which was reputed to be one of the best in the Kingdom of Prussia — although it was said that an inefficient schoolmaster who belonged to the Reformed religion was preferred to a sound Lutheran or Catholic teacher. Friedrich's parents wished to educate him to be subservient to convention, but a letter which his father wrote to his mother on August 27th, 1835 allows us to see how difficult they found it, although the boy was not yet fifteen. " Friedrich," says his father, " brought home middling reports for last week. As you know, his manners have improved; but in spite of severe punishment in the past, he does not seem to be learning implicit obedience even from the fear of chastisement. Today I was once more vexed by finding in his desk a dirty book from a lending library, a romance of the thirteenth century. May God guard the boy's heart, for I am often troubled over this son of ours, who is otherwise so full of promise."

The father was full of anxious forebodings for his son's future. He saw that the boy had considerable talent, but already he felt that his gifts were opposed to the unwritten laws of his orderly, conventional, pious family. The conflict was still shown in trifling matters — but how soon would it become more serious? Wide differences in outlook were arising to estrange father and son.

The boy unconsciously recoiled from those rigid conventions for whose existence he could see no justification. But at first he did not think of going outside the sphere of Christian ideals which surrounded him in Barmen, to seek satisfaction for his half-realized spiritual needs. In 1837, when he was confirmed, he still earnestly desired to find in the traditional faith of his family the "calm religious joy" for which he longed. Here is the text for his life which was given to him at confirmation: "*Forgetting those things which are behind, and reaching forth unto those things which are before, I press toward the mark for the prize of the high calling of God in Christ Jesus.*" These words were fulfilled, but not as the clergyman who chose them had imagined. In the world outside, Engels won for himself the spiritual satisfaction which he could not find in the faith of his home. He gradually *forgot those things which were behind* and *pressed toward a mark* which was new. As his strength and knowledge grew, he sought spiritual support more and more earnestly and at last found it in the movement which was endeavouring to construct a system of positive values such as would supersede revealed religion. But it was only through desperate endeavours that his spirit found its way from its old to its new home.

Besides authoritarian religion, there was another social force which determined the character of Engels's native town. His early thoughts were, it is true, chiefly occupied with the struggle against the Pietist intolerance of his home. But the glimpses which he got as a boy into the miseries of the working class had an infinitely greater effect upon his later intellectual development.

The district had been industrialized very early. Every day the boy went to school past factories where workers in

low-ceilinged rooms " breathed in more smoke and dust than
oxygen," where the children were imprisoned from the age
of six, to be " victims of capitalist exploitation "; past the
houses of artisans who worked at home, bent from morning
to night over their looms, their backs roasting before the
hot stove; past the "barrowpushers," the lowest dregs of
the proletariat, homeless wretches, blinded and ruined with
cheap alcohol, sleeping in empty stables and on dungheaps.
In 1876 Engels wrote: " I remember well how, when I was
just twenty, cheap spirits suddenly appeared in the industrial
quarters of Brandenburg and the Lower Rhine. In the Bergisch district especially, and above all in Elberfeld-Barmen,
the vast mass of the working population lapsed into drunkenness. From nine o'clock every evening, crowds of drunken
men, arm in arm, taking up the whole breadth of the street,
roaring discordantly, reeled from public-house to public-
house and at last home." Engels was always an acute observer, and he noted the effect of the new drink on the excitable proletariat. " The whole character of drunkenness
had changed. Drinking was once a jolly affair, which ended
in an amiable tipsiness and only now and then in excesses
in which clasp-knives were sometimes drawn. But now it
degenerated into a wild revel, which inevitably ended in a
row, always resulting in knife-wounds, and more and more
frequently in murder. The parsons put this down to the
increase in atheism, the lawyers and other philistines blamed
it on the pubs. The real cause was the sudden flooding of
the country with cheap spirits from Prussia."
    The boy could not feel himself a mere spectator of all this
misery. He himself was the son of a factory-owner. In early
youth he heard conversations which voiced the employer's
point of view. For many years before he became a communist or had even heard of communism he had expressed
the conviction that the factories were " idiotically " run by
the owners, that the rich manufacturers had very elastic con-
sciences, and that no Pietist would go to hell for the ruin of

one child more or less, "especially if the Pietist went to church twice on Sundays."

Thus, far more than Marx in quiet Trier and Lassalle in the economically undeveloped district of Breslau, Engels knew from childhood the real nature of the factory system; for its darker side, in those early days of capitalism, was plain to see. He grew up in a world which marked him out to show his countrymen the first complete picture of the revolutionary force of capitalism as it advanced towards its full development.

It is a tradition in Engels's family that he originally intended to study law and enter the Civil Service. Two different reasons are given to account for his change of mind. According to one, his father was opposed to Friedrich's attending the University, and commanded him to enter commerce, although he himself felt no inclination for it. According to the other, Friedrich himself gave up studying the law, because he had liberal opinions and did not wish to be a Prussian official. It seems to me that these versions combine truth and falsehood, and that the real facts are rather more complex. When Friedrich left school at Michaelmas 1837, a year before his final examination, the headmaster said in his leaving report that he "believed himself inclined to adopt as his external career" a business life, "in spite of his earlier plans for going to the University." In this formula the emphasis is on the words "believed himself inclined" and "external career." At seventeen Engels thought that his inner career, his real one, was literature. A young man of talent may feel that he has qualities which are yet to develop, an inward strength which has soon to reach its full expression. He will abandon the conduct of his life with a fatalistic resignation if he is forced to make some premature choice of an external career which he cannot harmonize with that inner calling whose commands he hears far more clearly. His inner powers are struggling for free development. In that struggle he cannot collect his thought to mould his distant future. That must have been the position of Friedrich Engels. Although the life of a writer, untrammelled by a definite preparation and discipline, attracted him strongly, it was made impossible by family tradition and the inevitable opposition of his father. His hot young spirit must have turned eagerly hither and thither before at last he resolved to enter business. But in those days a commercial career did not condemn an able man to the breathless, relentless industry of later times.

At first Engels appears to have had his business training in his father's firm. After a year there, it seemed desirable that he should continue it elsewhere. His father pondered long and deeply where he could send Friedrich in order to improve his knowledge of his vocation and — even more important — to discipline his rebellious character. His eventual choice seemed to make it certain that, both in his new home and in business, Friedrich would still be exposed to ideas closely akin to those of his family. In Bremen he was to breathe the same severe religious air as at home — a little mellowed, perhaps, by the sea-breezes: it filled both the home of Pastor Treviranus, where he was to live, and the export-business of the Consul Leupold, which he entered as an unsalaried clerk.

Numerous letters to his sister Marie and to old school-friends tell us of Friedrich's life in Bremen. They show the superb sense of humour which stayed with him throughout his life; but they also present a vivid and absorbing picture of the young man's internal struggles.

He was not overworked in the office. As soon as the manager left the room, beer-bottles and cigar-cases — even a book of poems or a half-finished letter — would be produced from the clerks' desks. And after lunch Friedrich generally managed to get an hour's smoke and a nap in the hammock which he had specially transported to the top floor of a warehouse. He spent many free hours on exercise. We see him fencing with great enthusiasm, and riding out

on Sundays far into the country round Bremen; we learn
that he once swam the Weser four times on one trip. Music
— the only art which really flourishes in a hard commercial
town — often held him in the evenings; he composed choral
pieces and was a member of the local choral society. He
also visited the Union Society, the meeting-place of all the
young business men; he could talk big there with other
youths like himself — enjoying it perhaps even more because the English and Scandinavian newspapers which lay
about could satisfy his thirst for knowledge and exercise his
exceptional gift for languages. Even then, in his letters to
his sister and friends, he inserted garbled phrases of Spanish, Portuguese, Italian, and Dutch, as well as French and
English; he boasted in jest of being able to converse in five-
and-twenty different tongues.

He was now eighteen years of age. As soon as he left
home he began to set in order the new opinions he was
forming, the impressions which crowded on him, all his new
poetic inspirations. He was a fluent writer, and he boldly
sent these early productions to newspapers and magazines.
They were so vivid and varied, so instinct with life and so
full of powerful thought, that though their author was quite
unknown they were not often refused. Even stronger than
his desire to be a great writer was his impulse to settle accounts with the religious spirit which had oppressed his
childhood. He paid off old scores against it in March and
April 1839, in the *Telegraf für Deutschland,* edited by the
distinguished Young German writer Karl Gutzkow, author
of *Uriel Acosta.* Engels used the pseudonym of Friedrich
Oswald and kept his disguise a secret from his family for
many years. *The Letters from the Wuppertal* made a great
sensation in Elberfeld and Barmen: the citizens racked their
brains to guess their author's name. No one thought of the
son of the manufacturer who was such a respectable member
of the church.

Engels had all the gaiety of the Rhineland. Despite his

BIRTHPLACE OF ENGELS IN BARMEN

love for the North German dialect, he found it hard to make friends with the " terribly formal " Hanseatic burghers. He felt their outlook to be no less " obscure " and " mystical " then that of his own native town. The most interesting of the new things he saw in Bremen was its seaport life — its shipping, its foreign trade, and its emigrant traffic. When he saw a ship of emigrants leaving Bremen harbour, he pondered deeply on the reasons which induced so many sturdy German country-folk to make the hard decision of leaving their fatherland for ever. His inborn social conscience stirred within him when he saw men, women, and children, sick and well alike, packed like herrings between decks.

Immediately he saw that the political conflicts existing in that mercantile aristocracy were really social conflicts. Bremen politics were much ado about nothing. They convinced him that such little states had no longer any justification for their existence. In later life, too, he could sympathize only with large countries.

As soon as he reached Bremen, he began to do what had been impossible at home — to read and reflect on the opinions of contemporary authors. He gave himself up freely to the new impressions he received from them. But his critical sense was soon awakened. He learned to find what would profit him even in works whose weaknesses and absurdities he saw clearly. He found his way from one author to another; he traced out the predecessors of a new writer who interested him: the smallest indication was enough for his sensitive taste. In this way he discovered the two men who were to be his masters for the next few years. From Gutzkow he learned of Gutzkow's master Börne;[1] and through Strauss he came under the influence of Hegel, which was to mean so much more to him. It was his study of Hegel that enabled him —

[1] Ludwig Börne (Löb Baruch), the first great modern German political journalist (1786–1837). In 1935 his monument in Frankfurt was removed and the street which bore his name was renamed.

after rejecting the security of his home religion — to set his
course towards a new and positive belief.

Engels's faith in the verbal inspiration of Scripture was,
like that of countless contemporaries, more and more deeply
shaken the longer he reflected on Strauss's *Life of Jesus.* In
his home he had known only the most rigidly orthodox aspect
of religion. For that very reason a flood of doubts must have
swept over his mind at the moment when he was brought to
realize that men, as well as God, had played their part in the
making of the Bible. Strauss convinced him that the obvious
contradictions in Scripture made the hypothesis of its verbal
inspiration by God utterly untenable. As soon as his clear
intellect mastered this thought, he was caught up in the whirl-
pool of German theological and philosophical dispute. He
saw in speculative theology a possible satisfaction of his need
for a firm foothold, and he saw that in theology only Strauss
and the left wing of the Hegelian school could lead him to
the certainty which he desired. He was intoxicated with their
immanent God.

CHAPTER II

ENTRY INTO POLITICS

ᔓ

In the eighteen-thirties there was one common thread which went through all that concerned the spiritual life of Germany and set it in increasing excitement: wherever opinions confronted one another, the war for or against authority raged fiercely. The conservatives who controlled the country had learned from the French Revolution that the revolt against authority — in society, in politics, and in the church — affected every holder of authority throughout the country. The Congress of Vienna had succeeded in re-establishing the old European order and in confirming the influence of the old authorities within each country. Soon after 1815 the forces of revolution again began to wrench at their iron chains, with a violence which astonished and terrified the rulers. The safety of conservatism must not be risked a second time; the ordinances of the congress, like a gigantic rock, blocked the pathway to destruction. To maintain the *status quo* in every sphere of life and conduct became the aim and object of Prussian and Austrian policy.

The first article of the conservative creed was the absolute interdependence of all existing forms of authority. And the most urgent clause in that article was the unshakable alliance of church and state. For the maintenance of order in the world, an almighty ruler in heaven was as indispensable as an absolute monarch on earth. Formulas were devised so that the two authorities might support each other — formulas which implied their complete interdependence. Thus the politicians and philosophers of the romantic movement were brought, by their reaction against the state run by the Enlightened rationalistic bureaucracy, to the ominous dogma of the Christian state.

But by now the repressed elements in the German Confederacy had realized the essential unity of authority in all spheres of human life. Rigid religious orthodoxy, absolute monarchy, and aristocracy — all were linked by common interests. There was a no less obvious community of purpose between all those who were striving to bridge the great gap between the rulers and the subject classes.

For ten years after the deaths of Goethe and Hegel the interest of Germany was most actively occupied by problems of philosophy and religion. From time to time among these questions isolated social problems emerged. But any avowed interest in politics was impossible: newspapers were not allowed to publish political articles, and political societies and meetings were forbidden. The reactionary attitude of governments towards the demands of liberalism turned the youth of Germany *en masse* to adopt radical beliefs. In literature and in theoretical discussions they forged the weapons with which they hoped to attack and overpower Authority in state and church. The creation of political parties was then, and for many years to come, an impossibility. But the belligerence of youth demanded some form of active organization and found it in the formation of literary and philosophical cliques. Hence arose the movements known as " Young Germany " in literature and Young Hegelianism in philosophy. Along with the liberalism of East Prussia which sprang from the school of Kant, and that of the Rhineland which expressed the claims of the most highly developed industrial region in the kingdom, these were the real spiritual forerunners of the middle-class revolution. Engels belonged in turn to both the former movements.

At first he admired the Young German movement in literature — he called it " the queen of modern letters." It presented him with contemporary ideals in their most modish form, and its piquant and worldly style made an astonishing contrast to the sugared piety to which he had been accustomed at home. He dreamed of preaching through poetry the new ideas which were revolutionizing his inner world; but later he was conquered by the impulse to action. He joined the ranks of the others, of those who dedicated themselves to bringing about " the day of the great decision." Engels admired the Young Germany movement for asserting the claims of a young generation against the political and social complacency of the generation before 1830. But although he ranked himself proudly among the Young German writers, he was compelled to admit that the real needs of his spirit must be satisfied elsewhere. With his craving for companionship, both in society and in the life of the intellect, he had often, since turning his interest to public life, desired a true comrade-in-arms, one to guide him through the strange labyrinth of contemporary life. In the inner circles of Young Germany he found no one who could fulfil these conditions. His disillusionment grew with his increasing interest in politics. When he read the works of Börne (who had recently died) he fully realized the spinelessness of the clique.

The younger generation, in its demand for real action and strong conviction, had been estranged from Heine by that individual outlook which raised him above party. Börne was the man after their hearts. Where else in Germany could be found another such independent soul, given up so single-mindedly to politics, attached so blindly to his opinions, and able to dedicate all his literary gifts with such unselfish abandon to support new ideas against the ruling class? Engels found him the best possible interpreter of the political ideas of Western radicalism. In letters and essays from 1839 to 1842 Engels never tires of eulogizing Börne as a " heroic fighter for Freedom and Justice," the man who had strengthened and upheld the nation during the dark thirties. He ranked Börne beside Lessing as a writer, and Börne meant as much to him in politics as Hegel did in philosophy. As he moved towards Hegelianism, he felt the task of the age to be " the synthesis of Hegel and Börne," the mediation between knowledge and life, between philosophy and modern tendencies.

Engels now saw the history of the previous decades in the light of his republican convictions: he looked on it no more impartially than did Börne; and, with Börne's revolutionary opinions in his heart, he despised the great ones of the earth. His sister Marie wrote from a high-class boarding-school, with schoolgirl pride, to tell her brother that she had been presented to the Grand Duchess of Baden. This was not well received. Friedrich crushed her by answering: " When you are presented to another of these notabilities, write and tell me whether she is pretty or not. I have no other interest in such persons."

We can get a glimpse into the mind of the twenty-year-old boy if we read his poetic cycle *An Evening*. He published it in the *Telegraf* in August 1840, under the characteristic motto "Tomorrow comes " — taken from Shelley, whom he was attempting to translate. Of all Engels's surviving verse, this work bears the strongest stamp of poetry. We find the young man at sunset in the Pfarrgarten on the Weser. Calderón's tragedies lie open before him. The evening light awakens in him the longing for that dawn of which he dreams, the dawn of freedom which will change the whole world into a radiant garden. In this fantasy the future apostle of the class-war shows us love as the link between all men — all men are members of one spiritual family; and he can still praise the peace which will one day encompass all mankind. But already he feels it necessary that, whenever " the oriflamme of Freedom waves," ships should carry grain " which grows to human happiness," and " no longer goods to profit one alone." Of course, this thought is still in the background, behind the dreams of peace and freedom and purer faith in God; yet it is an indication that Engels had already grasped the imperfections of the existing economic order. The ideals of Saint-Simonism [1] introduced to him by Young Germany had already struck root in his heart. The essay on Ernst Moritz Arndt, nationalist patriot, poet, and author, which he published in February's *Telegraf* rejects the idea of ownership implicit in the entail system, with the remark that it " no longer fits in with modern ideas." In the meantime few important consequences could be expected from the thoughts which came to the young poet as he searched the clouds " before sunrise " for the coming life. When he hopes for the " collapse " of the old régime, he is still thinking of the servitude of the intellect. He is fighting Börne's battle as a free-thinker against the parsons, as a democrat against nobles and princes, as a republican against the monarchy. He does not yet suspect that these great conflicts will one day appear to him as subsidiary elements in a still greater combat.

[1] The Saint-Simonists were the disciples of Count Henri de Saint-Simon (1760–1825), whose conception of history had a strong influence on Engels, who considered Saint-Simon a " utopian socialist." The Saint-Simonist school represented a much more pronounced socialism than Saint-Simon himself.

CHAPTER III

MILITARY SERVICE.
THE YOUNG HEGELIANS

$\backsim$

The government of Friedrich Wilhelm III had appointed many Hegelians to professional chairs, because the school of Hegel attributed more importance to the state than any other philosophers had done for two thousand years. Hegel himself had contrived to disguise the pitfalls in his speculations beneath the symbols of Christianity. His school, therefore, cared little if orthodox religion found theological improprieties in Hegel's conception of God. The Prussian bureaucracy held no very rigorous views on this matter, as long as the positions of authority in it were filled by men trained in the spirit of Kantianism and the Enlightenment. But more attention was paid to the warnings of reactionary writers after Strauss's *Life of Jesus* had shown that the left-wing Hegelians no longer believed in the absolute inspiration of the Bible. Since the year 1838 Arnold Ruge[1] had made the *Hallische Jahrbücher* a rallying-point for all who in theory or practice were striving to free the spirit of man from the immoderate domination of supernatural powers.

The significance of Young Hegelianism was political rather than philosophical. The young generation used its ideas as weapons in the fight against dualism in church and state. Hegel's doctrine that even thought-structures are subject to the law of development was soon (as Engels saw)

[1] Arnold Ruge (1802–80), Young Hegelian, bourgeois democrat, and forerunner of the League of Nations idea, was intensely opposed to communism. He lived in exile in England, quarrelled with Marx and Engels, and later returned to Germany and made his peace with Bismarck.

put to the test on his own philosophy. He had been led astray by the timid age of reaction into attributing an absolute character to transitory historical phenomena. But the younger generation had gained impetus from the Paris revolution of July: they were once more inspired with the belief that the individual's right to self-determination in religion and politics could be made a political reality. Although Hegel himself had not felt the power of this idea, his pupils attempted none the less to separate the timeless content of his teaching from the useless and impermanent residue. Accordingly, they freed the dialectic from the restraint which Hegel had placed on its advance, and they sharply distinguished religion and the state as historical phenomena from religion and the state as absolute categories. Thus, as soon as they had gone beyond the absolute character which the master had given to religion and the state and had once more set them up as objects of dialectic, they found that they could be regarded as products of the historical process. And so reason — which thus had mastered the state and Christianity — became in the eyes of these young philosophers once more the mistress of the world.

When the opponents of Hegelianism came into power in Prussia at the accession of Friedrich Wilhelm IV, Engels recognized that the ultimate victory must lie with "Hegel renewed." After living in Bremen for two years, he left it in the spring of 1841. He had often regretted the fact that while he was living there his opinions "were bound to remain so raw and undeveloped." His spirit craved to be allowed to mature without disturbance. He determined, therefore, to serve his year in the army, and to do it in a university town. Berlin seemed to him the most suitable place, for it was then the battleground of the spiritual conflicts in which he felt himself to be involved. The Hegelian radicals welcomed "Friedrich Oswald" with open arms. This group of young writers chose to call themselves "the Free," and under that name they acquired a certain distinction. (Bruno Bauer, a revolutionist in the field of ecclesiastical history, and Max Stirner, who achieved fame through his anarchist work *The Ego and His Own,* were the best-known of their bohemian circle.) They were not, any more than Young Germany, a closely organized association. Most of them were not distinguished by solid opinions or personal courage. They were real products of pre-revolutionary apathy. They never harmonized thought and action. Worshipping reason as they did, they felt themselves exempted from attacking their unreasoning opponents — however fiercely they might threaten them among trusted friends in their favourite taverns, when no government spy was about.

Although the opposition had known that the new King sympathized with orthodoxy and romanticism, they had expected him — gifted as he was — to institute an era of great reforms. Scarcely anyone had ventured to imagine that he could find courage or will to oppose the spirit of the age. Yet he did oppose it — by appointing to posts in the University of Berlin Savigny, the great jurist of the romantic movement, Stahl, the apostle of the Christian state, and finally Schelling, Hegel's most distinguished opponent. Until then the Hegelians had eulogized Prussia as the state in whose hands lay the keys of the future. Now, when Prussia renounced her calling, how could the Hegelians maintain the thesis that she was to be the realization of Hegel's ideal state?

The radical wing now raised the fiery cross. And since it was safest and easiest to express revolutionary sentiments in theoretical language, the first attacks were delivered in philosophy. Holding as the Hegelians did to the irresistibility of dialectic, they soon found that Bauer's criticisms of the Gospels released them from the necessity of accepting Christianity. Belief in God and belief in immortality became equally unnecessary. As above, so below. Along with the other forces of authority, absolute monarchy, constitutional monarchy, and finally (through the work of Stirner and Bauer) the state itself were all shown to be empty ideas. All that was left was the belief in Humanity; and it was this fact that Feuerbach preached. The young radicals were desperately anxious to make their theories compatible with reality as they saw it. Their theological conclusions had closed the gates of heaven to them. Feuerbach's philosophy gave them a new incentive to construct a humanist ethic and to busy themselves only with the things of this world. The problem of action was urgent upon them in their everyday life. It now became the *leitmotif* of their philosophical speculations, and, as such, opened their minds to socialist and communist ideas.

This violent spiritual revolution among the Young Hegelians was completed in the year when Engels approached its storm-centre. He was moved by the violence of the revolt, and played his part in furthering it. Just after he had entered the Household Artillery as a volunteer in the autumn of 1841, the first clash of opposing forces took place. The King had appointed Schelling with the express mission of breaking the influence of the Young Hegelians. Engels attended his inaugural lecture and was filled with passionate indignation to think that the philosopher of romanticism should condemn the new developments in philosophy as useless and misconceived.

But surely it was an enterprise of almost insane audacity for a young clerk to challenge a man like Schelling! Engels's inexhaustible appetite for work and his unusually versatile mind had enabled him to read widely and deeply and to profit from what he read. His powers of physical endurance and his excellent nerves allowed him to use every unoccupied hour for serious study. He had drunk deep of Hegel's philosophy; he had followed with earnest attention all the disputes of the master's disciples among themselves and with their opponents. But was the knowledge which he had thus acquired sufficient to back the challenge he now made? He knew little of philosophers before Hegel; and if we recollect that by this time, after hard struggles, Marx had mastered the Greeks and Spinoza and Leibniz, we shall realize that Engels's philosophical equipment was light indeed. Yet he did not incline to conceit and self-complacency: he drew his confidence from the maxim that "the sword of inspiration is as sharp as the sword of genius." And if he had something of David's audacity in facing his Goliath, he had a giantlike faith in the victory of his good cause.

In 1842 Engels issued two anonymous pamphlets against Schelling, with only a short interval between them. In the first he spoke from the depths of his personal conviction. In the second he put on the disguise of a Pietist — he wished Schelling to be compromised in the eyes of the philosophical world because a *soi-disant* Pietist exalted him to heaven. However, the first pamphlet is far more important. Its name was *Schelling and Revelation,* and for many years it was thought to be the work of Bakunin.

With the publication of these pamphlets Engels broke the last ties which held him to the faith of his childhood and his parents. There was still a long way for him to journey before reaching his final view of the world and of history. Yet here for the first time we can see the fundamentals of that view. Engels accuses Schelling of comprehending the whole history of the world merely as a series of external and fortuitous events, in which only God's hand averts evil. Schelling, he says, does not see God as Hegel saw him, in the development of the human species.

By this time Engels knew himself to be an atheist. But he imparted some of his old religious fervour to his cult of history. "The Idea" was for him still so weighted with the emotions which arise from religious experience that when Feuerbach guided him from the worship of God to the worship of human society he found the transition a happy rather than a painful experience. The Idea appeared to him in a supernatural light. Accordingly, when his heaven went up in flames, he was not conscious of a loss; he was rather thankful that out of the ashes of his old faith the new faith in humanity

THE PARENTS OF FRIEDRICH ENGELS

arose. He had as yet no suspicion that, if he followed Feuerbach further, he must find the perfection of the Idea in the everyday world of human relations.

Engels was now one of the boldest radicals among " the Free." Not long before he came to Berlin, they had lost the allegiance of a young scholar who had shown himself superior in character and intellect to all his contemporaries. Karl Marx was now in Bonn, working for the revolutionization of man's religious consciousness. A few months later he became the editor of the *Rheinische Zeitung,* the first great opposition newspaper which was allowed to appear in Prussia.

During the first months of his stay in Berlin Engels had been kept busy by his struggle against Schelling and his fight for Bruno Bauer, who had been deprived by the government of his tutorial post in Bonn. Now he began to contribute to the *Rheinische Zeitung,* where he was enabled to put forward certain claims which were common to the liberals and to the radical opposition which was then in process of formation. But the power and the glory of the *Rheinische Zeitung* soon passed: the editorial board and their radical Berlin correspondents uttered some sentiments which were too strong for the King's susceptibilities. Both the organs of German radicalism — the *Rheinische Zeitung* and the *Hallische Jahrbücher* — were sentenced to death in 1843.

Until now Engels had not shared the faith in the liberal mission of Prussia which the other Young Hegelians had embraced. He was a Rhinelander, true German in feeling — but as the son of an older land and an older civilization, he kept himself aloof from the real Prussia and from the Prussians. But he could condemn it and its new King savagely, when he was allowed to speak without fear of the censorship. This is shown by the essay on Friedrich Wilhelm IV which he sent in the autumn of 1842 to the radical German poet Georg Herwegh, who was attempting to found a revolutionary paper in Switzerland. In this essay Engels attacks with special force the new King's " fostering of 'true' historical traditions," and the "sophistry" of the romantic theory of the state. For this theory, with its notion of the "organic state," was simply a justification of hereditary aristocracy. Engels answers with an emphatic negative the question whether Friedrich Wilhelm IV would succeed in establishing his system. Of the two questions on which public opinion in Prussia was concentrating more and more intensely, Engels says this: the people will force the King, however he may try to evade it, to give them a free press — and as soon as it has a free press, a parliament will be created within a year. The position of Prussia, he says, is like that of France before 1789.

The man who wrote these words had lost the belief that Germany would ever become a free people by a process of peaceful transformation.

CHAPTER IV

TOWARDS COMMUNISM

Engels saw before him a clear path from the attack on the principle of authority to the revolutionization of the real world. He saw this path and recognized that it had been opened by Feuerbach's analysis of the speculative idea. But some time was still to pass before he saw communism to be the nucleus of the new realistic outlook. We have only a few statements by Engels himself to show the stages by which this process came to completion in him.

The young revolutionaries in German philosophy were called by Feuerbach to the renunciation not only of Christianity but of all religion. And the abolition of God and immortality led Feuerbach to still more important conclusions. He came to place force of will and richness of heart on a level with strength of thought. He no longer saw man simply as a thinking being; action always was for Engels the culmination of life, and it was action which now had a glorious resurrection in the philosophy of Feuerbach.

A short time before Feuerbach's *The Nature of Christianity*, a remarkable book called *The European Triarchy* had appeared. Its aim was to drive an even straighter path into the heart of the problem of Action. Feuerbach had ignored social questions; but in this book Moses Hess attempted to turn the attention of Germany from philosophy to the actual problems of society.

Hess was considerably older than Engels or Marx, but like them both he was a Rhinelander. He was of Jewish descent like Marx, and he was the son of a manufacturer like Engels.

49787   LIBRARY
College of St. Francis
JOLIET, ILL.

He was to throw open the world of socialism to them both; yet he approached it from a different side, and he did not long travel in their company. It has often been said that Marx both embodied and intensified the dialectical powers of the Jewish spirit. It could be said even more justly that all the emotional forces of the Jewish spirit, which for ever seek fulfilment and completion, vainly strove in Hess to attain some final form. He was an ecstatic visionary, far less stable than Marx and Engels and almost always groping among illusions. But throughout his spiritual wanderings he retained the old messianic faith in the future perfection of the human race. This was the dream which he nourished with his heart's blood — for which he sought fulfilment first in Christianity, then in communism, and at last in Zionism. He drew strength for it from the traditions of the ancient stock whose blood still flowed in the veins of the " communist rabbi."

Although Hess had a keen speculative mind, he was unable to write a logical exposition of his most vivid dreams — to bring his soul's aspirations into the clearer light of reason. But he could do something else. He could establish connexions which, in view of the needs of his age, were full of value and interest. On his travels as a young man in France and England, he had seen how in these countries the tide of economic prosperity was steadily rising while their political development continued unhampered. He grew convinced that the time had come for German philosophy to give up worshipping reason on a lonely pedestal. In his attempt to create a philosophy of action he found that he must marry the spirit of Spinoza to that of Saint-Simon. Thus, at the very moment when Feuerbach confronted the Young Hegelians with the problem of the Human Species, Hess introduced their radical wing to French sociology. Engels has left us (the date is November 1843) the express acknowledgment that Hess was the first to make communism credible and acceptable to him and his circle, as being the necessary development of Young Hegelian thought.

Revolutionary as was Feuerbach's effect in the field of German philosophy, this recluse was altogether incapable of grasping either the necessity for or the nature of the problem of action. Where he fell back, Hess rushed into the breach. He blamed the Hegelian philosophy of history for refusing the task of deducing the future from the past and the present and of proceeding to influence its formation. This is a typical Saint-Simonian idea, and later it was to become a corner-stone in the system of Marx and Engels. It is possible that it now presented itself clearly to Engels for the first time. Hess set up Saint-Simon by the side of Hegel, and he used the differences between his heroes to explain the differences between contemporary developments in France and Germany.

But now Hess saw that a third nation was to join Germany and France in bearing the burden of man's future on this earth. Prophesying the approach of the revolution in England, he assigned to it the task of synthetizing the German Reformation and the French Revolution, of establishing complete freedom in the world, of creating political and social liberty everywhere. Its mission was to abolish the opposition of pauperism and plutocracy and to bring to completion the great historical changes which were even then beginning to affect the relations of the governing classes and the governed.

Hess was therefore the first radical philosopher in Germany to see that the universal struggle against authority was a phenomenon common to all the great civilized nations. The Chartist movement was in full flood in England, and there political and social revolution was certain to come. But *The European Triarchy* did not look forward with the same certainty to any such violent manifestations of the class-struggle in Germany. When Engels read the book, he was deeply exercised to find out how Feuerbach's notion of complete human self-consciousness could be made a reality. At last, in a blaze of revelation, he saw that Feuerbach had indeed begun to liberate German philosophy from the one-sided intellectualism of the Young Hegelians, but that Hess had shown communism to be the next step in that liberation.

During his childhood in Wuppertal, Engels had seen the meaning of class-conflicts. In the bourgeois state of Bremen he had seen how they influence systems of government. These discoveries, however, remained mere isolated observations until they were brought into connexion with his struggle to form a philosophy of life. Then, and only then, they ceased to be purely theoretical and became springs of decisive action. Far earlier and far more clearly than Young Germany, the acute intellect of Heine had probed the social crisis; he had understood its far-reaching importance, and he had set down its meaning in lucid phrases. In the year 1821 Heine's *Ratcliff* had contained the idea of " two peoples," " the rich and the starvelings," fighting to the death within " one and the same nation." He recurred to this idea after the revolution of July had attracted him to Paris. There he watched — with fascinated, almost terrified eyes — the strange new phantoms conjured up by the revolution. He put much of what he saw into the account of the July government in France which he sent to the *Allgemeine Zeitung*. Engels was a keen reader, and Heine was already famous; it is probable that Engels saw the articles in which Heine described communism as the dark hero waiting in the wings for the cue which was to call him to play a brief but great part on the world's stage.

These new socialist ideas made a powerful impression on Engels. No less powerful was the impression created by the pictures of poverty which he found in the novels of Eugène Sue, George Sand, Dickens, and Disraeli. They blended at once with the indelible memories of his childhood in the industrial towns. It is clear in his *Letters from Wuppertal* that the scenes he saw daily on his way to school had awakened his social conscience once for all. We must remember the cries of pity which escaped the young man, the bitterness with which he pilloried the exploitation of children and the slavery of men and women. It is easy then to see how these memories kindled him with the fire of revolution as soon as he heard (in the summer of 1842) that the exploited workers of Lancashire had called a general strike. It seemed as if Hess's prophecy for England was being fulfilled to the letter. Engels must have seen as a gift of fortune the fact that his father was partner in a Manchester factory. He decided to visit the storm-centre as soon as he was released from military service.

In an essay written next year in England for the *New Moral World,* Engels asserted that Hess's articles in the *Rheinische Zeitung,* pointing the way to communism, had failed of their effect. But was this judgment justified? Surely nothing more could be expected of the articles than that they should awaken a few choice spirits to the thoughts which were so new and strange to Germany. Surely it was success enough for Hess to convince men like Marx and Engels of the importance of communism. At that time socialism was understood in Germany to mean the struggle for a peaceful reformation of society, communism to mean the effort to overthrow society — an effort led by secret proletarian associations. But the only distinction which Engels made in analysing the German situation was between philosophical communism, led by members of the educated classes, and communism, which was a working-class movement. He thought Hess the first apostle of German philosophical communism. And now he suddenly discovered a movement and a leader whose existence he had never suspected. While he was still in Berlin he met Weitling and recognized him as the founder of a genuinely spontaneous working-class communism; he tried to convince himself that the new gospel was the logical development of Hegelian doctrine.

At the beginning of October 1842 Engels left Berlin. On the way to Barmen he stopped at Cologne to visit the offices of the *Rheinische Zeitung.* There for the first time he met

Hess. " We talked of questions of the day. Engels, who was
a revolutionary to the core when he met me, left as a passionate communist " — in these words the " communist
rabbi " described their meeting to Berthold Auerbach a few
months later.

Engels left home towards the end of November 1842. His
father hoped that he would complete his commercial training at the mills of Ermen and Engels in Manchester. He
himself looked forward to studying the working-class movement at its centre — for he was coming to believe that the
movement was the most important thing in the history of
his time — and also to take part in the social revolution
which he saw hanging over Britain. On his way he revisited
the offices of the *Rheinische Zeitung* in Cologne: he thought
of sending them articles from England. However, a few days
before, the paper had entered on a savage dispute with " the
Free," who were their chief correspondents in Berlin. The
editor was suspicious. He considered that Engels belonged
to Bauer's clique, and imagined that he was sent as their en-
voy to him. Thus the first meeting between Marx and Engels
was cool, even unfriendly.

CHAPTER V

POLITICAL AND SOCIAL STUDIES IN ENGLAND

ᡧᢧ

By moving to England, Engels freed himself from the atmosphere of purely theoretical disputation which had surrounded him in Berlin without satisfying his impulse towards action. He was impressed by the reality and earnestness of the political and social struggles by which industrialized England was torn asunder. He was filled with envious amazement when he saw how every Englishman read a daily newspaper, went to meetings, paid a subscription to some organization — while Germany was sunk " in a state of primeval apathy." He must have counted it great good fortune to be enabled to plunge into this world of free and active politics.

At his arrival he was still influenced by Hess's conception of the three revolutions on which the progress of humanity depended. England, he believed, was to give humanity the social revolution — the social revolution which would take up and transcend the German philosophical and the French political revolutions and unite them in a higher unity. He hoped that political developments in England would fulfil his ideal of human progress. With these convictions, he could not look on events with an unprejudiced eye. He had, in a sense, the conclusion ready-made before he inspected the facts. From the moment he left the ship, he had eyes for nothing but the signs of approaching revolution. He had abandoned his exaggerated ideas of the value of abstract reason, but he still retained " a good deal of philosophic arrogance." This " arrogance" was enough to keep him

away from the narrow ideals of equalitarian communism
which distinguished the leaders of the German working-
class revolutionaries in London. Moll, Bauer, and Schapper
were " the first revolutionary proletarians " whom he had
met; they were " three real men," and he himself " had now
the will to become a man." They made an ineffaceable impression on him; and yet he felt that he should not for the
time being enrol in the League of the Just.

The naïve belief which these men had in natural rights
struck him as peculiar; but, fresh from the teaching of Hegel,
he was even more surprised by " the insistent empiricism "
which he noticed in all the talk of his English acquaintances.
He was ready and willing to admire the breadth of British
social and political life; he was therefore all the more depressed by the discovery that the British lacked the most
elementary philosophical training. When he saw how they
clung to tangible realities and ignored the principles which
conditioned them, he began to feel that they could not see
the wood for the trees. He was astonished by this " crude
empiricism." And he was not less astonished by the old-
fashioned devoutness of the British bourgeoisie. He found
it incredible that educated Englishmen should still believe
in miracles, and that even scientists should pervert the facts
of science to avoid direct insult to the Mosaic myth of
creation.

The effect of these discoveries made in his first weeks in
England was that he came to reflect constantly on the relation between material, political, social, and spiritual forces,
the chief problem of what was later to be his philosophy of
history. He did not, of course, attempt to force all historical
events and possibilities into one pattern. But he was eager
to discover the relations between these forces in the land
where his chief hopes of revolution lay. As long as the dialectical necessity of their connexion was not absolutely clear
to him, he remained true to his old philosophical outlook,
and felt uneasy to observe how ideal factors were subordi-

nated to material and how principles paid homage to facts. Yet the world around him was a glaring example of this simple truth. In Manchester he was daily compelled to see that economic conditions wield the decisive influence in the modern world, that it is out of them that class-oppositions arise, and that in countries where great industries have developed (especially in England) these class-oppositions dictate the composition of political parties, the nature of the conflicts between them, and therefore the whole of political history. Engels recognized these facts slowly and reluctantly. He had to acknowledge that in England progress depended not on the clash of principles but on the clash of interests; but he was still far from making this individual case into a philosophy of history. He went no further than the inference that economic interests were leading to the revolution and that principles must develop out of these interests at a later stage.

Engels enjoyed a lively argument. He was impressed by the long tradition of skilful discussion which prevailed among the English middle classes. But he was angered by the cool incredulity with which the prosaic English met his conviction that revolution was inevitable. He adduced every sort of argument against the universal conviction that the English political system was elastic enough to assimilate without vital derangement the change which was being thrust upon it.

Although he wished to see English political and social conditions in their darkest colours, he should not have seconded the complaints of Cobden and Bright, famous advocates of the English free-trade movement and the Anti-Corn-Law League. He came from Prussia, and yet he wrote in the *Rheinische Zeitung* that English freedom was despotism and that feudalism was more powerful there than on the Continent. Engels was always inclined to look at things in a broad, simple way. He did not respect the complexity and apparent disorder of a system with a long history of development behind it. Accordingly he saw in English law only a slough of confused and contradictory enactments. He saw the House of Commons as a body which was elected by corruption, estranged from the people, and powerless to influence the government in matters of principle. When he came to study English political history, he viewed much of it in a more favourable light. Then at last he could recognize what was a fact — that Britain had long possessed far greater freedom of the press and of political meetings than any other nation in Europe and — within certain limits — a liberal right of combination. But it is easy to see how reluctant he was to admit this. In spring 1844, a short time before he returned to the Continent, he wrote an account of the " Condition of England." It culminated in the assertion that contemporary England was enslaved by class-prejudice and that its legislative, administrative, and judicial system was permeated by the spirit of the ruling classes.

It had long been an open secret in England that the opposition of Whigs and Tories concealed a conflict between real property and finance capital. This was the first time that Engels had been able to examine a well-developed party system. He did so with prejudices imposed on him by the purely philosophical and theological party-struggles of Germany. But he came to discover the enormous influence of social and economic conditions on English politics. He learned from his study of English history to understand his own age. The Reform Bill of 1832 had transferred parliamentary power in the electorates of the large towns and most of the industrial districts to the Liberals. But in the country and in most of the small towns the power of the aristocracy remained unbroken. At first Engels thought the Tories were the same as Prussian nobles. But his natural hatred for Liberal industrialists led him to think of the Tories as the lesser evil. At the same time he paid homage to the small group of Tory philanthropists, followers of Antony Ashley Cooper, seventh Earl of Shaftesbury, and Disraeli, because they were defending the working classes from the exploitation of their employers. Although he considered these "romantics" to be aiming at the moon, he praised the courage with which they opposed the prejudices of their class. He agreed with the Whigs on certain important issues, but he shrank from them as being essentially the typical party of the employers. And he soon realized that the factory-workers who lent their huge numbers to the support of Liberalism should create a separate party for themselves as soon as possible.

Engels now settled in Manchester, the birthplace of the Anti-Corn-Law League and the centre of the free-trade agitation. There he found his attention drawn at once to the new problems; he became anxious to disclose "the contradiction latent in the idea of an industrial state." But he foresaw a gloomy future for England's industrial hegemony. French, Belgian, and especially German factories were already entering into competition with those of England in mass production and would ruin them as soon as she abandoned the tariff barrier which was destroying her finances. Her European markets were lost already. She still had markets in America and the colonies, but even America was no longer dependable and the colonies could not import enough to save England. German competition for the world's markets became stronger every day; for production was cheap in Germany, while in England the tariff wall had raised both prices and wages to a disproportionate height. The " enormous " agitations against the Corn Laws made a deep impression upon Engels, but his interest in the free-trade movement was limited by his expectations of revolution. He judged it necessary that corn should be free from import duties, but he saw it to be equally necessary that the Conservative government should be done away with, "peacefully or forcibly." He prophesied correctly that Peel would be obliged to commence the abolition of the duties on corn. But both from Peel and from the Liberals he expected no more than " *juste-milieu* legislation." Only the Chartists and the small Radical group made a resolute stand for complete abolition of the duties — he has left us a vivid picture of their fury against the food-profiteers. Actually Engels was convinced that this conflict would lead to the revolution which he awaited so impatiently. He considered it out of the question that the aristocracy would once more surrender of their own free will, as they had done at the passing of the Reform Bill. This time, he hoped, they would stand fast " until the knife was at their throat."

Engels saw the dominance of the aristocracy attacked not only by industrial agitation but by the tenant farmers. The Anti-Corn-Law propagandists had attempted to convince the farmers that their interests were opposed to those of their landlords. Engels decided that the political emancipation of the tenant farmers meant the disappearance of the Conservative majority in the House of Commons. He was grateful to the Anti-Corn-Law Leaguers for doing their part to abolish the Tory domination in country districts. But he lost all sympathy for the League when it came into conflict with the National Charter Association, as it did in Lancashire in 1843. At once he came to think of it merely as an association of rich textile magnates, aiming at creating good trade conditions for themselves by abolishing the protective duties on corn. When he turned his eyes to the country districts, he saw opposed, not great landlords and tenant farmers, but farmers and " the wretched class " of day-labourers.

Engels now saw the future of Liberalism in darker colours than a few months before. On May 23rd, 1843, in the *Schweizer Republikaner,* he wrote : " The reign of the *juste milieu* is over, and the power of the landowners has reached its zenith." The industrial proletariat was especially embittered by the Liberal refusal to support Sir James Graham's bill to limit the working hours of children in factories. Engels constantly attended the meetings in Lancashire in which the Chartists opposed the Whigs over this question. He was shocked to see that the police supported any Liberal manufacturer who got into difficulties with his audience.

At this time O'Connell was agitating in Ireland and had been rousing the Irish poor to frenzy ever since the famine of 1842. At first it seems surprising that Engels did not support him as strongly as did Bismarck — who greatly admired O'Connell. But Engels was repelled by the fact that the revolutionary energies of the " subtle demagogue " were directed only to the " wretched and petty " aims which inspired all the effort for Repeal — not to the abolition of human misery. Like the *Northern Star,* he considered O'Connell's nationalism as mere bungling compared with the real aims sought by the destitute wretches who flocked to the banner of Chartism. He thought that O'Connell was allied to the moneybags of Liberalism in order to overthrow Sir Robert Peel. O'Connell was not, then, a democrat by conviction. And Engels could never forgive him for warning his Irishmen of " the dangers of socialism." But his admiration for the revolutionary spirit of O'Connell's followers was unbounded. " What people ! " he cried. " They haven't a penny to lose, more than half of them have not a shirt to their backs, they are real proletarians and sans-culottes — and Irish besides — wild, ungovernable, fanatical Gaels. Nobody knows what the Irish are like unless he has seen them. If I had two hundred thousand Irish, I could overthrow the whole British monarchy." For many years Engels was intimate with an Irish working girl called Mary Burns. It was she who introduced him to proletarian circles in Manchester; and his relations with her added a special warmth to his sympathy for the Irish victims of " five hundred years of oppression " and made him permanently interested in their salvation.

The climax of the Chartist movement came in the famine year of 1842, when the north of England was paralysed by a general strike, centring on Manchester. When Engels reached that city in December 1842, the workers were still stirred by the events of the strike. His judgment on the affair tells us something of the attitude which he brought to the study of Chartism. In the *Rheinische Zeitung* he wrote that one-third, perhaps one-half, of the English people belonged to the destitute classes — the classes created by industry — which never acquired any property, but were constantly increasing in numbers. When a violent commercial crisis made them foodless as well as destitute, they had no remedy but revolution. Although their numbers made them the most powerful section of English society, they had not yet felt their power. But the rising of 1842 showed that they were beginning to feel it. The rising had failed chiefly because its creed and motive were impossible — a revolution on legal lines. This mistake had crippled the powers of the proletariat. After their savings had disappeared, they drifted back to work. But these weeks had taught the destitute workers that they could be saved only by the violent overthrow of the unnatural conditions which oppressed them and the eradication of the aristocracies of blood and industrial wealth. Even if the typically English fear of the law held them back from violent revolution, the still greater fear of starvation would push them into it. Engels longed for the revolution and therefore believed it was close at hand; his expectation of it was increased by the confident prophecies of Chartist propagandists.

He wrote to Germany to say that the Chartists knew " that before the storm of a democratic House of Commons, the whole rotten framework of crown, peers, and everything must collapse." Like Macaulay (who of course reached diametrically opposite views), Engels was convinced that no Conservative or Liberal government would concede to peaceful agitation a reform which would hand the state over to the propertyless masses. That is why Engels regarded the struggle for universal suffrage as the prelude to the social revolution. The crisis, he thought, was inevitable; he could prophesy its era, if not its exact time.

England's future belonged to democracy — Engels was assured of that — but it would not be simple political democracy. The German communist artisans had long asserted in print that political democracy was not strong enough to perform the task which the world was putting on its shoulders. Weitling's greatest work, *The Guarantees of Harmony and Liberty*, called democracy a useless and dangerous basis for the still unrealized principle of community. Engels himself thought that the democracy which was defined only by contrast with monarchy and feudalism had now outlived its time. He believed that another democracy was soon to come — that democracy which recognized its opponents to be the bourgeoisie and property. He had seen that the war of the poor against the rich could not be fought out upon the field of politics.

Engels now joined the Chartist movement. He was convinced that it must lead (of its own will or of necessity) to the social revolution, but he was at first astonished by the fact that it had so few supporters among the educated classes. He did not yet understand that this was due to the class-instincts of the property-owning bourgeoisie; he thought that the bourgeois did not believe the Chartist movement strong enough. Its quietly growing power would, he imagined, be ignored by the bourgeois as long as its representation in Parliament was negligibly small.

He had never believed in the definitions which made a fundamental distinction between socialism and communism; and when he now became connected with the English labour movement, he did not feel the necessity of worrying its members with such distinctions. They knew only Chartism and English socialism. They had heard nothing of German communism, and even French socialist thought was strange to them. In every great mass movement of the working classes the inequality of wealth is constantly under discussion. It makes an important difference, however, whether the abolition of private property is the chief purpose of a movement or is only a matter for occasional discussion, while political democracy is the real aim. The latter was the case with Chartism. The Chartist demands were based on natural rights. Now, such an argument is very suitable for bringing the masses to believe in the justice of their cause, but it cannot assure them of the certainty of their victory. In the philosophy of the Enlightenment Engels saw only the " penultimate step to the self-knowledge and self-liberation of humanity." He vowed himself to dialectical philosophy, for in it he saw a guide through the last stage of that self-liberation.

But in England at that time there was another socialist movement, opposed on one decisive issue to the proletarian movement. It bore the stamp of one man's genius — that of Robert Owen.

Engels credited Owen with all the real social progress which was made in England at that time and for many years afterwards. As is well known, Owen attributed all the misery of his age to the maldistribution of wealth. He did not believe that the class-war preached by Chartism was the means of conquering this misery. He was an unshakable optimist and always held that the warring interests of this world could be peacefully harmonized. Like Engels, Owen thought that the age of human unreason was soon to end, and both of them reached socialism under the same emotional impulses. But as to the road which history would take to the realization of socialism, the child of Enlightenment and the disciple of Hegel entertained vastly different ideas. He thought of Owen's idealistic belief in natural rights as a long-outworn creed. He was more interested in the practical success of Owen's social experiments. But he was most of all astonished that Owen dared to call " marriage, religion, and property the sole causes of all unhappiness since the beginning of the world." He admired English socialism for declaring open war on the English churches, and he praised it as far more practical, more fundamental than the French creed. The Sunday meetings in the Manchester Hall of Science (founded by Owen's supporters) were attended by thousands. Engels went to many of them and was enormously impressed by the strange picture there presented to him.

We have no exact information on the commercial duties
which Engels had to perform in the Manchester firm of
Ermen and Engels. We know more of his activities when
away from the office; they are more important for us, as
they were for him. With his vigour, his sure discernment,
and his natural desire to find his bearings, he gave up his
leisure to the study of contemporary English literature. The
newspapers and magazines which spoke so freely of public
affairs gave him much material for thought. And his earnest
reading of English history helped him to a deeper comprehension of contemporary England and to a clearer vision
of its future. In Bremen he had been chiefly attracted by
Shelley, because of his hatred for monarchy and Christianity;
he had begun a translation of *Queen Mab*. And now he read
all the literature whose inspiration sprang from the conflicts
of the day. The works of Carlyle, the novels of Disraeli, the
poems of Mrs. Browning and Tom Hood, spoke to him of
the vast social convulsions which were shaking England. And
more eloquent than any literature were the streets of Manchester.

As he came home from the Cotton Exchange or returned
from an expedition into the slums with Mary Burns, he realized that all the impressions he was collecting and all the
thoughts he was working out could not bear fruit unless he
studied the science of political economy, which was then
flourishing in England. Until now he had neglected that
branch of thought and relied almost entirely on philosophy,
but now he saw its necessity. His sensitive spirit was terribly
impressed by the spectacle of highly developed industrialism,
for Manchester was then the industrial capital of the world.
From his earliest years he had had a strong sense of social
justice. Now his new philosophy of history changed what had
been mere emotion into a scientific outlook upon the problems of the day. And the new science gave so complete an
answer to those problems that he felt it imperative to give
immediate expression to his emotions whenever they were

roused. He had an unselfish and idealistic nature. He would have preferred mankind to be inspired by motives which would have abolished all conflict and fostered community of spirit. But mankind is not so fashioned; and Engels had such an insatiable thirst for knowledge and such a keen, unwavering gaze that he preferred to see things as they really were. Coming from a gentler, more paternal country to the materialistic city of London, he was shocked by "the brutal indifference, the unfeeling egotism of the people, each concentrated on his own private interests." Here for the first time he recognized that "unyielding self-interest" was the basis of contemporary society. As in London, so in the industrial towns — "everywhere barbarous indifference, relentless self-seeking on one side and unspeakable misery on the other; social conflict everywhere, a general rush to rob one's fellows under the cloak of law."

The plight of the industrial proletariat could be seen and studied in Manchester and the neighbouring cities more clearly than anywhere else in the world. Sympathy with human suffering and hunger for knowledge alike spurred Engels on to study the position of the new social class. As he gradually came to see it as his task to free that class from its bondage, he felt more and more that he must write a book to express his new knowledge, for he knew that no other philosophically trained German was so widely acquainted with the subject. He intended to set down, not an impression of one locality chosen by hazard, but a general and typical account, from which positive conclusions could be drawn. He was coming to know Manchester more intimately than most of its inhabitants. He was a gifted observer, and he never ceased collecting material, but his first stay in England was not long enough to let him arrange that material in the way he had planned.

Even in Germany he had been convinced that without the abolition of private property the emancipation of mankind could never be completed. He found that the Chartists over-

FRIEDRICH ENGELS IN EARLY MANHOOD

estimated the effectiveness of political means to their ends, but he was sure that circumstances would soon convert them to socialism. As a convinced revolutionary, he could envisage no success for the peaceful tactics of English socialism; he was sure that in England the social revolution would never come except by force. And thus he was brought to wish that Chartism could be inspired with the spirit of socialism, and socialism with the energy of Chartism, for he felt that the one movement was superior in theory and the other in practice. He hoped for their amalgamation. He read the *Northern Star* and the *New Moral World* with equal eagerness, and he cultivated the acquaintance of the leaders of both movements.

Among the socialists his chief friend was John Watts, the Manchester tailor. Watts gave many lectures, and theorized much on the existence of God. Engels, straight from the German philosophical schools, sought in vain to convince him that God's existence could be proved by other means than by inference from material fact. He cared little about the question of the existence of God, but he was exercised to vindicate the dialectical principle, for Watts would not admit its *a priori* necessity. Among the Chartists Engels sought out James Leach, whose wide knowledge of facts and healthy common sense gave him much influence in Manchester labour circles. But Engels made a more important connexion when in the summer of 1843 he visited the offices of the *Northern Star* in Leeds, for there he met George Julian Harney, who was directing that important paper under the ægis of Feargus O'Connor, famous leader of the left wing of the Chartist movement. Only three years older than Engels, Harney had a stormy political career behind him. At first he had been a left-wing Chartist, but he had been deeply shaken by the failure of the general strike. Although he had none of the innate force of O'Connor or Lovett, outstanding figure of the moderate wing of the Chartist movement, and although he had none of their influence, and no eloquence comparable to theirs, he was the only man among the leaders of his movement who had made himself conversant with political and social conditions on the Continent. The impression made on him by Engels at their first meeting had not disappeared fifty-four years later, when Engels died — " a slender young man with a look of almost boyish immaturity, who spoke remarkably pure English, and said he was keenly interested in the Chartist movement." So Harney described him, and said that even at seventy-two Engels was just as modest and retiring as he had been when he first called on the *Northern Star* at the age of twenty-two.

From his acquaintance with Watts and other socialists Engels learned that the English had not the vaguest idea of the work of their comrades on the Continent. He determined, therefore, to explain to them the position of Continental socialism. In November 1843 he published an essay in the *New Moral World,* called *The Advance of Social Reform on the Continent.* This essay shows that Engels felt that, not only in England, but in France and Germany also, society must soon undergo the revolutionary transformation which the abolition of private property was to achieve. Observing that social movements in all these countries were converging on communism by different paths, he was convinced that modern civilization was bound by its structure to travel in that direction. Since the ultimate aim of all these movements was the same, differences of opinion between them were bound to disappear in time. But meanwhile Engels thought that the establishment of friendly relations among their leaders and followers was a paramount necessity, and he felt himself bound to help in forming them. Individual members of the Chartist movement had previously thought it necessary that the proletariats of different countries should become conscious of their community of interest. But it was Engels who before all others, and more eagerly than all others, devoted himself to the task of uniting the " communists " of every country in Europe.

He wished to shake the English faith in law and order. Accordingly he called French history to witness and explained from it why French communists were republicans, belonged to secret societies, and did not shrink from using force. He praised Proudhon's polemic against private property as the most important achievement of French communism; for Proudhon, he said, had revealed the true nature and the contradictions of the idea of property far more scientifically than any other writer. At that time Engels's belief in " the approaching collapse of the state " was strongly influenced by Proudhon's anarchism, but his belief was strengthened by his new and surprising discovery of the supremacy of economic over political forces. He saw that private property was the most important factor in history, the central issue of all revolutions; accordingly he no longer saw society as subordinate to the state, but the state as subordinate to society. He formed the belief (which was from now on his consistent view) that the state was not a social category which had always existed or must remain in existence for ever. Writing in Owen's paper, he dealt chiefly with working-class communism in his discussion of Germany; but even there he said with great emphasis that he expected more advances would be made towards communism by German intellectuals than by German workers.

Engels saw the blank demoralization of the English workers. And yet he expected England to be regenerated exclusively by this " part of the nation still unknown on the Continent." He had nothing but contempt for the English middle classes, who held egoism to be the one force uniting mankind, and he was confirmed in this judgment by the picture of Britain which had just been drawn by a distinguished author. Engels recognized Carlyle as the only cultured man in England who was really troubled by the moral problems of the society he lived in. He was deeply stirred to read the words in which " the great rhapsodist " described the lamentable state of Britain and emphasized that things could not remain as they were. Carlyle's condemnation of the vanity of his time and the corruption of all social institutions was loudly applauded by Engels in his fine essay on *Past and Present*. But Carlyle's practical proposals were not enough for him. He found it incredible that such a bold writer could pitilessly condemn the system of open competition and still not realize that private property was the root of all evil.

About this time Engels wrote his *Sketch for a Critique of Political Economy* — a still bolder and more brilliant work than his Carlyle essay. He had been terribly impressed to see that in the metropolis of the world's industries production was rising to an amazing level through mechanical inventions, while the masses were still ground down by poverty because they could not obtain or consume the products of their own labour. Carlyle had called this the curse of Midas. As soon as Engels understood the full absurdity of the paradox, he began as usual to look about for precursors and companions in the same line of thought — he could learn from the former and discuss with the latter how the evil might be scotched. He was much moved to find that " the unreasoning, unfeeling mechanism of open competition " was deified by Adam Smith and the whole classical school of economists, and that the English bourgeoisie therefore considered the system of private property to be necessary and indestructible. It is yet another proof of Engels's courage that at the age of twenty-three he ventured to make an independent attack on the political economists and sought by use of the dialectical method to expose their theories as a tissue of contradictions. He turned with special passion to attack the Malthusian theory of population as a " hideous blasphemy against nature and humanity," whose purpose was to make men accept as a law of nature the consequences of the faulty structure of society.

These two essays are the first which show Engels's historical genius fully developed, and they are the first works which he published under his own name. During his stay in

England he had acquired a deep insight into the relation of classes and state, an expert knowledge of the social consequences of the industrial revolution, and an acute perception of the trends of capitalist development. By this time there was scarcely anyone on the Continent who could match his understanding of these problems; outside Britain their development was slow. Engels had now chosen his career. He knew the task to which his life was to be dedicated. It was time for him to meet that still greater man at whose side he was to fight.

CHAPTER VI

FRIENDSHIP WITH MARX

ᘒ

Engels left Manchester for his home towards the end of August 1844 and travelled through Paris to Germany. After long months beneath the "frightful leaden sky" of Lancashire, his gay spirits quickened again in the bright life of the boulevards. But the great experience of the ten days he spent in Paris was neither the dissipations of the town nor his tour of the places hallowed by the memories of Babeuf, Marat, and Robespierre: it was his new friendship with Karl Marx.

Marx and Engels now at last came to understand each other. They saw that they were meant to complement each other, and that their spiritual development had been along the same lines. And they were happy to realize that they would be companions on that path in future; because, independently of each other, they had formed the same views of their goal and their route towards it. They knew that they could achieve their common end only by sharing their knowledge and their strength. Friendships are not made only for a time and a season, yet few friendships withstand the laws of change. It is not surprising that both Marx and Engels now felt that they were entering upon a permanent partnership and that they would always learn and fight side by side. But it is amazing that this partnership remained stable throughout the changing years; and it is unparalleled that the achievement of two such men should be so complete, so vigorous, such a living unity.

We need not here investigate the life and spiritual development of Marx, but it is important for us to know how his character contrasted with that of Engels. If the urgent active spirit of Engels was like the mountain torrent, Marx was like the storm which blows unheeding whether it destroys or builds. Engels felt himself safe as soon as he had left the Pietist atmosphere of his home for the clear air of speculative theology and philosophy; he was satisfied that he had boarded " the train for the future." But Marx struggled with the spirit of his time as Jacob wrestled with the angel. His work came slowly, painfully to birth; his thought was profound and searching, because it was at once destructive and constructive. Engels was naturally a more practical man, quicker at finding his bearings. He had a feeling for " what was in the air "; he could take up material which lay ready to hand and select and combine until he had found a new connexion, but he lacked dialectical originality.

The different attitudes of Marx and Engels are reflected in the difference of their styles. Engels's phrases bear no marks of a struggle with their form or their thought. They run rapidly and unhesitatingly; transparently clear, fluent and graceful, they answer to every idea which their writer cared to express. His letters are lit by a healthy sense of humour. His early writings contain many vigorous poetic figures of speech. But the sentences of Marx are always filled to overflowing with thought; they are receptacles, and inadequate at that. The antitheses of which he was so fond were riveted around the conclusions which he had reached after long intellectual labour; his intention is always to make those conclusions the permanent possession of reader and writer alike. Brilliance and clumsiness and occasional obscurity are fused together in his writing, but it always glows from the anvil of thought.

Of the two friends, Engels was far less nervous, far more equable, than Marx; he had a brighter, less contorted, and more harmonious disposition; physically and intellectually he was more elastic and resilient. He often reproached Marx

for allowing his temper to " dragoon " him, for never re-
laxing and never being satisfied with himself. Both were
equally capable of resistance, tenacity, and persistence, and
both possessed an inexhaustible love and capacity for work.
Throughout their lives they were earnestly and selflessly
given up to their task; they pursued it with fanatical devo-
tion and an indomitable rejection of personal vanity. They
supported each other in disrespect for tradition and contempt for emotional display. The tone of the letters which
they exchanged is genial, brisk, free and easy; it reflects
the modesty which in both of them was combined with savage
ruthlessness towards themselves and others.

In one of these letters, Engels mentions that Marx " knew
his indolence *en fait de théorie*" which kept him deaf to the
complaints of his better self and prevented him from reaching the root of everything. Engels knew his own nature well.
It was necessary for him to find one point from which to
view the complex spectacle of history, but he could not reduce
his perceptions and thoughts to a scientific system. Marx's
powers of synthesis made Engels deeply indebted to him.
Engels helped in marking out the foundations — he brought
valuable material — but he could never have raised the building, however much he craved for a spiritual home. The elder
Liebknecht, who knew Engels well, speaks of the piercing
glance of his bright blue eyes. We know already his sharp
hunter's instinct, his sure sight and relentless grip on the
truth; we have seen how his quick and unfaltering sense of
direction served him throughout the perplexities of his
youth, helped him to teach himself and at last to find the
goal he had sought. He was always able to discard the useless and choose the useful, by an instinctive process of selec-
tion. But the sting of controversy was necessary before his
full powers of criticism could be aroused. And even then
intellectual criticism was seldom the motive force in his own
soul; the ultimate decisions had already been taken, for they

were immediate and perhaps unconscious. Yet if criticism were necessary, he fell to it with much pleasure and adroitness, for he was a natural fighter. And in his younger days, when his sharp judgments and quick temper offended others, he did not avoid occasional challenges to duels, while later his passionate interest in military science won him the nickname of "the general," and his friends thought of him as the Carnot of a future German revolution.

Engels's outlook on life was fresh and unacademic. He chose to learn from facts as they came into his view; he preferred to detect rather than to study, to improvise rather than to systematize. But where Engels failed, Marx was strong. He later admitted to Bebel that Marx had taught him the meaning of scientific work. Although he loved books, it was not natural for him to spend a lifetime in libraries, industriously collecting material to confirm his view of society and history. It was more to his taste to make friends with other men and learn from them, to find connexions and start associations which should further the sacred cause he had in view. Within his athletic frame there moved a constant impulse to action: he was an enthusiastic rider and huntsman, so that even his fierce social and political enmity to the English gentry did not prevent him from riding to hounds with them. And in the same spirit he did not shrink from "hunting over the high fences of abstract thought." But he was always happier when he could exercise the practical capabilities which he had inherited from his ancestors — even in the intellectual sphere. And after he had met Marx and realized that his friend excelled in the qualities which he himself lacked, he confined himself with an easy conscience to the exercise of his real talents.

Although he had a fresh and receptive mind, we must not forget that his unsystematic education had given him certain dilettante traits. But even if he had had time and opportunity to study philosophy with more exactitude, his special gifts would never have come to light in the realm of abstract thought. He could never have mastered the knowledge of past generations, analysed it and reconstituted it, with the freedom and mastery of Marx. It was wise of him to recognize that his spirit needed a pilot if it was to visit new lands. Although he had a sure sense of direction, he did not trust himself to steer alone. After Strauss and Börne he had turned to Hegel for guidance. When he reached Feuerbach, he felt spiritually strong enough to make an independent excursion beyond the bounds of that lonely unsociable philosopher's doctrine. And then he met Marx, who was moving in the same direction. He joined him at once, and gladly began to do what he "was meant for, to play second fiddle" — glad that he had found a first fiddle and could follow his lead. Did he never aspire further? Did he always remain content with his subordinate status? Engels himself would have brusquely refused to answer such a question. No words of his exist to prove any tragic conflict in his soul. His thought was never centred on himself, and he was not self-tortured by ambition. At eighteen he had been content to recognize that he was not a poet. And in the same way in later years he was content not to expect figs from thistles, but to enjoy the exercise of the rich powers which he actually did possess. In 1880 he wrote to his disciple Edward Bernstein, with reference to Marx, that he did not understand how one could be jealous of a genius. "Genius is such an exceptional thing that we who have it not always know that we cannot attain it." We shall be well advised, then, not to imagine that Engels was sad and resigned; he himself left no grounds for such a view.

But the most important fact about the new friendship was the contribution which each could make to the thought of the other at the time when they met. When Marx had been editor of the *Rheinische Zeitung* in Cologne, he had recognized that philosophy does not stand "outside the world." Disappointed in his political aspirations, he had turned to criticism of politics. He saw the significance of the material world, and the necessity of a revolution in it; he realized that every political revolution was limited, that democracy itself was an incomplete thing. But at the time when Engels was turning to communism, Marx knew no more of its doctrines than this. It is no more than truth when he says to Engels, twenty years later: "You know that I am slow to grasp things, and that I always follow in your footprints." The overwhelming importance of socialist doctrines for the development of his ideals of humanity first dawned on him when he migrated to Paris. As soon as the problem of the masses presented itself to him, he began to realize its importance in history. He plunged eagerly into the study of the French Revolution.

In France, as in England, there was a widespread belief that the political conflicts of history concealed what were really class-conflicts. Under such influences Marx soon realized that in every purely political revolution "one class attempts — from its own special point of view — to emancipate society." He had confidence in his own genius for productive criticism; refusing to dogmatize about the future of the world, he preferred to develop his new position out of the criticism of the past. He saw the need of his age to be ruthless criticism of all existing things — ruthless criticism which did not shrink from its own conclusions or from conflict with authority. Like Engels, he aimed at changing the outlook of his fellow-men; but he aimed straighter. He did not see the solution as "a great division between the thought of the past and the thought of the future," but as the recognition by the age of its own conflicts and desires.

Engels had early interested himself in the problem of action. Could he have found a more complete solution for it than that proposed by Marx in his contributions to the *Deutsch-Französische Jahrbücher*? He must have been overwhelmed to find there in such astonishing novelty and grandeur the complete unification of thought and action, the perfect reconciliation of theory and practice, and an uncompromising declaration that it was the course of history that would emancipate humanity. Did he not also call history his Alpha and Omega, did he not also expect that it would bring the victory of the revolution? Engels believed that the English proletariat was the shock-troops of the world revolution. Marx had his gaze still fixed on Germany; he had left it in order to avoid the bonds of censorship and "to make the petrifaction" of Germany "dance perforce" by piping its own music to it. We must remember the eagerness with which Engels tried to show that communism naturally grew out of Hegelian philosophy, the anxiety with which he asked why socialist leaders sprang from the educated classes in Germany, but not in England, the difficulty and eventual success of his search for the connexion between politics and economics. Remembering these things, we shall easily understand the immense effect which Marx's essay had upon him. We can see from the contributions of both Marx and Engels to the *Deutsch-Französische Jahrbücher* that they expected the abolition of the proletariat to lead to Feuerbach's ideal of the future of humanity. Marx called this the resolution of the "conflict between the sensual existence of the individual and the existence of human species," and Engels described it as the "reconciliation of mankind with nature and with itself." Engels wished to bring the processes of material production under the conscious control of mankind; only thus could man conquer private property, which had dislocated the social order. Marx hoped that "the existing world-order would dissolve" when the material interests of the masses coincided with the intellectual interests of the philosophers — as they were bound to do. But both Marx and Engels saw clearly that the liberation which they desired went far beyond the realm of politics.

In England Engels had recognized that the economic and social worlds were independent of and prior to the state. But it was Marx who first showed him that politics and history are explicable only in terms of social relations — the principle which became the lever of their whole conception of history. Marx gave Engels both the final proof of his assumption that communism was the continuation and completion of German philosophical thought, and a convincing solution of the apparently irreconcilable conflict between mind and the mass. In this vigorous thinker, who could systematically demonstrate to him with penetrating dialectic that which he himself had only glimpsed in outline and but sketchily set down, Engels found his spiritual master. But Marx himself found much of vital significance in Engels's *Carlyle* and his *Sketch for a Criticism of Political Economy* and even more in the opinions and facts which he heard from Engels's own lips. His own thought had always been abstract; until he became editor of the *Rheinische Zeitung,* he had never entered the world of practical affairs. Even then he had not the knowledge of fact which was necessary for a man who thought that economics played the principal part in history. It was Engels who taught him the technique he needed for the study of economic facts. Engels helped him to know the living realities; and Engels was the right man to do this, since he had personal acquaintance with industry, commerce, and capital and had been in personal contact with the modern proletariat. At first Engels could teach him lessons even in political economics. Marx was deeply impressed when he understood that Engels had used the science which was so neglected by the Hegelians to show that all economic categories are merely different forms of private ownership and thus to evolve a dialectical proof of the inevitability of communism. Since Marx held that history turned on material facts, not on ideas, he was forced to concentrate his attention on the economic world. Maintaining as he did that the progress of civilization depended on the abolition of the proletariat, he was compelled to investigate the laws which had brought the proletariat into being, and the tendencies which were making for its abolition. And here Engels's suggestions were of inestimable value to him. He saw things in a clear new light when his friend pointed out the opposition between the kindly phrases and the inhuman practice of *laissez-faire*. Engels's accounts of financial crises and the accumulation of capital were a revelation to Marx. Years later, when he re-read it, he spoke with admiration of the "genius" which he found in the *Sketch for a Criticism of Political Economy*. In 1862 he declared that Engels had already discovered the decisive objection to Ricardo's theory of ground-rent.

It was inevitable that the friends should discuss the progress of German philosophical thought, and the Berlin philosophical circle of which they had once been members. Marx found it easiest always to make intellectual progress by opposing his present beliefs to beliefs he had held and discarded. Engels did not feel bound to do this. It would not have occurred to him to compose a large work devoted exclusively to an attack on the Berlin Hegelians, who, secure on the lofty heights of abstract theory, were bombarding their earlier comrades with pamphlets — simply because they had felt they must go down into the world and learn something of the toiling masses. The book which he wrote with Marx was aimed at the Berlin group which centred on the "Bauer family," and it poured ridicule on their belief in the transcendent existence of Spirit. Its name originally was *A Critique of Critical Critique*. Engels was unpleasantly surprised when the other title, *The Holy Family* (which they had used in conversation), was clapped on to the book by the publisher. He was afraid of "unnecessary rows" with his devout father, already irritated by his conduct. And he was angry that his name appeared beside that of Marx on the titlepage. "I wrote hardly any of it," he said, "and anyone can recognize your style. Anyhow it is ridiculous, for I have perhaps a dozen pages in it, and you have several hundred!"

But we can see what Engels could achieve alone, from his

book *The Condition of the Working Class in England, from personal inspection and authentic sources.* He wrote it in Barmen in the autumn of 1844 and the winter of 1844–5. It is the chief work of his early life. He succeeded astonishingly well in blending his own opinions with the facts he describes. When in later years he was called the founder of descriptive political economy, he pointed to Petty, Bois-guillebert, and others, and he added that Frenchmen and Englishmen had described the position of the proletariat before him. He said that he had been fortunate enough to be the first man in the centre of modern industry who " had opened his eyes to the facts, at least to the most obvious ones." But was that a small achievement?

The book was dedicated, in English, to the working class of Great Britain. In the dedication Engels mentions with pride the documents he has studied and the personal observations he has made in order to give a true picture of their struggles against the social and political strength of their oppressors. He says he is glad to think that he spent his leisure hours in Manchester, not at the rich tables of factory-owners, but in the company of poor working folk and in the study of their lives. The English middle class had never produced a readable work dealing with the situation of the majority of freeborn Britons; they had left it to a foreigner to tell the civilized world of the unworthy conditions in which the English workers lived.

In the German preface Engels explains that the causes which were responsible for the subjection of the English proletariat must eventually have the same effect in Germany. Meanwhile, he observes, the description of the misery of England may bring others to see what misery there is in Germany, and indicate the danger which threatens Germany's peace. He adds an introductory survey of the history of English economic development in the early days of the industrial revolution. He holds the rise of the modern proletariat to be the most important result of this vast process, and he pillories the stupidity of the English bourgeoisie, who do not see that the ground beneath their feet is bound to swallow them up, with the inevitability of a mathematical law.

Most of the book is taken up with a description of the position of the proletariat in its various strata — first industrial workers, then the miners and agricultural workers. Special chapters deal with the Irish immigration, the great cities, and the effect of competition on the proletariat. Chartism and English socialism are treated under the heading of *Working-Class Movements*. A concluding chapter investigates the relationship of the middle class to the proletariat; and, after a full diagnosis of the social disease, closes with a prognosis of its outcome — the prophecy which we know.

But this rich mass of material did not remain merely descriptive. It gained an extraordinary unity through the consistency with which Engels articulated it under his general principles — principles which sprang from deep-rooted personal convictions. It would be wrong to accuse Engels of painting too black a picture of the misery of the English proletariat in that first period of capitalism. The official inquiries, and the writings of countless Englishmen who were far from being revolutionary communists, show us the appalling barbarism which existed. Still, it is a matter of great importance whether the author of such a book conceives it possible to reform those conditions or thinks of a peaceful reform as out of the question.

Engels was sick of the magical formulas repeated by Hess and the " true socialists " — Humanity, Real Humanity, and so on. In this book he deliberately turned his back on such language. To do this he found strength in the redeeming idea that the imperfections of the present system were bound by inner necessity to produce a better system. Even though the English social revolution still tarried, he looked forward to the time when the concentration of capital and the devastating effects of commercial crises would reduce the whole nation (with the exception of a few millionaires) to the proletarian level and drive them to action. He now saw that the class war was the moving force in the revolt of the proletariat. But how was he to recognize this brutal fact as a historical necessity, without coming into conflict with the humanistic creed of German idealism? As long as capitalism continued, he realized, there were only two alternatives for the vast mass of mankind — to abandon themselves to fate or to take up arms for their rights as men. And thus the class-war was a stage on the way to the ideal aim of the humanists. When Engels wrote a new preface to this book, three years before his death, he felt himself compelled to justify himself for the emphatic assertion that communism was not a party-cry of the working class but actually aimed at the liberation of all society. After half a century of fighting the bourgeoisie he granted that his assertion was still true "in the abstract," but, he added, in practice it is "worse than useless." But in youth he was inspired by the belief that communism was "not an affair of the workers, but of the human species."

Engels had returned to Barmen with the determination to abandon a business career as soon as possible, in order to devote himself unhindered to scientific research and communist propaganda with Marx. But he was forced to recognize that he must wait some months at least to make his resolve seem plausible to his family, for it cut across all their traditions. Marx and he realized that they must live and work together; they had to create a new communism by their own powers, both a party and a philosophy. Engels's first meetings with those who called themselves communists in the Rhine district convinced him that the future of the cause depended on the construction of a theoretical basis for communism. He felt it especially urgent to counteract the doubts of its practicability which he everywhere met. He promised Marx that within three days he would write a pamphlet covering this point. Shocked by watching the death struggles of the home industries, a few chosen spirits among the German bourgeoisie had turned, for the moment, to a modified socialism and had actually founded associations for promoting the welfare of the working classes. This movement was not displeasing to the governments of the various states — they were glad that the attention of the public should be thus diverted from more awkward questions such as representative government and the freedom of the press. But such associations were not a soil in which communism should be allowed to grow.

Engels soon found that it was far harder to make direct contact with the working class in Germany than in England. The dye-workers and bleachers of Wuppertal were splendid material for a communist movement. But how was he to reach them, hampered as he was by the ubiquitous police supervision? "If one could only show the fellows the right road!" he lamented to Marx, after making numerous unsuccessful attempts. At the time he was working in collaboration with Hess, although certain discords made themselves felt at times. They were compelled at last to make what use they could of the educated classes, some of whom were at that time showing themselves receptive of new social ideas. It was possible to call meetings without the permission of the police if their purpose was to found associations for the betterment of the working class. At such meetings Engels met people who had some radical ideas; he was always a sanguine man, and he wrote to Marx: "Wherever one goes, one runs up against a communist." He had at first much too hopeful views of the prospects of the movement, as is shown by his article in the *New Moral World* of December 14th, 1844, called *The Rapid Progress of Communism in Germany*.

Engels and Hess planned to found a monthly review, which, without risking immediate suppression by indulging in open communist propaganda, would print accounts of the situation of the working class in Germany. This plan was described by the distinguished Christian-socialist writer V. A. Huber as "an undertaking which might, in worthier hands, have satisfied a real need and spread the knowledge of possible improvements." It was published in Elberfeld. The editors persuaded the publisher that they intended to found a non-political popular magazine, whose purpose was to print simple facts, and to be the organ of the new associations for the betterment of the working class. Its title was the *Mirror of Society*. The subtitle, "An Organ for the Representation of the Propertyless Classes and for the Analysis of Contemporary Social Conditions," was meant to persuade the government that it would discuss, but not champion, the interests of the proletariat. However, the government was soon convinced that the new undertaking was dangerous. It had been unable to take any steps against Engels's book, but "when its contents were disseminated through these channels, the position was different." The *Mirror of Society* was soon broken.

In the eyes of the factory-owners of Elberfeld and Barmen charitable work was founded on Christian ideals. Accordingly, in the first meetings which were called to found an association for the betterment of the working class, there were fierce disputes between parsons and rationalists. Engels and Hess took advantage of the excitement to give publicity to their own more radical demands. There were some officials and young merchants who wished further information about the aims and practicability of communism. For their benefit Engels and Hess agreed to hold a private meeting in one of the better restaurants. There were more present than they had expected. A few days later, when the discussions were continued, they were speaking to an audience of more than a hundred. At a third meeting the crowd was so large that the authorities forbade such assemblies to be repeated.

We have an eyewitness account of these, perhaps the first

socialist meetings in Germany. " In order to make the thing
look harmless, some harpists had been engaged. At the beginning of the meeting, poems based on social themes were
read. Then Hess and ' Friedrich Oswald' began their
speeches. In the audience were manufacturers who had come
for a thrill; they expressed their annoyance by laughter and
jeers. The defence of capitalist society was left to the director of the local theatre. The more violently he attacked the
possibility of communism, the more enthusiastically the no-
tables drank his health."

While Hess eulogized communism as the law of love,
Engels felt it more appropriate to appeal to the intelligence
of his hearers. In lucid phrases he analysed the absurdities
he had seen in the system of free competition in England.
He contrasted the present system with communism, which
would remove the differences between social classes and
banish financial crises. He said that there were various ways
of bringing it into reality. The English would found a few
communist settlements and leave it to individuals to enter
them if they wished. The French would bring in state communism by legislation. How the Germans would introduce
it one could not yet say. After the second evening's discussion it was objected that he had not stated convincingly
enough the economic necessity of communism in Germany,
although he had explained its inevitability in France and
England. In answering this objection on the third evening,
he realized that he was making his last speech. Determined
as he was to leave Germany at once, he now ventured to
assert that the social revolution was necessary in Germany
also. One of his chief arguments was the future commercial
rivalry between Germany and England. It was held that if
the Germans could manage to strengthen their industries by
high tariffs and thus compete with England in neutral markets, the German and English industries could exist side by
side in perfect peace. Engels disputed this. He pointed out

that if an industry was not to be left behind, it must find new markets. If there were no more new markets, England was bound to protect its own industries by repressing those of other countries. The result would be a life-and-death struggle between German and English industry; Engels considered that England would win it. If it did, the depressed industries of Germany could no longer feed the proletariat which they had artificially created, and the social revolution would come at once. But even if Germany won, she would still be where England was at the moment — on the brink of social revolution. And it was still more probable that England's ruin would hasten the revolt of her proletariat and that the English revolution would extend to the whole of Europe.

It was good for Engels to speak for once in public. He confessed to Marx that this damned abstract penpushing was a very different matter from standing up before real men and preaching directly to them, face to face. Engels was not a born speaker. If he had been later, it would have been more difficult for him to restrain, as he did, his impulse to make direct political contact with the proletariat.

Since his first absence from home he had never spent such a long period in his parents' house. For the first time he saw, and saw every day, the impassable gulf which separated him from the convictions and feelings of his home. It would seem that until then his father had not realized the extent of Engels's activities as a propagandist of subversive ideas. And now Engels was forced to come to some understanding about his future. He was unable to carry consideration and respect too far. The anxiety of his parents had persuaded him to take up commercial work again in his father's office; but a fortnight after his arrival he found that this was impossible. He wrote to Marx on January 20th, 1845: "This penny-grabbing is too horrible, Barmen is too horrible, the waste of time is too horrible; and above all it is too horrible to continue to be — not only a bourgeois, but a manufacturer, a bourgeois in active opposition to the proletariat. I needed only a few days in the old man's factory to realize the horror of all this; I had rather overlooked it before. Of course, I had planned to stick at the penny-grabbing as long as it suited me and then to write something which the police banned, so that I could make a graceful exit over the frontier. But I can't wait for that. I think I should have been petrified already if I had not had to write the most hideous stories about English conditions in my book every day; that at least kept my indignation hot. One can be a communist and still hold the position of a bourgeois and a penny-grabber if one does not write. But industry, penny-grabbing, and extensive communist propaganda all together — impossible!"

Hothead as he was, he found the "enervating life of a radical Christian and Prussian family" more and more intolerable as the disputes between himself and his father increased. His father was willing to give him money to study in Bonn; but he resolutely refused to support him if he was preaching communism. He had learned that Engels did not shrink from receiving communists in his own house. The disputes came to open war when Engels hurt his father's pride (as a leading manufacturer and elder of the church) by preaching communism at a public meeting. On the 17th of March Engels complained to Marx of the "dog's life" he was leading at home. "You cannot imagine," he wrote, "the malice of the Christian witch-hunt which is whooping after my soul." He said he would not start a row, for he was leaving "in a fortnight, one way or another." But "if it were not for the sake of my mother — who is really kind and human (though she has no independence where my father is concerned) and whom I really love — I would not think for a moment of making any concessions to my fanatical and despotic father."

At last the relations of father and son became so intolerably strained that the police did Engels a real service by showing a special interest in him. An arrest in Barmen meant a scandal which would mortally wound the proud father. So he could not raise much opposition when Engels went to Brussels for safety. Marx had been expelled from Paris and had been living in Brussels since February.

CHAPTER VII

IN BELGIUM AND FRANCE

In Brussels Engels felt himself free from all restrictions. There was no detestable business career to hamper him, no social considerations to respect. For the first time, in the close contact of daily life, he and Marx learned to understand each other's intellectual character and to know each other as men. They lived next door to each other in a working-class suburb. Never again did they work in such complete harmony as in those years before the revolution, when they were working out their final position both in philosophy and in practical politics.

In the summer of 1845 the two friends travelled together to England. Engels wanted to re-establish his relations with the Chartists and to fetch Mary Burns, who from now on remained his constant companion. Marx wished to receive his first impressions of England under Engels's guidance and, now that he had immersed himself in economics, to study the earlier English writers on the subject. The weeks of their stay were rich in experience. Long afterwards, in 1870, Engels reminded his friend of the bay in Manchester Library, from which they had gazed out through bright-coloured panes on bright summer weather. Engels became a regular contributor to the *Northern Star*. In September 1845 he attacked in its columns the opinion which he had advanced earlier, in the *New Moral World*, that in Germany the revolution could be the work of the intellectuals. "The working classes will carry it through unaided. We do not count on the middle class," he wrote.

On their return to Brussels, they started on a new book which was to develop and complete their economic conception of history. Once more they took up the cudgels against their "former philosophical conscience," attacking Bruno Bauer, Stirner, and even Feuerbach and the "true socialists." The book was to be called *German Ideology,* and between September 1845 and August 1846 they brought it almost to completion. It had a singular fate. Owing to the severity of the censorship no German or Swiss publisher dared to issue any of their work. Meanwhile Marx had finished his polemic against Proudhon, and for this also he failed to find a publisher. In March 1847 Engels wrote to him: "If the appearance of our book is going to hurt yours, then for heaven's sake shove ours into a drawer — it is more important that yours should be published." And they did in fact leave their *German Ideology* to the "nibbling criticism of the mice"; it is only now that this comprehensive exposition of their conception of history has been printed. Marx had also asked Engels whether he might, in his work on Proudhon, use some of the ideas expressed in their joint work; and Engels had replied: "Of course!" The friends always shared their intellectual property. They thought only of the end in view; and from now on, that was a common end. Although they resented any attempt by a third person to appropriate their ideas without acknowledgment, they never thought of explaining to posterity the difference between their individual achievements. It is therefore always difficult to distinguish between the work of Marx and that of Engels, and at this period it is supremely difficult. Most of the *Ideology* was written down by Engels and amended and supplemented by Marx. Part of it is copied out in the hand of Joseph Weydemeyer,[1] a former officer in the Prussian artillery, who became a firm friend of theirs in Brussels. So handwriting cannot be used as a test of authorship.

[1] Weydemeyer (1818–66) came to the United States in 1851, where he fought in the Civil War as an officer in the Federal army.

Marx's writing was illegible, so it was often Engels who made the fair copy of a passage which they had both worked out beforehand. Engels was the less inhibited of the two, and it is probable for this reason that many sections are the work of his hand alone. We know that he could write with amazing rapidity long articles and even whole pamphlets, which he later discarded or for which he found no publisher. It is impossible, then, to understand the part of either man in the joint work unless we clearly understand their respective characters and education. Engels repeatedly said that Marx presented to him the basic principles of their conception of history in a fairly complete form when they met in Brussels. But he acknowledged that he, too, had gradually approached the idea several years before 1845. That this was in fact so has been shown earlier in this volume.

Although the manuscript of the *German Ideology* did not become effective during the lives of its authors, one should have some idea of its contents to understand the development of their political ideas. In all they wrote independently later, there was something of the consciousness that they had previously given combined expression to a common conception of historic development. For this reason, perhaps, it seemed to neither of them essential or urgent to repeat a work of this character. It is true that in some of his later writings — in *Anti-Düring,* in his booklet on Feuerbach, and in several letters written in his later years which were meant for publication — Engels gave expression to his conception of society and state and the forces of historic development. But nowhere as thoroughly as in *German Ideology.* When Marx and Engels wrote this book they had only just fought their way to freedom out of the primeval thickets of German ideology. It was their purpose to find a point of departure for new research based on empiric realities and not arrived at through abstractions. The longer they reflected, the more clearly these two " practical materialists " perceived that " real individuals, their actions, and their material living-conditions " were the only possible hypothesis from which realistic ideas could be developed. They concluded, in other words, that " Nature and the modifications it undergoes in the course of history through the instrumentality of man " are the foundation of all social change. Thus the production of food, which first differentiated man from the animal world, became to Marx and Engels the elemental fact of all historic interpretation. Morals, religion, metaphysics, seen from this point of view, lose all appearance of reality and all claim to a separate history.

Up to that time historians had taken no account of the materialist basis which Marx and Engels now believed to have discovered, or had regarded it as a complementary phenomenon bearing no relation to the total course of events. German historians especially had been wont to regard as historically important only those forces which stood above and were separated from ordinary day-by-day life — religion and philosophy — while the English and the French had at least made an attempt to write the history of bourgeois society, its commercial and industrial growth. But they, too, had taken each passing epoch at its own estimate, believing what it said and thought of itself instead of asking to what extent these concepts were dictated by class-illusions.

With the development of civilization, thus the authors continue their work, there came an increasing division of functions. This division created conflicts between the interests of individuals and in the common interests of society as a whole. It created the domination of class over class. All struggles within the state, the struggle between democracy, aristocracy, and monarchy, the fight for suffrage and other rights were only the illusionary forms in which the real struggle between the classes found expression.

Every class which aspires to domination must first win political control. To do this it must interpret its interests as being representative of the interests of society at large. Since it always faces a class, the revolutionary class appeals for support, not as a class, but as the representative of society as a whole. The liberals do not admit that their phrases are actually nothing more than the idealistic expression of the concrete interests of the bourgeoisie. The class which controls the nation's material resources dominates the instruments of intellectual production as well. The ideas which predominate in each successive epoch are therefore merely the reflex of material conditions as they exist in that epoch. Just so the form of government is always the expression of the jointly practical and idealistic interests of a specific class. The more developed capitalism becomes and the stronger the influence of the state on property forms, the more does the last pretense of a state, independent of bourgeois society, disappear.

According to the *German Ideology* the earliest important type of the division of function was that which divided city from country and brought about the inflexible division between material and intellectual effort. In his book on *The Condition of the Working Class in England* Engels had already pointed out that an isolated agrarian population which had no contact with the rest of humanity, developed "labouring machines," not human beings. To Engels it seemed that this rigid division must of necessity be overcome. Only so could the coincident separation between capital and land, which in his eye was the cause of all capitalist development, be eliminated.

To destroy this separation, however, private property itself would have to be abolished. In an as yet sketchy review of the history of economic development in the civilized world, the two authors of *German Ideology* tried to prove that all progress moves towards the destruction of private ownership. It was the victory of the city over the land, of large industry over more primitive industrial forms, that created the same basic relationship between the classes of society in different lands.

It destroyed, too, specific national characteristics. While

the bourgeoisie still has separate national interests, there arises the modern proletariat, a class with identical interests in all nations. With no peculiar national interests to enforce against the ruling class, because it has rid itself of the old world and is hostile to it, it is the standard-bearer of that revolution which will put an end to all classes and to all class-rule. This revolution of the proletariat will transform human dependence on economic forces into deliberate control and conscious mastery of these forces. It will be a communist revolution because this division of functions can be abolished only by social co-operation and because the individual will have an equal chance to develop his capabilities in all directions only after this division has been removed. Only in a communist state will the free development of the individual be no mere phrase. The workers themselves will have to abolish that which was heretofore fundamental to their own existence and fundamental to the existence of the state: the wage system.

Beyond that they will have to abolish the state, since it is inconceivable in its present form without class-rule. Then and later Engels always held firmly that the state, "this temporary contrivance," is incompatible with a communist society and would, therefore, disappear. This great change, the *German Ideology* contends, can come only through revolution, since no ruling class will willingly relinquish its power and since the rising class becomes capable of creating a new social order only in the course of a revolution.

Communism differs from all previous movements in that it overturns the foundations of all previous conditions of production and distribution. For the class-movement of the proletariat, it is not a hindrance that the great industries are unequally developed in the different countries and within the same country. The backward nations are subject to the influence of the more advanced. They are caught in the network of world trade and dragged into the international competitive struggle. Within each land the industrial workers sweep the other elements of the population before them the more irresistibly since those workers who are not employed in the large industries are condemned by the rise of large-scale production to accept a diminishing standard of living. The authors object to the identification of proletariat and pauperism. Pauperism is the condition of a proletariat ruined by and incapable of resistance against the pressure of the bourgeoisie, while a revolutionary proletariat which understands its condition and is determined to change it is a forward- and upward-striving force, a class with a revolutionary mission which changes with the external circumstances that surround it.

In *German Ideology* Marx and Engels put themselves forward as the leaders of a German communist party. This is the first we hear of it. So far they were its only members, with perhaps two or three other intellectuals. They had as yet no working-class supporters. Despite this they maintained that the program of the new party was not to embody the opinions of a few secretaries, but to be the product of the real day-to-day struggle of a class which was now mustering its strength for political conflict. The utopias of Fourier and Cabet might have been well enough suited to the undeveloped consciousness of the early proletariat. Weitling adapted French ideas to the narrow outlook of the German artisan. But if a theoretical writer wished to help the proletarian cause, he was bound to record the actual conditions in which the workers lived. Every day in Germany the opposition between the propertied class and the poor was being more sharply defined. Marx and Engels expressed their indignation that the " true socialists " — a small group of idealist disciples of Feuerbach — should blur this clear-cut line with phrases like " the Human Species " and " Mankind," instead of ruthlessly proclaiming the complete opposition of communism to the existing world-order.

Now, how were Marx and Engels to explain the new communist doctrine to its proper audience, the German workers?

For this task they needed the help of the numerous German journeymen who were spending the usual years abroad to complete their training. Many of these belonged to the revolutionary League of the Just. The League gravely distrusted all intellectuals, and Engels saw that his and Marx's next task was to overcome its distrust. It was also necessary to win over the French and English workers to the new conception of history and the new policy which was based on it. These workers were to be reached through their leaders. Engels knew some of them in England; he now sought similar friendships in France.

Now that Engels had worked out (with Marx) a firm theoretical basis for the revolutionization of society, he considered as enemies of communism all who thought the proletariat could be emancipated by any other path than the one he had discovered. In Germany there were two rivals to the new communism: Weitling's artisan communism, and philosophical socialism ("true socialism"), whose protagonist was Karl Grün.[1] Both these movements had a considerable following among the German journeymen who met from time to time in Paris. Paris was still the chief centre for all communist activities; and in those years when the bourgeois monarchy was tottering to its fall, there were always new socialist creeds arising, to find more or less support. Engels had treated " true socialism " with a mixture of contempt and derision, ever since he had become convinced that only the class-war could emancipate mankind. If anyone thought — with or without Christian prejudices — that universal love could regenerate humanity, Engels looked on him as a sentimental reactionary. If such a man tried to attain influence over the masses, Engels considered him a dangerous windbag. If such a false apostle called his vapid enthusiasm " communism," Engels held it absolutely necessary to attack

[1] Karl Grün (1817–87), German journalist and writer on historical subjects. Through Feuerbach he came to his conception of socialism, which was a mixture of Feuerbach and Proudhon and was sharply condemned by Marx and Engels in their *German Ideology* and in the *Communist Manifesto*.

a movement which would dissipate the revolutionary energy of the workers.

At the beginning of 1845 a student called Kriege had presented himself at Engels's house with an introduction from Feuerbach and had been sent on by Engels to Marx. From Brussels this crazy fanatic journeyed to New York, eager to preach his gospel in the New World. There, with money supplied by rich Americans, he founded a journal which he himself declared to be a continuation of Babeuf's *People's Tribune,* but which was in fact only a poor copy of " true socialism." Marx and Engels had long meant to disassociate themselves from this movement. They now determined that their " party " must secede from it at once.

But who were the members of their " party "? The steps which Guizot had taken against the German radical writers living in Paris had made Belgium the chief meeting-place for German communists. Marx was the first arrival, and gradually almost all the leaders of the movement gathered round him. Besides Engels and Hess, there was Weitling, who was no longer in agreement with the German labour leaders in London. There were also Seiler and Weydemeyer, and Wilhelm Wolff, who had seen the inside of so many Prussian fortresses; Georg Weerth,[1] and Freiligrath.[2] With the addition of a few intelligent working men, the whole group might amount to twenty people.

Engels had always done full justice to the historical importance of Weitling's thought. But soon after he came to Belgium Marx and Engels had to admit that no profitable collaboration with him was possible. He had neither philosophical training nor historical sense; he was no longer open

---

[1] Georg Weerth (1822–56), German poet and satirist, with strong socialist leanings, imitator of Heine, countryman and friend of Engels.

[2] Ferdinand Freiligrath (1810–76), noted German poet, author (1848–9) of the most powerful revolutionary lyrics in the German language. During his exile as director of a German bank in London, he severed his contacts with the revolutionary cause. This had a cooling effect on his friendship for Marx and Engels. Later he returned to Germany, where he sang the praises of his Fatherland's achievements against the French in 1870.

to new ideas; he was quite given up to his own barren and cranky theories. Also, he was filled with distrust of the two young intellectuals who would not recognize him as the appointed leader of German proletarian communism; he held them to be nothing but " cunning intriguers " who " blackened " all those whom they thought to be dangerous rivals. He could not realize that these presumptuous youths believed the realization of communism must be preceded by a bourgeois revolution, that they despised secret propaganda, and that they defined all emotion as " dust in the eyes." On the other hand, Engels saw in Weitling only a " big man," full of his own conceit, who carried in his pocket the recipe for establishing heaven on earth and who suffered under the delusion that every man's intention was to steal it from him. Between such men a break was inevitable. It came in May 1846, at a party conference, when Marx and Engels moved that a pamphlet against Kriege's activities should be circulated. Their motion was carried despite Weitling's opposition. This reverse, and the poverty which crushed him, drove him to fury. He saw that his part in the German working-class movement was over, and decided to join Kriege in America.

Hess had not attended the council in which Kriege was outlawed, but later he criticized the severity of the decision. Marx and Engels felt that any wavering was dangerous, and a coolness appeared in their relations with Hess. Engels attached no importance to reconciliation with him, although he owed him a great deal. He showed Hess that he was being put on the shelf — and in so doing made sure of Hess's hatred.

As we have seen, Engels had always chafed at the fact that his and his friend's " sole strength " lay in theory. Now that Weitling's star was waning among the German workers abroad, Engels saw that the time had come to convert them to the new doctrine. He determined to press on with all his force. There was little time to lose. Grün, who had advised Proudhon on German philosophy after Marx left Paris, was trying to win the allegiance of the German proletarians living there. Since Marx was officially exiled from France, Engels decided in August 1846 to go and live in the French capital. However, the tailors and cabinet-makers and leather-workers whom Grün was trying to convert had nothing in common with the proletarian type on whom Engels counted for the realization of his ideals. Paris was the headquarters of fashion and of the arts and crafts; most of the German workers had come there to better their position in the trade and then to return home, become worthy master-craftsmen, marry, and have apprentices of their own. Engels's mind was still full of the conditions he had seen in Lancashire, so that he at first under-estimated the difficulties which confronted him. They arose, of course, from the fact that handicrafts were still paramount in Germany. His speeches to the German workers in Paris were based on the more highly developed conditions of England; they had therefore little attraction for the Germans, since it was still possible for them to attain economic independence and a life of comparative happiness. They were bound to look with more favour on Grün's theories of human felicity, the universal harmony of interests, and so forth. Still, Engels did at first make every possible effort to convert them.

Grün had lauded to the skies the co-operative schemes which Proudhon had recently developed in his *Contradictions in Economics*. And then Engels appeared and derisively asked them whether they really hoped to buy up France and the whole world with their savings. This " plan for world liberation " which promised to be the " philosophers' stone " was discussed for three evenings. At first Engels had the whole group against him. He preached the necessity of armed revolution and accused Grün and Proudhon of fostering an anti-proletarian and petty-bourgeois ideal. The opposition which met him, and the many attacks on communism which he heard, infuriated him: he proposed that a vote should be taken to decide whether they met as communists or as a debating society. If they met as communists, attacks on communism should be discontinued. If not, he need not waste any more time upon them. Grün's supporters were horrified. They explained that they met " to further the good of humanity " and were not biased doctrinaires. Before they could make up their minds about communism, they must be told exactly what were its aims. Engels thereupon gave them " a clear and simple definition." " I defined," he says, " the aims of communism thus :

" 1. To achieve the interests of the proletariat in opposition to those of the bourgeois;
" 2. To accomplish this through the abolition of private property, and the substitution of common ownership;
" 3. To recognize violent democratic revolution as the only means of accomplishing these ends."

On the third evening Engels succeeded in convincing the majority of his listeners. He expected to be their recognized leader thenceforth. But Grün did not intend to leave the field to the newcomer without some resistance.

In January 1847 a young composer called Stephan Born, who later played an important part in the German workers' movement during the revolution, visited Engels and soon became his aptest pupil. They quarrelled later, and Born in his *Memoirs* drew a caricature of his former friend as " the rich young bourgeois " who never hit it off with working men. Engels was in fact not a demagogue. His honesty and the natural pride of one who was the son of an old family, unaccustomed to dissembling, prevented him from fawning on men of inferior education and character. He was irritated by the backwardness of the artisans, and he may have let them feel his superiority more clearly than was prudent. Yet that was not bourgeois arrogance, but the inexperience of youth.

Engels had another purpose in going to Paris — he wished to establish closer relations with the leaders of the French workers' movement. Another means to this end was a Communist Correspondence Committee, which Marx and Engels now created. (This body was the earliest Communist International; its English branch was the Fraternal Democrats.) The French must now be won over. Engels found it hard to convince them that his efforts were backed by valuable and powerful confederates. It was obviously impossible to convert Proudhon. Cabet also turned his back. And it was impossible to establish any connexion with the *Réforme* group. Louis Blanc could not imagine a human being without religion; when Engels expounded his point of view, Blanc replied: " So your religion is atheism! " Engels was in constant collision with the national arrogance which breathed in every word uttered by this French state-socialist.

Even if Engels's successes were not great, he was very happy in the life and movement of Paris, which he praised as " the heart and head of the world." He admired the Parisians for combining the power of enjoyment with that of action. None of all the great men he met made a stronger impression on him than Heinrich Heine. The time was long past when he had worshipped Börne, the tyrannical spouse of liberty, as opposed to Heine, her peevish lover. He was now full of sympathy for the poet of the revolutionary " Weavers' Song " (which he had translated and abridged for the English workers), for the prophet who foretold the approach of the revolution, and for the satirist who could jest so brilliantly about the rotten state of " the dear old country." And his sympathy was divided between admiration for the man of genius and compassion for the sufferer. " It is absolutely horrible," he lamented to Marx in September 1846, " to see such a fine fellow dying piecemeal." He thought it one of Heine's worst symptoms that when he visited him Heine spoke kindly of his acquaintances: that was a sad change!

Engels and Marx were now compelled to struggle for the soul of the German proletariat against the efforts of " true

socialism " and of handicraft-communism. It was the eve of
a revolution, and the revolution depended on the masses. But
the masses now supported bourgeois democracy, which was
sweeping through Germany like an avalanche. What attitude
they should adopt to it could best be seen if they first turned
their gaze on the common enemy, Reaction. Since the
weavers' revolt of 1844 the reactionary press had never
ceased to tell the proletariat that they received more sympathy from the feudal landowners than from their natural
enemies, the liberal employers. Engels and Marx opposed
this attitude in a joint manifesto, which appeared in the
Deutsch-Brüsseler Zeitung on September 12th, 1847. They
always referred to this manifesto later when they saw some
danger that the Prussian government might enlist the workers against the liberal bourgeoisie. The proletariat, they said,
does not ask what the bourgeois *want* to do, but what they
must do. " It asks whether the present situation — bureaucratic rule — or the bourgeois rule for which the liberals are
striving will offer it more opportunity of obtaining its own
ends." The German proletariat can see from England,
France, and America that the supremacy of the bourgeois
would give the masses new weapons for the struggle against
the bourgeoisie itself; and also a new position: that of a recognized party. Their manifesto was directed against the al-
lurements of the church as well as those of the existing state.
Had Christian social principles ever prevented Christianity
from justifying slavery in ancient times, from praising serfdom in the Middle Ages, or from defending (somewhat rue-
fully, no doubt) the oppression of the proletariat in modern
times? Did these principles not explain away every vile oppression either as the just punishment for original or later
sin or as the trial which the Lord in his wisdom inflicted upon
his redeemed? Engels and Marx asserted that it was useless
for the monarchy to try to tempt the people once more. The
people would insist on its rights — universal suffrage, freedom of the press, the rights of assembly and combination,

and other equally unpleasant demands. When it had obtained them, it would use them to deprive the monarchy of its power at the first opportunity.

As they approached the hour of reckoning with the forces of conservatism, Engels and Marx felt it vital to establish their position with regard to bourgeois democracy. They were bound to show why it could never realize the aims of the proletariat, however revolutionary it might at first sight appear. But they had also to make it absolutely clear that they felt the democrats to be their closest allies in the approaching revolution. Engels found occasion to drive home this point in answer to a democratic attack on himself and his friend. Its author was the boorish bourgeois republican Karl Heinzen (who, from 1870, carried on in the United States an active newspaper campaign against socialism) ; it appeared in the *Deutsch-Brüsseler Zeitung,* which was at that time the platform of Marx and Engels. Engels replied early in October 1847, by a direct contradiction. Heinzen had said, and Engels now denied, that the desperate state of Germany was due not to general conditions but to the princes — that is, to certain individuals. Engels added that Heinzen could never hope to divert the hatred of the bondman for his overlord, and of the worker for his employer, against the princes and potentates. Heinzen's opinions were, he said, a gallimaufry of provincial, sentimental utopianisms. In all party matters the communists considered themselves to be democrats. They knew that in all civilized countries democracy would inevitably lead to the rule of the proletariat, and the rule of the proletariat was the necessary preliminary to all communist measures. But until democracy had conquered, the differences between democrat and communist were purely abstract and could be discussed without hindering common action.

When the Combined Diet was summoned, Engels in a frenzy of excitement hailed the act as the beginning of a new era. In the *Northern Star* of March 6th, 1847, he asserted

Ich und Mein Haus, Wir wollen dem HERRN dienen.

Extra Beilage zur Deutschen Brüsseler Zeitung (vom 6 Mai 1847.) Se vend séparément au prix de 40 c.ᵗˢ Rue Botanique Nᵒ 33 à Bruxelles,

Zur froh... meiner Siegel... freund, in... au bureau du Journal... Friedrich Crueger.

ENGELS'S CARTOON OF THE OPENING OF THE
PRUSSIAN DIET:

*Friedrich Wilhelm IV Saying: " I and My House, We Wish to Serve
the Lord."*

that Prussian history was repeating the events of 1789. Financial stringency was compelling the government against its will to summon the Estates, and that was the prelude to the revolution. The liberal majority would not ratify the loan unless their most important demands were granted. Until the bourgeoisie had captured the state, the working classes must fight its battles as though they were their own. But when the old powers had been overthrown, then the struggle between bourgeois and proletariat would begin.

In his speech from the throne on the 11th of April, the King said with great pathos: " We and Our House intend to serve the Lord." Engels, overcome with angry contempt, seized his pencil and caricatured the scene in the White Hall. Marx reproduced the drawing in the *Deutsch-Brüsseler Zeitung* of May 6th. In March Engels had begun a pamphlet on the government of Prussia, which he gave to Marx " to keep or throw away " as he wished. It never appeared, but a sketch of it was found among his papers after his death. In it Engels gave reasons for his opinion that in the approaching German revolution only the middle class could take the lead successfully.

Engels knew well that the rising wave of revolution would not overwhelm Germany alone. Political excitement was increasing everywhere, and the *Deutsch-Brüsseler Zeitung* became more and more willing to print the views of Marx and Engels as political passions rose higher. Engels took the chance and in fiery phrases expounded the conditions of other countries throughout Europe, where popular feeling had broken loose or was tugging at its chains.

CHAPTER VIII

THE *COMMUNIST MANIFESTO*

ॐ

Throughout central Europe there was now a violent political ferment. Its violence was increased by repeated bad harvests, by a dreadful economic depression, and by the widespread poverty which ensued. In 1847 there were bread riots in many countries. The horizon was dark with the clouds of revolution. Everywhere in Europe the forces of democracy knew that it was time to unite; national and international unity was indispensable; the future of the whole movement depended upon it. And, as the proletariat awoke to class-consciousness, its leaders also felt the need of unity. Since the middle forties both movements — democratic and proletarian — had been growing steadily, and Engels had played a prominent part in both. Now if the leaders of German democracy wished to achieve any success, they were compelled to act from beyond the frontiers. But their propaganda from Switzerland, France, and Belgium was frequently countered by the German government, who procured their deportation from these countries. Only England was safe from the forces of Continental reaction. But here, too, there were difficulties. The insularity of the English and their ignorance of Continental affairs made it hard for the German exiles to attain a real sympathy with their political sympathizers in England.

Engels seems to have played a part in the foundation of Harney's association, the Fraternal Democrats, in 1845. The moving force in that innovation was a very active German association in London, the Workers' Education Association. It was closely connected with the secret League of the Just: both the Association and the League were headed by Karl Schapper, Heinrich Bauer, and Joseph Moll. They had tried to make Engels a member of the League of the Just in 1843, but he had been repelled by their crude philosophy of " natural rights." Yet since they were long-tried revolutionaries and convinced communists, he did not break off his friendship with them, and he was glad of it later. When he visited London in summer 1845, he found them ready to become the English representatives of the Communist Correspondence Committee. Like Engels, they had all been dazzled by the struggles of the industrial proletariat of Britain; and they had come to see the insufficiency of Cabet's and Weitling's interpretation of social and economic conditions as applied to England. Engels's work *The Condition of the Working Class* was the first to give them a satisfactory explanation of the social transformation for which the machine was responsible. The new insight which they owed to that book was increased by the circulars which Marx sent from Brussels to the London committee. Soon they were convinced that they must no longer struggle to establish a utopian system, but must rather " play a conscious part " in the social changes which were proceeding under their eyes. The circulars which they sent out in 1846 and 1847 were proof of their abandonment of " system-peddling " and their growing desire to unite all the forces of communism in one organization. They had already been sorely disappointed by Weitling's visit. They were not less disappointed by their talk with Cabet in 1847. The countless revolutionary intrigues which they had fostered since 1830 aimed at something greater than his ideals — to found a communist colony in America on the eve of a new European rising!

Even before Cabet's visit, the central executive of the League of the Just had resolved that Moll should visit Marx in Brussels and Engels in Paris to ask for their assistance in the reorganization of the League and the reconstruction of its policy. But it had not been easy for the executive to get the approval of the majority of the Leaguers for this decision, and the wording of Moll's mandate clearly shows their deep-rooted distrust of intellectuals. Moll explained to Marx and Engels that the League was convinced of the general truth of their beliefs and had determined to abandon the underground policy to which they objected. It now envisaged a complete reorganization. If the two friends wished to take part in that reorganization, they must accept Moll's proposal: they must become members of the League and change the Communist Correspondence Committee into a section of it. Only by accepting these terms would they be permitted to attend the congress at which the new proposals would be discussed. They could not form a new society themselves, and the only existing society was the League of the Just. They had for long sought to grasp the hand of the German proletariat — now that it was outstretched, would they refuse to take it?

Marx and Engels gladly became members of the League. The decisive congress was fixed for June 1847. Engels held it to be vitally important that he should attend as a delegate from the German community in Paris. He managed to do so because Stephan Born was in the chair when his name was discussed and called for the noes without asking for the ayes.

Marx had no money and could not make the journey, so that it was left for Engels to win the first real victory for their common cause. After long and heated discussions he took the lead in making the League an openly propagandist association. One of his most vital proposals was that the new statutes should break with the whole tradition of " decisions from above." A secret society was bound to be dictatorially ruled by a central committee, but in a public association the officials must be elected by the whole membership. The League of the Just now became the Communist League. Its principal task was stated in Engels's words to be the " overthrow of the bourgeoisie, the rule of the proletariat, the abolition of the old bourgeois society based on class-conflicts, and the establishment of a new society without classes and without private property."

According to the new principles of the League, its statutes and program were distributed to its several branches for discussion. On the agenda of the congress the future program appeared as a " communist creed." Schapper and his friends would gladly have undertaken to compose it, but they saw that their grasp of theory was inadequate for the task. They decided to make a first draft and submit it to their " friends on the Continent " and to incorporate any amendments which they suggested, before publishing it. They announced this in a solitary issue of a *Kommunistische Zeitschrift* in September 1847. How powerfully Engels could influence the minds of those who were ready to hear him is shown by an appeal which was also printed; many sentences of it might have come from his own pen. The Fraternal Democrats had borrowed the motto of the League of the Just: " All men are brothers." The *Kommunistische Zeitschrift* offered a new motto: " Workers of the World, Unite." The new war-cry was not a direct contradiction of the old; but there is a deep historical significance in the fact that the Communist League substituted, for a general assertion of brotherhood, the defiant rallying-cry of the proletariat.

From London, Engels went to Brussels. There, until October, he represented Marx in the democratic movement. That movement had greatly increased its strength during 1847, although the majority of its new members were not Belgians. An international democratic association was founded, on the model of the Fraternal Democrats; and here Engels was successful in preventing the editor of the *Deutsch-Brüsseler Zeitung* from keeping Marx out. (The editor was Bornstedt, a shady character who had once been an officer in the Prussian Guard and could not bear to see himself used as a tool by the communists.) The new association was keenly interested in the welfare of the working classes and their international unity. These ideals were even more exclusively the principles of the German Workers' Education Association, founded under the influence of Engels. "This at least is certain," he wrote to Marx on the 30th of September 1847: "you, and I after you, are the recognized representatives of the German democrats in Brussels."

If an agitator is to achieve lasting results, he must speak as the representative of a body of opinion. Even important men attain little if they speak merely for themselves. Engels must have realized this during his first visit to Paris. At his second he found that the doors at which he knocked were more easily opened. French socialism still refused to have anything to do with political struggles. Therefore he could look for allies in the coming battle only among the state-socialists connected with the *Réforme*. These men, like Marx and Engels, held that it was necessary to obtain political power before attempting any social transformation. Engels was ready to work with any democratic movement; he could not refuse to associate himself with this party in France, although he despised Louis Blanc's belief in the magical power of "organization." He attempted, therefore, to link himself with the left wing of French democracy, as closely as he had done with the Chartists. He had learned from experience; he presented himself to Blanc as "the official delegate of the German democrats in London, Brussels, and on the Rhine" and "the agent of the Chartist movement." He did not find it hard to come to an agreement with the "little sultan" on the tasks of the coming revolution, for he concealed his contempt for Blanc's theories. Speaking for Harney, he asked Flocon, the editor of the *Réforme,* and member of the French government in 1848, why it paid no attention to the *Northern Star*. Flocon told him that none of the editorial board knew English; whereupon Engels volunteered to write a weekly report on conditions in Germany and England for the paper. "If this works," he wrote to Marx, "we shall have won the whole party in four weeks."

The second congress of the Communist League, which was to complete the work of the first, was fixed for the 30th of November 1847. Schapper's and Moll's sketch of a " creed " had been discussed by some branches of the League, and others had debated its contents without actually seeing it. The Paris branch took as a basis for discussion an " amended creed " written by Moses Hess, but the criticisms of it offered by Engels were so deadly that he was asked to undertake a new version. This time he was elected as a delegate without dispute. The second congress fulfilled all the hopes of Engels and Marx. They were officially requested to put the party program into its final form. We must pay special attention to the way in which this famous document was composed. In great haste, just before his journey to London, Engels jotted down the " creed " which the Paris branch had asked him to compose. He objected to the term " creed," and he decided that the question-and-answer form which was usual in such programs was unfitting for a document which " must contain some history." Accordingly, on the 24th of November, he proposed to Marx to call " the thing " by the name of " Communist Manifesto " — a name which had been made familiar to French political literature by the *Manifesto of Equality* of 1796.

A few days before he met Marx in Ostend, he wrote to him that his own draft was " nothing but narrative, and desperately badly put together, in a frightful hurry." In the same letter he warns Marx: " Think the creed over a bit " — which shows that he did not expect Marx to produce a version of his own. Unfortunately, Marx's letters to Engels during these weeks are lost; they would have been illuminating.

How did the *Communist Manifesto* finally take shape? In later life Engels used to say that both Marx and he had produced drafts independently, and that the definitive version had been made after that. Engels condemned his own sketch as badly put together even while he was working on it. But the *Manifesto* itself gains its power by the colossal urgency of its message. Its style is highly wrought and shows that it was not rapidly conceived and written, but that its authors — conscious of their historical mission — intended to make their work perfect before it left their hands. The book is intended for advanced readers. Engels had been compelled to respect the journeymen in Paris whom he represented; this fact tied his hands in the early " creed." But Marx was addressing a more modern audience, the Workers' Education Association of Brussels. And as soon as Engels could cast off the bonds which hampered him, he also refused to adapt the *Manifesto* to the mentality of a backward section of the proletariat. The first sketch could presuppose no historical or economic background in its readers, whereas the language of the *Manifesto* shows that its authors did not belong to the working classes. In " the Principles " are expressed the real needs and hopes of the proletarian: the *Manifesto* unfolds a terrific panorama of past, present, and future; it deploys, with the power of genius, a vast mass of facts, reduced to form by laborious thought. " The Principles " had been confined to questions and answers. The *Manifesto* teaches, prophesies, inspires, converts.

In its definitive form the *Manifesto* bears the stamp of Marx's genius: he had a genius for coining phrases of wide significance and suggestiveness, and in the *Manifesto* we can see him guiding words like molten metal into the mould of his thought. But although it was chiefly Marx who coined the gold, Engels had not been behind him in collecting the ore. There is in the *Communist Manifesto* scarcely one thought which cannot be found in the manuscript (then unpublished) of *German Ideology*. If that work had found a publisher, it would have anticipated the *Manifesto* in all its accounts of the history and tendencies of economic life, the origins and future task of the modern proletariat, the function of the class-war, the shrinkage in the functions of the state, and the inevitability of the communist revolution.

Apart from the difference in form, there is little variation between the *Manifesto* and Engels's earlier sketch. The lesson of both documents is the same : that the age of capitalism, free competition, and bourgeois rule is bound to change into an age of communism, consciously directed community of ownership, and proletarian rule, owing to the forces inherent in the means of production. Both books examine, with penetrating insight, the development of large-scale industry in the Continental states of western and central Europe; in both books those tendencies are signalized as primary factors in the future political developments of these states. Both books greatly under-estimate the powers of survival possessed by the older types of organization and by the corresponding forms of government. In discussing the steps to be taken to realize communism after the victory of democracy, the *Manifesto* goes further than the sketch by demanding the expropriation of the land without expressly asserting that expropriation must be gradual and partially accompanied by compensation. And the *Manifesto* recommends the abolition of the right of inheritance, while Engels's sketch merely proposes to restrict it. If we used the methods of classical scholarship to discover what part Engels bore in writing the *Communist Manifesto,* we should gain little. He always spoke of it with great modesty. We on the other hand should do well to remind ourselves that he anticipated Marx in understanding modern capitalism, in defining the position of the proletariat in opposition to it, in attempting to synthetize German philosophy and English political economy, in accepting communism as his own creed, and in demanding and assisting the international unification of all communists.

The *Manifesto* was completed in January 1848. On the 25th of January, the central executive in London sent Marx an ultimatum demanding its delivery on the 1st of February on pain of " further measures." It was printed in London and sent out to the branches of the League a few days before the outbreak of the February revolution. It had no appreciable influence on the movements of 1848–9. It was never on sale, and few read it apart from some hundred members of the Communist League. But posterity sees in it a document of incalculable importance. It was published on the eve of a revolution inspired by liberal and national ideals — that is, by political ideals. But it called the workers of every civilized country to fight for common interests which had nothing to do with nationality. In the name of the first militant international organization of their class it preached the subordination of national ideals to the future solidarity of the workers of the world. At the moment when political and national conflicts were everywhere coming to a head, the *Manifesto* proclaimed the primacy of the class-war, both as a sociological factor and as an instrument of policy.

The *Manifesto* declared that the communists were not a special party, different from other labour parties. Marx and Engels adopted these tactics partly from regard for the Chartists, partly because they knew how tame the French socialists were and how undeveloped were social and political conditions in Germany. They demanded the conquest of power by the proletariat; but since they could not attain their aims through the approaching revolution, they declared themselves whole-heartedly on the side of democracy. Engels still believed that the rule of the bourgeois would last for only a short transitional period. He warned the bourgeois that the proletariat stood behind them everywhere, sharing their efforts and sometimes their illusions. " But you should realize it is for us that you are really working," he wrote in the *Deutsch-Brüsseler Zeitung* on January 23rd, 1848. " Fight on bravely, then, gentlemen of capital! We need your help, we even need your rule on occasions. You must clear from our path the relics of the Middle Ages and absolute monarchy. You must abolish patriarchalism, you must centralize, you must change all the more or less destitute classes into real proletarians, recruits for us. Your factories and trade connexions must lay the foundations for the liberation of the proletariat. Your reward shall be a brief time of rule. You shall dictate laws, you shall bask in the sun of your own majesty, you shall banquet in the royal halls and woo the king's daughter — but remember! the hangman's foot is on the threshold!"

CHAPTER IX

THE GERMAN REVOLUTION

∽

The February revolution in Paris alarmed the Belgian government. To prevent any such rising in Brussels they expelled many foreign revolutionaries from the country. Among others, Marx and Wilhelm Wolff were sent over the French frontier. They had wished to enter France in any case. Engels had been the last to be deported by Louis Philippe's government; but he was not molested in Brussels, because his passport had been issued by the Belgian authorities. However, he soon followed Marx to Paris. When the revolution broke out in France, and was followed by great political excitement in Germany and Italy, the Communist League decided to transfer its headquarters from London to Paris. Meanwhile the revolution had broken out in Germany also, and Marx and his confederates immediately began to work out a plan of campaign for the German communists. The seventeen demands of the German communist party were in the same tone as the *Communist Manifesto;* but they were suited to conditions in Germany, where there were not many factory-workers and a democratic victory must depend on revolutionary activities of the farmers and petty bourgeoisie. Engels had already realized what effect the peculiar social structure of Germany would have on the balance of political forces in a revolutionary situation. He understood that the nobility were still powerful, that the upper middle class was not nearly so large or so concentrated as in England and France, and that most of the workers were the dependents, not of modern industrialists, but of little master-craftsmen.

He placed little reliance on the artisans and the democratic party which represented them. Accordingly he was at first confident that the upper middle class (which was the nucleus of the constitutional or liberal party) would usurp the position which had been held by the old nobility.

This class, though temporarily the ally of the Communist League, was its natural and final enemy. And the League did not need to safeguard its interests in its plan of campaign. For the middle classes were bound to oppose the demand that Germany should be a single indivisible republic. They were even more likely to oppose the proposal to confiscate (without compensation) the large landed estates and to nationalize transport, mines, and banks. Nor could they accept a uniform salary for all officials, the restriction of the right of inheritance, and a guaranteed living-wage for all workers. The declaration which Engels helped to compose proclaimed it the common interest of all German workers, petty bourgeois, and farmers to strive for the passing of these measures. If they were carried, it announced, the millions of workers who had been exploited by a small minority would attain the powers and rights which belonged to them as the producers of all wealth.

Engels was eager to see his homeland now that it had at last risen in revolt, and to proclaim the aims of his party in a country which was free from censorship. Like him, thousands of German workers in France were burning to re-enter Germany. Marx and he felt bound to ensure that they were enabled to do so; they did not, therefore, leave France until the second half of April. But where in Germany could they influence the course of the revolution most freely? They were advised to return to their native cities, and there stand as candidates for the National Assembly of Prussia. But neither of them was a natural orator; they did not feel impelled to become the Mirabeaus of Prussia, and they were not in contact with the masses of Berlin. But they had many connexions on the Rhine, and some supporters, though few as yet. The Rhineland was politically and industrially the most highly developed district of Germany. They resolved, therefore, to start a new *Rheinische Zeitung* there; the press was free at last, and they could put forward the demands of radical democracy. They would enrol themselves in the army of democracy and at the same time disseminate among the masses the principles of their new conception of history and the inferences which they drew from it. Three years later, in the *New York Tribune,* Engels explained the situation as he had seen it when he reached Germany. He had found the upper middle class in an awkward position. If the Prussian revolution had not been carried through in the train of the revolution in France — where the proletariat was already voicing its demands for a transformation of society — the German bourgeoisie would perhaps have joined the people in the total overthrow of feudalism. But they saw that the French government was headed by men who were known to wish the abolition of religion, family life, and private property. Their revolutionary ardour was cooled, and they saved themselves from these more dangerous enemies by compromising with the monarchy.

When Marx and Engels reached Cologne, plans were already afoot for the foundation of a great democratic paper. Its sponsors disliked the idea that the communist leaders should return from abroad to deprive them of the management of a plan which was intended to be a local and provincial affair. But, as Engels says, " in twenty-four hours we had cleared the ground — Marx did most of the work; the paper was in our hands." The editor of the old *Rheinische Zeitung* of 1842 was entrusted with the new journal, on the assumption that he would make it a democratic paper, and Marx had no more scruples than Engels in accepting this condition. It was difficult to raise money for the project, since many of the capitalists to whom they appealed knew something of their social ideas and intentions. Marx collected subscriptions in Cologne, and Engels in the Wuppertal. Thence he wrote to his friends: " If a single copy of our Seventeen Points gets into this district, our cause is lost. The outlook of the bourgeois is really contemptible." He added that even the radical bourgeois considered them to be their future enemies and were careful not to help in forging a weapon to be used against themselves. Marx advised Engels to ask his father to take shares. But Friedrich Engels senior thought that even the tame *Kölnische Zeitung* was an agitator's rag. His son complained that " he would rather put a thousand pellets of shot into us than send us a thousand dollars." During his stay in Wuppertal, Engels translated the *Communist Manifesto* into English for Harney and founded a branch of the Communist League. But when the *Neue Rheinische Zeitung* made its first appearance on June 1st, he went to Cologne. The Communist League had settled there too, and Schapper and Moll offered their services for agitation among the Rhenish workers. Marx and Engels did not expect that the still undeveloped German working-class movement would greatly influence the revolution. They therefore took no active part in it except in the Rhineland and left it to Stephan Born to organize the workers elsewhere in Germany, who were of course still influenced by mediæval ideas of guild organization.

The *Neue Rheinische Zeitung* collected a brilliant staff in order " to produce the most radical, the most spirited, and the most individual journalistic enterprise of the first German revolution." Even at seventy Engels loved to recollect the pleasure he had had in his daily work on the paper, at a time when he and his confrères could see the effect produced by every word they wrote. Like a true artilleryman, he said that each article struck and burst like a shell! For the first time events within and without Germany were reviewed from the point of view of the revolutionary proletariat of all countries. As Engels himself acknowledged, the policy of the paper was under the unquestioned control of Marx. If Marx was away, Engels took his place; but Wilhelm Wolff, Weerth, Dronke, and the rest of the staff did not submit to his dictation so naturally. Marx followed and analysed every stage of the German and Prussian agitation for a constitution. Engels's special task was determined by his gift for languages and his knowledge of foreign affairs, especially in western Europe — it was to follow the course of the revolution abroad. His task was no less important than that of Marx. The two friends already knew how closely foreign policy and internal affairs are connected, and they realized that the future of the European revolution would not be determined by the efforts of one country alone.

The friends were now working in the closest collaboration. They were constantly confronted with decisions and demands admitting of no postponement, and every day gave fresh proof that they were made for each other. Marx, tortured by inhibition, admired Engels's powers: " he can work at any hour of the day or night, fed or fasting; he writes and composes with incomparable fluency." He was astonished at the rapidity with which his friend reviewed and utilized the material he found in the English, French, Belgian, Danish, Austrian, Italian, and Spanish papers. After Marx had sat over an article for a whole day without bringing it into a reasonable shape, he could listen without offence to Engels's suggestion that he was not born to be a journalist. But he was clearly a better political strategist. Engels was now and then led to see things as he wished them to be, but Marx's cool and certain judgment kept him from hasty conclusions. Engels regretted that he never had Marx's gift of sizing up the situation at a critical moment and reaching the right conclusion. Later he admitted that he had sometimes been right and Marx wrong in periods of tranquillity, but at revolutionary moments Marx's judgment was unassailable.

When the first issue of the paper appeared, the heavens had opened to smile on the German bourgeoisie. It was not yet a fortnight since the constituent assemblies had for the first time met in Frankfurt and Berlin; almost every German expected miracles from their deliberations. Germany had scarcely an inkling of the power of survival and the urge for domination which the old powers still retained, despite their momentary paralysis. When the *Neue Rheinische Zeitung* expressed some contempt for the new German parliament (which the liberal press was lauding to the skies), it lost half its stockholders immediately. The other half left the paper when it attempted to glorify the June revolution of the Parisian proletariat. Its editors did not wish to abandon their work; accordingly they decided to forgo their salaries. The petty-bourgeois democrats hoped for a federal state, but the platform of the *Neue Rheinische Zeitung* was a united republic. Accordingly it reproached the German parliament for not having shaken itself free of the past and consolidated the achievements of the revolution. Its editors were resolved not to let the turmoil of the past few months die down, for they were convinced that nothing could realize the aims of the bourgeois revolution (and *a fortiori* their own) but a decisive struggle at home coupled with a war between the revolutionary and the reactionary states throughout Europe.

To Engels was entrusted the paper's foreign policy. He made it fundamentally different from that of the liberal bourgeoisie, inasmuch as he laid the emphasis on class-struggle; from that of bourgeois democracy, inasmuch as he preferred force to the magic wand of political catchwords; from that of the Right, inasmuch as his hopes were its fears, his fears its hopes. Engels's judgments on events were based on realities, especially economic realities. He held " iron reality " to be the mistress of all " moral categories." During the Polish debate in Frankfurt he condemned Ruge's " naïve theorizing " in the words: " Theory proposes; business disposes." Like Marx, he was convinced that the League of Nations which Ruge preached would be nothing but an empty phrase while the capitalist property-system continued to exist. Originally, the *Neue Rheinische Zeitung* hoped that

Germany would impart some of its revolutionary enthusiasm to its neighbours. Much depended on the attitude adopted by the new central authority to the aspirations of the nations that bordered on Germany and Austria and were partly their subjects. Engels knew that the German people had committed many crimes against revolution. German mercenaries had taken English gold and fought against the independence of North America; German troops had shot down the French revolutionaries; in Holland, Switzerland, Hungary, and Portugal, Germans were detested as the executioners of liberty. And now in Italy too! Engels pointed out that the French had won sympathy even from their enemies, but no one loved the Germans. This, he said, was justified. Throughout their history they had been the instruments of oppression in other countries; before they could find sympathy they must show that they had really revolutionized their nature and their country.

But in the foreign policy adopted by Berlin, Vienna, and Frankfurt there was no trace of a will to recognize the independence of the other nations. When Engels heard that the Austrian Emperor's troops were bombarding Prague, he wrote that the German nation had already contributed " a bloody soldiery " to aid in the oppression of Italy and Poland and was now doing the same for Bohemia. But genuine revolutionaries could not fight in the cause of a fallen monarch. An alliance of the western powers to fight Russia — that was the international policy which the *Neue Rheinische Zeitung* most strongly recommended. In such a war the German nation would be compelled to centralize its power, and thus, Engels believed, a real and final break could be made with the ignominious past. He consoled himself for the dangers of this policy by reflecting that the war must mean the destruction of the two German monarchies — Prussia and Austria — a consummation devoutly to be wished for the sake of Germany. He held that Austria would be broken up by the internecine struggles of the various nationalities composing it, and Prussia by the split between the people and their dynastic rulers — a split which would be final if the King joined the Czar against the German people. Engels demanded that Prussia should grant to Poland not only the district along its great rivers but their estuaries too, and a large slice of the Baltic coast-line; and he reiterated this demand as long as he thought that an agrarian revolution in Poland would rouse the whole of eastern Europe. But when he was disappointed in this prediction, he acknowledged that Germany would be in a dangerous position if its " painfully weak frontier " were " completely ruined from a military point of view."

At first Engels had no doubt that the February revolution would spread to England too. His disappointment was great when the Chartist Assembly proved itself powerless, and when Wellington showed the workers' leaders that the simplest military measures were enough to nip in the bud any proletarian demonstration, however huge. With a heavy heart he acknowledged that the fall of the free-trade and high-church tyranny was not imminent. He saw that — outside Russia — the European revolution had no stronger enemy than the " unshaken counter-revolutionary rock in the sea." England's decision to side with the powers of reaction was dictated by her wish to preserve her monopoly of trade and the existing social system. The English bourgeoisie were determined as a class to oppress the bourgeoisie of Germany, France, and Italy, just as individually they oppressed the individual English proletarians. But the German revolution alarmed England — perhaps the English could no longer exploit the German markets if Germany became a united nation.

Disappointed in his hope of a revolution in England, he consoled himself by the expectation that France, true to its traditions, would once more take the lead in Europe. In June came the first news of the sanguinary struggles on the boulevards, and Engels began to hope that the bourgeoisie was fighting its last battle in that great " duel to the death between bourgeois and proletariat"! But the news grew daily worse: it became certain that the bourgeoisie had won. Many years afterwards Engels proudly told how the *Neue Rheinische Zeitung* had taken the part of the " victims of the first decisive battle waged by the proletariat." He did not at first recognize that the fighting in June was the death-blow to the European revolution. He still hoped, although he was forced to admit that in the summer of 1848 the move-ment was not taking the course he had expected. The bour-geoisie was vacillating and leaving the reactionaries time to muster their forces. And while the splits in the bourgeois ranks daily widened and the crowds in Berlin and elsewhere grew daily more and more uncontrolled, the King of Prus-sia (as we now know) was wondering whether it would not be wisest to compel " the Reds to deliver a premature attack " before " the red flag of civil war " was hoisted in Germany.

These hopes were fostered by the rising excitement in democratic circles during the critical month of September in Berlin and Frankfurt. In the middle of August, at a meeting of the Democratic Union of the Rhine Province in Cologne, Engels had given full vent to his hatred for bureaucracy and Prussianism. Now the political excitement of the province drove him to speak again. In order to smother any attempt at armed revolt the government had concentrated a strong force of troops on the Rhine. Engels and Marx did not wish to play into the hands of the reactionaries by encouraging a hopeless rising. The *Neue Rheinische Zeitung* cautioned the workers not to be drawn into a random attempt at a putsch. Everything depended on the question whether the King would bring himself to dissolve the national constituent as-sembly on his own authority. On the 13th of September a large public meeting in Cologne unanimously passed an ad-dress proposed by Engels; it called upon the national assem-bly not to yield even to bayonets if an attempt was made to dissolve it. On a proposal of Wilhelm Wolff, seconded by Engels, the meeting resolved that a Committee of Public Safety should be created to represent that part of the population of Cologne which was then without constitutional representation. Engels's address was also approved at a huge meeting which took place on the next Sunday, in a field at Worringen on the Rhine. It was attended by many from Cologne in great barges flying the red flag at their bows instead of the usual " black, red, and gold." The delegation from Düsseldorf also carried the red flag. They were led by a young man of twenty-three — Lassalle, whom Engels now met for the first time. Engels was among the speakers; they all declared themselves for a social, democratic republic. On his instigation the meeting sent an address to the Parliament at Frankfurt, promising to fight heart and soul for Germany against Prussia. Every day the excitement grew; although the *Neue Rheinische Zeitung* called the workers to wait until the counter-revolution had thrown off the mask in Berlin, it could not prevent the riots which broke out in Cologne on the 25th of September.

On the morning of the 25th, the chairmen of the Workers' Association, Schapper and Becker [1] (who, with Moll, constituted the central committee of the union of Rhenish democratic associations) were arrested. That afternoon at a meeting in the Old Market (which had been forbidden by proclamations posted on the walls) Moll demanded their release. Meanwhile the chief of police was arranging for Moll's arrest and was summoning troops. Towards evening, when Moll was again speaking in the same place, there was a rumour that the soldiers were coming. Barricades were started, but the troops did not appear, and there was no bloodshed. But the commandant of the fortress declared Cologne to be under martial law. The right of assembly was suspended, and the *Neue Rheinische Zeitung* was banned.

---

[1] Hermann Becker (1820–85), member of the Communist League, later Oberbürgermeister of Cologne and member of the Prussian House of Lords.

Every one of its editorial staff who had appeared in public was prosecuted for high treason. But revolutionaries dislike being in prison while a revolution is proceeding. Engels had to find safe hiding. His father had been deeply hurt by his son's appearance as a rebel. However, when his parents were away for a few days, young Engels seized the chance and hid in Barmen. His father got wind of his coming, and there was a painful meeting; his mother vainly warned him not to pursue a course which would in the end estrange him for ever from his family.

He now went to Brussels. But the Belgian police remembered his previous activities and sent him over the French frontier as a vagabond. He was in Paris on the 12th of October, when the *Neue Rheinische Zeitung* was allowed to resume publication. Paris was sadly changed since that spring day when he had left it with bright hopes in his heart. In a diary meant for publication on the literary page of the *Neue Rheinische Zeitung* he wrote: " Between the old Paris and the new lies the most frightful battle which the world has ever seen, a sea of blood, and fifteen thousand corpses." It would have been natural for Engels to wait in Paris until his business was cleared up and meanwhile to send to his paper reports of the struggles which preceded Louis Napoleon's election as President. But he could not bear the " dead Paris " which was preparing for the resurrection of Bonapartism. He felt that he must go somewhere else — anywhere! He decided to travel in Switzerland. " I had not much money, so I walked. And I didn't take the shortest road; no one likes to leave France." So we find Engels, healthy and cheerful, on a walking tour through the most beautiful districts of eastern France at a time when the counter-revolution was preparing its last blow in Berlin, when Hungary was breaking loose from the Habsburg domination, and the revolution was breaking out once more in Vienna. The loving care with which he describes the people and the country in his diary shows us what pleasure he took, after the storm and stress of the preceding months, in the enchanting French landscapes. He was delighted by the hospitable welcome which he received from the peasants in the district between Seine and Loire, but he was shocked to see how strong was their sense of proprietorship in the land which their fathers had won from the clergy and the nobility. In France, as in Germany, he wrote, the peasant is the "barbarian living in the midst of civilization," and his point of view is as limited as it could possibly be in the modern world. Great historical developments pass over his head; sometimes he is swept along by them, but he never understands the nature, the origin, or the direction of the wave on which he is borne.

Engels firmly believed that the future of the revolution in France, and even throughout Europe, depended on the attitude of the French peasants; accordingly he paid careful attention, as he met them day by day, to the motives which had influenced them since the fall of the bourgeois monarchy. Wherever he went, he was told that only the country-people could save France. Was it not the land that produced everything? Did the cities not live from its grain, were they not clad with its wool and flax? Who but the country-people could put things in order again? When Engels asked what they meant by all this, he discovered that they meant the election of Louis Napoleon as President. He could not but see that the nephew of the great Napoleon would certainly be elected in December. His tour in France taught him that the French peasants were the great obstacle to the victory of the French proletariat, and that nothing could permanently postpone a violent clash between the two classes.

When he left the valley of the Loire, he entered Burgundy and enjoyed "the sweetest of grapes and the loveliest of girls." His time in France was a lyric intermezzo in the mad year of 1848, and in it he sang a hymn to the wines of France. And the women! The German women might hold it against him; still, he was charmed by the slim Burgundian girls, with whom he lay in the grass, laughing and talking, and eating grapes and drinking wine.

Yet at that very time Windischgrätz was storming Vienna, and Jellachich was entering the devastated city in triumph with his Croats. How could Engels pass his time in such peaceful meditation when he knew that the cause to which he was sworn was being decided? Marx knew that his friend could cheerfully spend his time and strength and knowledge on some passing whim. Such irresponsibility was foreign to him, and he often reproached Engels in a friendly way for spoiling his efforts for mankind by dissipating his talents. Yet Engels was no less devoted to the cause than Marx; when the time demanded (as it soon did), he did not shrink from risking his life for the revolution. But he was so fundamentally modest that he never believed his presence to be an essential factor in making or hindering great events. He had excellent nerves and great mobility of character, and he was sometimes content simply to take things as they came. He never believed that he was indispensable. If he was involved in a movement, if he had taken up a task, he worked at it with astounding energy. But he was not tortured by the demon of restlessness which prevented Marx from surrendering to the gay variety of experience which this world has to offer. Marx was driven by the harsh goad of genius; Engels lived under the gentler domination of his rich humanity.

At the end of October 1848 his wanderings ceased and he reached Geneva. A letter from Marx told him that during his absence efforts had been made to break their friendship. Engels's brother-in-law Griesheim believed that he would be more docile if he thought Marx was turning away from him. But that was all labour lost. Engels soon found idleness and exile unendurable. He asked Marx to let him know exactly how matters stood for him — he said he would face ten thousand juries, but " smoking is not allowed when one is a prisoner on remand, so I shan't become one." In order to occupy his mind, Marx advised him to write articles in Berne " against the federal republic " and upon the " Hungarian sauce." An article of that kind appeared in their paper on the 13th of January 1849, by which time Engels had already resumed his post as co-editor. The examining court informed him that there was nothing against him. His flight in September had been well advised, but since then the authorities had decided that the police reports which had started proceedings against him were exaggerated.

CHAPTER X

THE ISSUE OF THE GERMAN REVOLUTION

During Engels's absence the *Neue Rheinische Zeitung* had boldly opposed the rising tide of reaction. In his review of the year 1848 Marx wrote that the shooting of the French workers in June had resulted in the triumph of the East over the West. Meanwhile the Czar was ubiquitous. But Europe would free itself again, and the steps in her emancipation would be "the overthrow of the French bourgeoisie, the triumph of the French proletariat, the emancipation of the working class in all lands." On his return Engels agreed with this "Forecast for 1849." But he had more hopes for the influence of the Hungarian revolution on Germany. In later days he criticized Kossuth, at that time dictator of Hungary, severely, but at that time he admired Hungary's dictator as "a combination of Danton and Carnot." Every day he studied the complicated campaigns of the Hungarian revolutionary war, and through them his lifelong interest in military problems was first awakened.

He could no longer hope that northern Italy would be freed by the valour of revolutionary German-Austrians, now that the Imperial armies of Austrian Slavs had won back Vienna. But what if the Austrian Slavs were to demand freedom as their price for betraying the revolution? Engels held that if a nation were so backward as to sabotage progressive peoples in the decisive hour of their struggle for freedom, that single action determined once and for all its

present and its future destiny. Hegel had ruled the Slavs
out of his consideration, asserting that they had not played
a sufficiently active part in the development of the human
spirit; he had actually described the Balkan Slavs as " scattered dregs of barbarism." Engels went further than his
teacher: he saw no future for any Slavonic people except
the Russians and the Poles. In his revolutionary fury he
would allow even the Czechs no function except that of
disappearing " in the world-wide revolutionary upheaval."
At that time Bakunin was raising the cry of a " democratic
national and social revolution," and demanding that the
brotherhood of all nations should be built upon the ruins
of the Habsburg and Romanov monarchies. But Engels said
that it was absurd to make such demands " without regard
to the historical position and social development of individual nations." In sharp contrast to Bakunin he proclaimed
the alliance of the revolutionary against the counter-revolutionary peoples. He did not accept without qualification the
right of nations to self-determination — the guiding principle of bourgeois-democratic international policy. It seemed
to him absurd to take a sentimental interest in " narrow national prejudices " when it was a question of " the existence
and free development of great nations." The Pan-Slavists
were demanding Slavonic unity; that meant to Engels
" either mere sentimentalism or the Russian knout." Con-
sistently enough, he refused to admit any attempt to cut
Germany and Hungary off from the Adriatic in order to
patch up an independent nation from the " rags and tat-
ters " of the southern Slavs. In his opinion it was not moral
categories that turned the scale; they " proved nothing
whatever." It was " facts of world-historical importance "
that mattered. The United States of America had just
robbed the Mexicans of the lately discovered Californian
gold mines. This was quite unjust — Engels admitted that.
But he approved of the annexation because the " energetic

Yankees " were better able than the " lazy Mexicans " to develop the latent forces of production and to open the Pacific
Ocean to civilization.

But during the early part of 1849 Engels did not look to
Hungary alone to revive the revolution. When Radetzki's
victory had reconquered northern Italy for the Emperor,
Engels wrote that France could not allow the Austrians to
hold Turin and Genoa. The people of Paris would rise and
would be joined by the French army. A new French revolution would rescue Hungary from the Russian forces which
menaced it and would involve the whole of Europe. The
revolutionaries would not lay down their arms until they had
avenged all the treacheries and atrocities of the last nine
months. The European situation did in fact seem once again
to justify his rosiest hopes. During recent months Engels's
political barometer had shown him two storm-centres, one
over France, the other over Hungary; it was over Germany
that they would join, if they joined at all. A general explosion throughout Europe was inevitable if only the revolutionaries could now win Germany for their cause.

The German bourgeoisie had confidently expected that
German unity would be created in Frankfurt. When their
hopes were frustrated by the opposition of the various
states, they clung to the constitution of the Reich which
Prussia, Austria, and Bavaria had rejected; it was the only
standard under which bourgeois, peasant, and worker could
still unite to save something from the rout. The *Neue
Rheinische Zeitung* had nothing but contempt for a constitution headed by Friedrich Wilhelm IV as Kaiser. But it
suited the policy of the paper to help every agitation which
intensified the revolution, aggravated conflicts, and turned
public opinion towards radicalism.

In the second half of April and the first week of May,
Marx went on an advertising tour in order to recoup the
paper's finances. Meanwhile Engels wrote the leaders on
German politics. He thought it was a hopeful sign that Ger-

many was so affected by affairs in other countries. Taking into consideration the victory of the Hungarians, the languid policy of Austria, and the rage of the Prussian people over the dissolution of the Chamber, he hoped that Frankfurt and South Germany might become the temporary nucleus of a new revolution based on Hungary — if they rose in open revolt on behalf of the German constitution. For this to happen, however, it was necessary that the German parliament should not shrink from declaring civil war and should at least prefer a united indivisible republic to the restoration of the Federal Diet. He did not credit the delegates in Frankfurt with much revolutionary energy, but he thought their attitude would change if the Hungarian hussars and the Viennese proletariat gave them a lead.

The heads of the Prussian army had taken extensive precautions to crush any armed rising on the Rhine; almost one-third of the Prussian army had been drafted into the province. Accordingly, the *Neue Rheinische Zeitung* warned its readers to avoid " disorganized rioting " and cautioned the workers of Cologne against becoming the cat's-paw of the bourgeoisie. It advised them to wait for the decision of the Rhenish town councils, which had been summoned to an extraordinary meeting by Cologne. The excitement in the province, however, increased from day to day. It reached boiling-point when the government called up the militia and thus exposed the bourgeoisie to a conflict of loyalties. The militiamen were willing to march against foreign foes, but not to be used for the repression of the movement to which all Germany looked for the defence of the new constitution. On the 5th of May the town councils of the Rhine province passed a resolution that the mobilization of the militia in these circumstances was a grave danger to the peace of the country, and that the continued existence of Prussia in its present form would be endangered if the order was not withdrawn. Simultaneously they called on the German parliament to support the resistance of the people with that unity and decision which were necessary if the armed counter-revolution was to be defeated. This revolutionary address was passed by the councillors from some thirty Rhenish towns — a fact which tended to make the petty bourgeois think that the upper middle classes sympathized with them. The upper-middle-class *Kölnische Zeitung* said that the " treacherous counter-revolution " was responsible for any blood which might be spilt, and, on the other hand, entreated the citizens not to take the law into their own hands. But how could soldiers under the colours uphold the law and simultaneously refuse to shed German blood? Engels was probably right in asserting that hostilities had been opened by the mobilization of the militiamen.

In the chief towns of the Bergisch-Märkisch industrial area the reluctance of the militia grew into an open revolt. Since March 1848 the undisputed supremacy of industrialists and clergy had ceased, even in Engels's birthplace. But it was there that the conflict first came to a head. The mobilization of the militia was the final incentive for a violent rebellion — the way had been prepared by widespread unemployment and the rising political excitement. Barricades were thrown up in Elberfeld on the 9th of May. The prison was stormed. Peace was maintained in Barmen, but from it and other places the unruly elements streamed into Elberfeld. The municipal authorities disappeared, and the administration of the town was taken over by a Committee of Public Safety headed by bourgeois democrats. Simultaneously with the news that his home town was in revolt, Engels heard that the rising in Dresden was holding its own, that there had been fighting at the barricades in Breslau, that the revolutionary movement in the Palatinate was growing, that in Baden a military rising had forced the Grand Duke to flee, and finally that the Hungarians were about to march into Austria. Since March 1848 prospects had never been brighter for the general success of the revolution. At such a moment it was imperative for Engels, despite his inevitable scruples, to try to raise the Rhineland in revolt. If this could be done, the revolution would be irresistible.

Just before throwing down his pen and joining the insurgents in Elberfeld, Engels communicated to his friends a plan of campaign. The left bank of the Rhine must support the right. Something must be done in the smaller towns, in the industrial areas, and in the country districts, to keep the garrisons busy. In the forts and larger garrison towns all unnecessary disturbances must be avoided. All available forces must be thrown into the districts on the right bank which were already in revolt, in order to spread the revolution there. And lastly the militia must be used in an attempt to organize a revolutionary army. The plan was not ill conceived; but, like all plans advanced by determined revolutionaries in such a situation, its failing was that its creator judged the willingness of the people by his own passionate sincerity. The polite middle classes and the backward proletariat could not be transformed into an army at the sound of the trumpet. The revolutionary groups had no cohesion; their energy was dissipated before the rising had even attained a unity of command. And so the rebellion on the Rhine was easily suppressed.

Engels saw that republicans and communists must enrol themselves in the great constitutional party which had developed under democratic leadership. It was difficult enough for him to put aside his real objective; it was still harder to accommodate himself to the petty-bourgeois mentality which remained philistine, even in the act of revolution. He found conditions in Elberfeld quite different from what he had supposed. True, he had not persuaded himself that the proletariat, so recently saved " from the slough of gin and cant," would be the mainstay of the movement. And yet the irresolution which confronted him was a disappointment — the deep suspicion which he encountered among the leaders of the movement was a source of amazement. He was assigned by the Committee of Public Safety to the Military

Commission which was looking after the defences of the town. The commission entrusted him with the inspection of barricades and the completion of the fortifications. He got together a company of engineers, set up cannon, and requisitioned the necessary labourers. It was on his advice that von Mirbach, a former Prussian artillery officer, was appointed commander-in-chief. On his arrival Engels was asked by the Committee of Public Safety what his intentions were. He replied that as a native of the place he regarded it as a matter of honour to be at his post on the first armed rising of the Bergisch people. He wished to confine himself to military activities and to take no part whatsoever in the political side of the movement, since he fully realized that in Elberfeld a Black-Red-and-Gold rising was the only possibility. Despite this statement by Engels, the news that he had been given a position of authority caused widespread alarm among the bourgeoisie. They feared that the "communist gang" might get control of the movement, and the result was that the Committee of Public Safety took the first opportunity to rid itself of the "young visionary" who demanded that the Civil Guard, which wished to remain neutral, should be disarmed, that its weapons should be distributed among the revolutionary workers, and that a compulsory levy should be imposed to cover the cost of the workers' maintenance. At roll-call on May 14th, the young hothead was informed that his presence was highly disturbing to the bourgeoisie and that they demanded his withdrawal. On the same day the Committee of Public Safety announced on placards: "While fully recognizing the value of the services he has hitherto rendered, we request Citizen Friedrich Engels of Barmen (recently resident in Cologne) to leave the city boundaries today, since his presence might give rise to misunderstandings of the nature of this movement." Engels, however, refused to leave until he had received the demand in writing from the committee, with the countersignature of Mirbach himself. Under pressure from all quarters, Mirbach gave his endorsement on the following day, and Engels returned to Cologne. This incident aroused considerable indignation among the armed workers, and Engels shortly published his advice to them in an article in the *Neue Rheinische Zeitung*. "This movement," he wrote, "is just the prelude to that real revolution in which the vital interests of the workers will be at stake. When that comes, you will find me at my post, and no power on earth will move me from your side."

Engels's memories of the days he spent with the heroes of the barricades were shot with flashes of his characteristic humour. His stay in Elberfeld, however, was memorable for another chain of events which made a far deeper mark upon his future life. On the morning of the only Sunday which he spent in the Wuppertal, he went as inspector of barricades to see that everything was in order on the bridge between Elberfeld and Barmen. Or perhaps he meant to stir up the workers of Barmen, who were held down by the factory-owners' Civil Guard. He was met by a deputy called Pagenstecher, who has left an account of the incident. Engels, full of gay enthusiasm and wearing a revolutionary sash, was directing the gunners on the Haspeler bridge when his father (no doubt on his way to church) met him. The painful encounter between "worthy old Engels" and his "rebel son" roused the indignation of all right-thinking folk. We know none of its details, but we can see from letters exchanged in the succeeding years that it had a dramatic climax. The memory of it was ineffaceable. Engels could never forget the gulf which then opened between his father and himself.

After the suppression of the revolt the victorious military party refused to tolerate the existence of a paper which had so loudly preached secession from Prussia. The *Neue Rheinische Zeitung* was suspended. The last issue was printed in red. In it Engels reviewed the events in Elberfeld and regretted that the armed working classes had not used their power more relentlessly for the " complete overthrow of a spineless and yet more treacherous bourgeoisie." Happily, the south-west of Germany had " become a pill which would not be easy for God's elect to digest." In German history of 1849 the place of honour was held by the soldiers of Baden and the Palatinate, who had broken " the oath which they had been compelled to swear to the enthroned crooks." The volcano of European revolution was on the eve of eruption. Soon its red lava-streams would submerge for ever the whole system of prayer and plunder. The whole infamous bourgeoisie, cowardly, corrupt, hypocritical, and arrogant, would be hurled into the blazing crater — the expiatory sacrifice of a proletariat which had at last attained wisdom and unity.

Engels did not wait in Prussia for the appearance of the red number. The warrant which followed him on the 6th of June proved that he had been wise. Instead, he went to Frankfurt with Marx, in the hope that the German parliament, when faced with a decision between the existing government and the constitution which the people demanded, would turn towards revolution. But the friends soon saw that to talk thus in Frankfurt was only ploughing the sand. Few of the delegates understood that a revolutionary assembly was lost if in such a situation it stayed on the defensive. Most of them never dreamed of summoning the army of Baden and the Palatinate to their defence. In Frankfurt, Marx and Engels found no trace of the spirit which stakes all to win all. They hoped to find it among the rebels of Baden. But as soon as they crossed the frontiers of Baden, they realized the amateurishness of the military commanders. When they reached Mannheim, they saw that the first impetus was spent and that the movement lacked vigorous direction. In Karlsruhe they offended the district committee by calling it a capital error not to have marched the revolutionary troops on Frankfurt at the outset, and by complaining that little had been done to draw the whole of Germany into the movement. In the Palatinate, just as in Baden, they found that the rising

in south-west Germany was not a serious force; its whole atmosphere was too foreign to them for any official co-operation by the little communist party to be of much avail. On
their way back from the Palatinate they were arrested by
soldiers in Hesse under suspicion of being implicated in the
revolution. They were transported to Darmstadt and thence
to Frankfurt, where they were set free. Meanwhile they had
made up their minds about their plans for the future. Marx
went to Paris, with secret authority from the Democratic
Central Committee then in the Palatinate. Engels went back
to the Palatinate, to watch developments in Germany from
this land of revolution.

Engels was a distinguished democratic refugee. As such,
he was offered many military and administrative posts in
Kaiserslautern. However, he refrained at first from taking
part in this " self-styled revolution." In order to prove his
goodwill he agreed to write for a little paper published by
the provisional government. But, as he had foreseen, his
first article discouraged those easy-going gentlemen from
making further demands on his services. In it he defended
the people of Baden and the Palatinate against the counter-
revolutionary charge of high treason. They had not rebelled,
he said, in order to support the despots in the decisive struggle yet to come between the free West and the despotic East.
If the despots of Prussia, Austria, and Bavaria could still find
soldiers who would fight under the same flag as pandours,
Bashkirs, and suchlike brigands, these mercenaries would not
be welcomed as fellow-Germans in the Palatinate. " In a few
weeks, perhaps even days, the armies of the republican West
and the slavish East will move against each other to fight
their great battle on German soil. But Germany will not be
asked for her consent, and for that we must thank our princes
and our bourgeoisie. It will not be a German war, or even a
war fought with the approval of Germany, but a war on
German soil which Germany can do nothing to prevent. We
cannot speak of German interests, German freedom, Ger-

man unity, German prosperity while the liberty and well-being of all Europe are at stake. All nationalist questions are set aside. There is only one issue at stake — will you be free or Russian? "

But what if the decisive battle between West and East never came about? What if the fires of revolution — so difficult to revive — had in France been exhausted by the struggles of June 1848? What if all Engels's hopes were to be disappointed?

In the Donnersberg inn where he stayed, his exceptional sense of humour found some compensation for the gravity of the preceding weeks. The whole Palatinate seemed to have turned into an enormous pot-house. He saw in it none of the sedate pedestrian honesty which had marked the revolution in Baden. The folk of the Palatinate were serious only between times. " Scarcely anyone believed that the Prussians were coming, but everybody was sure that if they did they would be beaten back again with the greatest of ease." The easy-going government allowed its citizens to make fun of their " potty little regulations." Thus they disarmed even so severe a critic as Engels. He did, of course, point out how much invaluable time had been lost and how much was yet to do — but always over a glass of wine in an atmosphere of friendly ease.

This idyllic situation was rudely interrupted by the Prussian invasion. Engels discovered the weakness of the local intelligence service when one day he informed them — much to their surprise — of the concentration of twenty-seven Prussian infantry battalions, nine batteries of guns, and nine regiments of cavalry between Saarbrücken and Kreuznach. He had found this important information quite by chance in a back number of the *Kölnische Zeitung*. When the Prussians did arrive, he could not resist the temptation of taking part in the war, as the representative of the *Neue Rheinische Zeitung* in the army of Baden and the Palatinate. He became A.D.C. to August von Willich. Apart from Techow, the chief of the Palatine staff, Willich seemed to Engels to be the " only one who was worth anything " among the Prussian artillery officers who had joined the rebels. Although his talents were not those of a great general, he was the ideal commander of six or seven hundred volunteers. He was " a steady, cold-blooded, clever, far-sighted fighting man, but off the battlefield he was a rather tedious visionary, one of the ' true socialists.' " These words are from a letter of Engels to Jenny Marx. He added that after four battles he himself had found that the courage required for hand-to-hand fighting was the most ordinary quality in the world. The whistle of bullets was nothing to talk about. During the campaign, in spite of a lot of cowardice, he had not seen a dozen people behaving like cowards in the field; but he had noticed that where every man was a hero individually, the whole battalion bolted with one accord.

Engels held his post at Willich's side in the battle for the Murg line, which gave the finishing stroke to the revolt. He always remembered as a charming holiday episode the retreat through the flower-decked hills of the Black Forest. In Wolfach they heard with indignation the news that the revolutionary government was resolved to surrender Freiburg without a battle. In order to prevent this, they determined to march upon it without delay. But in Waldkirch they learned that the headquarters had already been moved to Donaueschingen. Willich and Engels in vain urged the commanders to use the survivors of the army and their considerable force of artillery in a last battle. On the 12th of July, Willich's troops, " the last of the army of Baden and the Palatinate," were forced to retire from German soil.

During the previous autumn Engels had visited Switzerland with the confident expectation of seeing his home before long. At that time the final victory of the revolutionary forces was still undecided, and he himself was less of a marked man. But even then his brother-in-law had pestered him with banal exhortations; now he again heaped unsolicited advice and reproofs upon him, instead of sending the money for which Engels had asked. " You seem to me to be behaving like a hunted dog which can find nowhere to rest. You need not tell me that this revolution does not suit your tastes. In fact, it has been of incalculable harm to the realization of your hopes. It has shown the most intelligent of us that our dear Germany is still terribly crude and undeveloped, and that any social transformation would be followed by a positively Russian terror. I understand that you cannot appeal to your father, but why will you not turn to your mother? If you had a family to worry you as I have, you would have to change your restless way of life, and in the narrow circle of your own home you would make more of this short life of ours than you ever will among a gang of cowardly and ungrateful tub-thumpers. I think you must still have the thankless idea of sacrificing yourself for the incorrigible human race — of setting yourself up as a Christ to save society and of becoming a complete egoist for this end. But you are not lost to us yet. You can still, without humiliating yourself, see to it that you do not isolate yourself completely, like a whining hypochondriac." Thus Engels was tempted by the philistines. But he felt that " the world was in travail with a new era "; he had hailed it in print at the beginning of the year. He thought it fair that each individual who had not shrunk from the act of creation should have his share of the birth-pangs. He himself shared the agony with a joyful heart, because he felt that the future was in league with him.

CHAPTER XI

REACTION AND PROSPERITY. THE BREAK WITH BOURGEOIS DEMOCRACY

In Switzerland Engels spent his time in Vevey, Lausanne, Geneva, and Berne. In Geneva he met for the first time his future disciple Wilhelm Liebknecht. Liebknecht was fascinated by Engels and astonished by the sovereign contempt which he showed for the campaign in which they had both taken part. In Vevey Engels at last got into communication with Marx, who had been greatly worried to know where he was. Marx encouraged him to write a pamphlet or a history dealing with the rising in Baden and the Palatinate. Engels began at once. Originally he meant to publish his work in pamphlet form in Switzerland, but at the end of August, when Marx told him he was expelled from France and was on the way to London to start a German paper, he determined to keep his manuscript to be published in that paper.

The work is a masterpiece of narrative prose. In vividness, scope, and accuracy of observation it is far above any other account of the campaign for the new constitution. Engels considered that the revolutionary movement of 1848 was as important in the social and political history of South Germany as the June rising in the history of France. He pointed out that the predominant class in the revolution had been the petty bourgeois, to whom its official leaders had belonged. He had now realized that the petty-bourgeois class had little power of revolutionary action: it could not show real energy unless other classes joined the movement and, where possible, took charge. If the proletariat of the towns or some of the peasants chose to do so, the most extreme wing of the petty bourgeois would join them for a time. In Baden and the Palatinate it was those classes (headed by the proletariat of the larger towns) who had driven the petty bourgeoisie to an open breach with existing authority. At first the movement had been joined by the more resolute section of the upper and middle classes. But the German bourgeoisie retreated in terror from the battlefield as soon as they saw the slightest prospect of the return of anarchy — " that is, the really decisive struggle."

Engels had foreseen the failure of the rising, and this was some consolation to him. The disaster of the 13th of June in Paris, and Görgey's refusal to march on Vienna, would have been enough (he believed) to destroy its chances of success even if it had spread to Hessen, Württemberg, and Franconia. Ever since the June fighting in Paris (he now recognized), civilized Europe had had only one choice: either the supremacy of the revolutionary proletariat or the supremacy of the classes which had been supreme before February. Compromise was no longer possible. In Germany especially, the upper bourgeoisie had shown its incapacity to rule when, in order to assert its mastery over the people, it had allowed the nobility and the bureaucracy once more to become its own masters. In demanding the new constitution the petty bourgeoisie had been attempting to stave off the final struggle by an impracticable compromise. Their defeat had clarified matters. In the future, victory would lie either with the real revolution or with a mildly constitutionalized feudal and bureaucratic monarchy. But the revolution could not be won in Germany until the proletariat had achieved its supremacy.

In the middle of August, Marx sent Engels his opinion of the prospects of the revolution in France and England. This opinion later proved to be utter nonsense, but it may have comforted Engels at the time. His optimism needed strengthening during those weeks when — after the failure of the Rhenish, Saxon, and South German rising — he saw the collapse of the Hungarian revolt, a much more powerful movement, on which he had rested boundless hopes. Marx declared that Bonapartism was compromised for ever, that public opinion in France was once more anti-reactionary, so that another revolutionary rising could be expected soon; he added that in England the free-traders and the Chartists were joining forces to oppose reactionary forces abroad through English foreign policy. Engels did not wish to believe that the revolution was about to fail; when he heard all this, he allowed himself to hope that it would be fought out by the industrial workers of the more highly developed Western countries. It was therefore no sacrifice for him to follow Marx's wishes and cross to London at once. Marx had assumed that his friend would get a " transit-permit " to London from the French embassy in Berne. But Engels decided it was pleasanter and perhaps safer to go by sea. He boarded a sailing ship at Genoa, and spent five weeks at sea. Always keen to learn, he used this " great circumnavigation " to learn something of seamanship. Among his papers there is a diary in which he recorded the changes in the position of the sun, the direction of the wind, the condition of the sea, and the coast-line.

At last he joined Marx, and from autumn 1849 till the autumn of 1850 he shared with him the double task of starting a monthly magazine, the *Neue Rheinische Zeitung, Politisch-ökonomische Revue,* and reorganizing the scattered forces of the Communist League. Their daily paper in Cologne had as its subtitle *The Organ of Democracy;* but the monthly which they ran during their exile opposed bourgeois democracy. In their prospectus they expressed the hope that their paper might soon be able to appear in Germany as a daily. It never did. Even as a monthly it could not survive the year 1850. It was their last attempt on their own to run a paper. In it Engels published a short study of the English ten-hour day, and also *The German Constitutional*

Campaign and *The German Peasant War;* the last appeared in book form afterwards. He still considered that the events of the previous two years were only the skirmishes before a final struggle which would be more complicated and take longer to decide. But he and Marx firmly believed that that struggle would be botched and useless as long as it was led by the petty bourgeoisie. He was now eager to settle accounts with the bourgeois revolutionaries: he had fought side by side with them longer than he wished. Their attitude to past and future was determined solely by their personal wishes and their subjective point of view; in opposition to this, Engels and Marx now attempted to assert the superior grasp of theory which they themselves derived from their conception of history. They held that they had penetrated the secret of historical change, and that they were thereby qualified to see the inner meaning of events as they occurred and to recognize the course which they must take.

It was not until they settled in London that they realized how strongly political events (even during the storm of the revolution) had been influenced by economic factors. They saw that the commercial crisis of 1848 was the source of the revolution of February and March, and they inferred that the state of the world markets would determine whether another outbreak was near or remote.

In the same journal Marx used the class-war in France (1848–50), and Engels the campaign for the new constitution in Germany, to demonstrate that political events were in the last resort determined and conditioned by economic causes. Engels moreover made a detailed study of the Peasant War, hoping thereby to pierce through the outward forms of political events and to reach the economic forces which are the beating heart of history. This, he thought, would enable him to throw light on the recent revolution by comparing it with the greatest revolution in the history of Germany. He still hoped that the new movement was not yet dead, and he intended to quicken men's perceptions and redouble their energy by pointing out the numerous resemblances between the old and the new revolutions. " We shall find that the classes and factions which played the traitor in 1848 and 1849 did the same in 1525, at a lower stage of their development." That is one of the leading principles in the discussion. Another is connected with the tragic fate of Thomas Münzer, radical revolutionist in the German Reformation and peasant leader in the great Peasant Rebellion. " The worst thing which can happen to the leader of an extremist party," says Engels, " is that he should be compelled to take over the government at a time when the political movement is not sufficiently developed either to maintain in power the class which he represents or to carry through those measures which the situation demands. He is then in an insoluble dilemma. For he is compelled to stand, not for his own class or party, but for the class to whose domination the political movement is at the moment suited. The man in this unhappy situation is utterly lost." We shall have to recall Engels's judgment in this matter when we reach his criticism of the policy of Lassalle and Johann Baptist von Schweitzer, a declassed intellectual aristocrat, who became leader of the party organized by Lassalle and, after the latter's death, was the first Social-Democratic deputy in the German Reichstag.

Now that the forces of reaction had recovered, the Communist League was again compelled to keep its activities in Germany secret. The members of the General Board had almost all assembled in London. They considered it to be vitally necessary that in the revolution which would shortly break out once more in Germany there should be an independent working-class party which would not again depend on the bourgeoisie. Heinrich Bauer undertook to canvass any workers', peasants', labourers', and gymnastic associations which still existed in Germany, in order to start branches of the League within them. In March 1850 Marx and Engels together drew up the program on which he was to base his operations.

In it they reminded the German proletariat that the bourgeoisie had no sooner gained control of the state than they used their power to relegate their allies, the working class, to their former depressed condition. To do this they had united with the feudal party they had conquered, and in the end they had been forced to relinquish control to them. Now the new revolution was imminent. This time the petty-bourgeois democrats would play the traitor as the liberal upper classes had done in 1848. But the democratic party was far more dangerous to the workers than the liberals had been. It included not only the small factory-owners, the tradesmen, and the master-craftsmen, but the peasants and (for the time being) the agricultural proletariat. Far from wishing to revolutionize the whole social system in the interest of the destitute classes, they wished merely to modify it in order to make it more tolerable for themselves. For this they needed a democratic constitution for both central and local government. The workers were to be kept quiet by more or less disguised charities, and their revolutionary power was to be broken by a temporary amelioration of their conditions.

But a program of that kind could not satisfy the party of the proletariat. The petty bourgeoisie wished to end the revolution quickly — but *they* must strive to make the revolution a permanent thing, lasting until all the property-owning classes had been deprived of their supremacy, until the workers had grasped the government, and until the proletariat (not only in one country, but in the chief countries of the world) was united, and controlled the main forces of production. They must not be content with redistributing private property; they must aim at abolishing it. Class-conflicts were not to be slurred over; they were to be removed. The final aim of the party was not the improvement of the existing society, but the establishment of a new society.

But what attitude were the communists to adopt towards the petty-bourgeois democracy so long as it, too, was suffering under oppression? What dealings should they have with it during the imminent revolutionary struggle — or indeed after the revolution, when the petty bourgeois would stand supreme over the old rulers and the proletariat alike? At the moment they were inviting the co-operation of the workers in the task of creating a great opposition party. But there must be — of course! — no mention of the workers' specific demands. Marx and Engels, however, maintained that the proletariat must this time refuse to play the lackey to bourgeois democracy. The workers, headed by the Communist League, must create an independent organization (both secret and public) alongside that of the official democrats. They must make every town the centre of workers' associations in which — without interference from bourgeois influences — the position of the proletariat should be discussed. For the moment the interests of both parties were united in the struggle against reaction, and, as before, a temporary alliance must automatically arise. But immediately after victory the workers must oppose the pacific attitude of the bourgeoisie. They must demand guarantees and, if necessary, extort them. They must make sure that the new democratic government should compromise itself by concessions and promises. Side by side with the official democrats, they must set up their own revolutionary workers' organizations, in the form of town councils, workers' clubs, or workers' committees. Thus the bourgeois democratic government would immediately feel that it had lost the workers' support and that it was watched and threatened by officials who were backed by the whole force of the working class.

If the workers were to offer an energetic and threatening resistance to the victorious democracy, they must be armed and organized. Steps must be taken immediately to supply the whole proletariat with arms, for the bourgeois democratic government would begin the battle against the workers as soon as it had established itself. The abolition of feudal landlordism would be the first occasion for a conflict. The petty bourgeoisie would hand over the estates of the nobility to the peasants as freehold property and thus ensure the continued existence of a proletariat on the land; the workers' party, on the other hand, must demand that feudal estates when confiscated should remain the property of the state and be worked by the agricultural proletariat as a co-operative concern, retaining all the advantages of large-scale agriculture. Again, the democrats would attempt to make the new Germany a federation of small states; the workers must demand not only one united German republic, but also the most determined concentration of power in the hands of the central authority.

The democrats would be compelled to propose certain measures, more or less socialist in tone. As long as the workers could demand no directly communist measures, they must compel the democrats to interfere with the existing order of society at as many points as possible, to disturb its equilibrium and thereby to compromise themselves. Moreover, they must attempt to concentrate all possible factors of production — transport, factories, railways, and the like — in the hands of the state. The workers must push all proposals made by the democrats to extremes, so as to transform them into direct attacks on private property. If the petty bourgeosie proposed to buy railways and factories, the workers must demand that the railways and factories should be confiscated by the state without compensation, as being the property of reactionaries. The German workers could not attain power without passing through a long period of revolutionary development. But this time they would know for certain that the new revolution would begin with the direct victory of the French proletariat and that this would accelerate their own. Still, they themselves must do most of the work, by learning to understand the interests of their class, by adhering to the independent organization of the proletarian party, and by following the battle-cry: " The Permanent Revolution ! "

When Marx and Engels sent this *Plan of Campaign against Democracy* to Germany, they still expected that the revolution would shortly break out once more — that, in fact, the proletariat of Paris would start it by rising in revolt during a European war. As late as February 1850 they were still convinced that within a few months Russia, Austria, and Prussia would attempt to use their armies for the stabilization of the old governments.

At the time when the whole Continent was torn by revolution and counter-revolution, England (as reported in the *Revue der Neuen Rheinische Zeitung*) was making the most of its prosperity. Marx and Engels did not believe it could last. They prophesied that by the end of spring 1850 (or at latest by August) the economic crisis would arrive, and with it the revolution in England. But soon all political groupings in Europe were overshadowed by an event which Engels considered more important than the February revolution — the discovery of gold in California seventeen months before. Until then commercial jealousies had prevented the cutting of the Panama canal, but now the Pacific trade could no longer be conducted round Cape Horn. The gold of California was flooding America and the Pacific coasts of Asia; it was drawing the most backward native peoples into civilization and world commerce. In ancient times Tyre, Carthage, and Alexandria had been the markets of the world. In the Middle Ages they were replaced by Genoa and Venice and later by London and Liverpool. The new world markets would be New York, San Francisco, San Juan de Nicaragua, León, Chagres, and Panama — the centre of gravity of world trade was now the southern half of the North American continent. European trade and industry must strain every nerve if they were not to decline as

Italian trade and industry had declined after the sixteenth century. If the Atlantic Ocean became a mere inland lake like the Mediterranean, nothing but social revolution would prevent England and France from falling into the industrial, commercial, and political subordination which was the present plight of Spain and Portugal. While there was still time, they must alter their technique of production and distribution to suit the demands created by modern inventions. Thus they would create new factors of production which would ensure the supremacy of European industry and thereby compensate the handicap of their geographical position.

Engels and Marx were better prophets of the distant future than of immediate events. In France the abolition of universal suffrage was not followed by revolution. The prosperity of England continued to grow. The offensive of the Holy Alliance did not materialize. By the summer of 1850 the revolutionary party in every country in Europe had been forced into the background. In Germany the forces of reaction enjoyed a new access of power, and capital (as Lassalle wrote to Marx) " like a vulgar lackey jumped up again behind the coach of the great landowners." The time had come when Engels and Marx must make an objective examination of the situation.

The more carefully they studied the economic depression which had followed the shortlived boom of 1843–5, the more plainly they saw the causal connexion between the movements of world trade and the fluctuations of politics. The Universal Exhibition which was to be held in London in 1851 seemed to Engels to be infinitely more significant than all the diplomatic and party congresses on the Continent. It displayed side by side all the productive forces of modern industry. It was an exhibition of the material produced in the midst of the decaying capitalist system, but destined for the construction of a new social order. The bourgeoisie was building its Pantheon when its glory was already on the wane. A new phase of the trade cycle had begun in 1850; if it followed the same course as that of 1843–7, a crisis would arise in 1852. The discovery of the Californian gold meant more than a mere increase in gold-production; it was also a stimulus to world capital to seek new channels. Most of the Californian gold flowed to New York. Through the growing interest in transatlantic shipping, and the cutting of the Panama Canal, New York was becoming the centre of speculation and therefore the centre of the next big slump. Even if many companies were ruined, there would still remain the shipping lines which connected Australia, New Zealand, Singapore, China, and America and which went round the world in as little as four months. Engels published these speculations in the *Revue*. Although he thought it probable that America would win the economic hegemony of the civilized world, he still believed that England was " the demiurge of the bourgeois cosmos." Even the economic crisis which produced revolutions on the Continent would (he thought) always have their causes in England.

Although he believed that the world crisis and its revolutionary sequel were not far off, he found bourgeois society at the moment so vastly prosperous that the conditions for a real revolution were lacking. He and Marx announced in the last volume of the *Revue* that " a revolution can hope for success only when the modern factors of production and bourgeois technique of production are at variance. A new revolution is possible only after a new crisis. But the revolution is just as certain to come as the crisis."

Engels produced his new theory at a New Year festival held under Harney's chairmanship in London and attended by political exiles of all nationalities. It upset them all — but he did not mind that. Doctrinaires as they were, they believed one and all that revolutions could be *made*. Now Engels and Marx openly opposed this idea, and thenceforth any connexion between them and the exiles was impossible.

Engels, despite himself, was repelled by the " dissolute

habits " of these wandering *émigrés*. The traditions of his family were too deeply rooted in him to allow him to accept the standards of Bohemia. It is true that in Antwerp, on an earlier occasion, he had introduced his friend Mary Burns to a gathering of the German colony, knowing perfectly well what reactions he would arouse. It is true that he despised bourgeois marriage so much that he did not trouble to have his relationship with her legitimized. Yet fundamentally he recognized objective authority for what it was; he respected its strength when he found it strong, and tried to undermine it if he thought necessary. But he had only contempt for the arrogance and self-importance of individuals who had lost contact with society and did not see the true nature of the drama in which they were playing their minor roles.

CHAPTER XII

LONDON AND MANCHESTER

ॐ

In London it was the adherents of the *Neue Rheinische Zeitung* and the German Workers' Education Association who first grappled with the task of providing for the political exiles. Engels was a dependable and enthusiastic worker for any cause which he adopted, and he now became secretary of the social-democratic committee for the welfare of the exiles. The committee found that its funds were steadily decreasing, while claims on its attention were increasing. It therefore rented a large house in Great Windmill Street, where the poorest exiles could find board and lodging and (when they cared) work in the neighbouring workshops. These "wretched *émigrés*" had only one wish — a speedy return to their own country — and they idolized Willich, who promised them the fulfilment of their desire. Marx and Engels fell out with them as soon as they disputed the idea that the revolution would soon break out again. There was an open breach at the meeting of the Central Board of the Communist League on the 15th of September 1850. Engels and Marx stood almost alone in their opinion. Accordingly they proposed and carried a motion that the Central Board should be transferred to Cologne. In London there were thenceforward two sects in the communist party. The larger was led by Willich and Schapper; it was for action at all costs, even for a putsch. The smaller was composed of Engels and Marx and their closest friends.

In the same way Marx and Engels found themselves at odds with the bourgeois democratic exiles, both those from

Germany and those from other countries, as soon as they openly declared that they did not believe a recurrence of the revolution to be imminent. All the others believed what they wanted to believe, and clung to the hope that the hour of the new revolution would soon strike, when they would be called back to their beloved homes; they grotesquely exaggerated the importance of their past achievements in Germany and of their speeches and writings in London. They were taken seriously by no one except each other. Engels could not realize that there was a constant supply of fools whose highest ambition it was to enter some sort of government on the morrow of the first successful rising — only to be discredited and discarded a month later.

Among the exiles a wide variety of opinion existed; they were divided by national peculiarities and personal ambitions. But they were almost all united by their faith in the magic of democracy and their conviction that the coming second revolution would finally realize it in their native countries. Even the socialist minority who demanded some reform of the class-structure were still prepared (with the exception of Marx's tiny group) to form a united front with the other exiles for the attainment of democracy as the first stage on the way to socialism. But the authors of the *Communist Manifesto* would have nothing of this. Refusing to play the conspiratorial game, they remained to all appearances quite inactive, and sneered at the hustle and bustle of *émigré* life. The others could neither understand nor forgive this, and soon Engels and Marx were the most unpopular of all the exiles. They heartily reciprocated the hatred of the " lousy democrats." Bourgeois democracy was the enemy they must fight tomorrow. They cared not to bridge, but rather to emphasize, the gap between it and them. Viewing these crowds of empty theorists with contempt, they lost all chance of influencing them. If the two friends could find no intellectual understanding among their own sympathizers,

how much less could they expect it from men who believed
that when the existing governments fell, there would be no
more war and no more change, for " the Golden Age of the
European Republic " would dawn!

The various national groups had many reasons to desire
a united front. We must examine them and their activities
with some care, for Engels saw a great deal of many of
them and usually quarrelled with them. Among the Italian,
Hungarian, and French exiles were men whose names were
famous throughout Europe. The German contingent had
no one to compare with Mazzini, Kossuth, Ledru-Rollin, or
Louis Blanc. But Gottfried Kinkel and Arnold Ruge (who
had both been on the staff of a university) felt themselves
equal to Mazzini and the others.

Kinkel, the poetaster-don, who had been liberated from
Spandau prison by Karl Schurz in such romantic circumstances, was the " lion of the season." Engels despised him
for an " empty, affected, mincing ape." Kinkel himself could
not forgive Marx and Engels for dismissing him contemptuously in their *Revue* as a " harmless fellow " while he was
in prison. Engels had fought side by side with Ruge in the
Young Hegelian movement, but had quarrelled with " the
prosperous bourgeois " when he ceased philosophizing and
became a confessed communist. He had little love for the
dons who headed the German *émigrés,* and even less for the
ex-officers from Prussia who were trying to take the centre
of the stage. Ever since the rising in Baden, he had resolved
to make a systematic study of strategy and tactics as soon as
circumstances allowed. The " military gang " were to find
that " at least one of the civilians " was a match for them on
their own ground. We already know Engels's opinion of
Willich. Willich thought himself to be the leader whom
Germany needed. The nucleus of his " army of the future "
was the " men of principle " who sat at his feet in Great
Windmill Street and in German beer-shops. After the success

of the great stroke on which he affected to be brooding night and day, he would rise on the shoulders of his "army" to be dictator of Germany.

Engels and Marx were alienated from the other *émigrés*, just as from the Germans, by their belief in the power of economic factors rather than the human will. This deeply offended Mazzini, the apostle of action, who preached that republicanism and nationalism should go hand in hand. A mystic through and through, he expected salvation only from "the holy Act," and found it demoralizing merely to deny the existing order. With his creed of national self-determination (he was nicknamed by Marx "the Pope of the Democratic Church *in partibus*"), he founded a European Central Committee with Ruge, Ledru-Rollin, and others, with the idea that the *émigrés* who believed in action (that is, almost everyone but Marx and Engels) should co-operate at first even if they had to part company later. Engels knew that his own instincts impelled him to action. For that very reason he felt himself justified in describing Mazzini's "abstract passion for revolution" as pointless and silly.

However, he had more respect for Mazzini's disinterested nature than for the disgustingly theatrical Kossuth. He soon lost his admiration for the ex-dictator when he studied the history of the Hungarian revolution and read through the mass of "revelations" which participants in it began to publish. Both Mazzini and Kossuth declared that socialism was not a problem which concerned their countries. They thought it deserved no attention from them, since they were interested only in immediate action. Engels and Marx, on the other hand, could pay no heed to any but a social revolution affecting all Europe. At the end of November 1851 Marx explained in a Chartist paper that the English, French, and Germans held revolution to mean the crusade of labour against capital; they did not care to lower themselves to the intellectual and social level of a half-civilized race like the Magyars. Engels agreed with him.

The leadership of the French colony was disputed by Louis Blanc (christened by Marx " the Napoleon of socialism ") and Ledru-Rollin, who had been destined by himself and his numerous supporters to be the President of the Republic. Ledru-Rollin's pamphlet on the impending collapse of England had not increased Engels's admiration for him and his bourgeois democracy. Engels felt that a wide gulf also separated him from Blanc. He had always despised Blanc's belief in France as the messiah of civilization and revolution, and he was shocked that he should try so earnestly to gain support among the bourgeois *émigrés*. The only French exiles with whom Engels and Marx felt themselves in sympathy were the adherents of Auguste Blanqui, French revolutionist and follower of the Jacobin tradition. With them and Harney and Willich they planned a " World League of Revolutionary Socialists " before the Communist League broke up. Its aim was to be " the overthrow of the privileged classes under the dictatorship of the proletariat, through the permanent maintenance of the revolution until the achievement of the communist state." The plan was still-born. But we must notice it because it was the first occasion on which Engels proclaimed the necessity of the dictatorship of the proletariat " in order to attain the final form of the organization of human society." Since the revolution Marx and he had realized that if communism was to be attained, the dictatorship of the proletariat was a necessary preliminary stage. How elastic this notion was, however, we can see from the fact that in his article on the English Ten-Hour Bill Engels still declared that universal suffrage was sufficient to give the working class supreme power in England.

We have a record of a political discussion which took place shortly before the schism in the Communist League. The parties were Marx, Engels, and Techow, who had once been a lieutenant in the Prussian army and whose support they would have been glad to enlist. Techow criticized them heavily afterwards, but the account he then gave to his comrade-in-arms Schimmelpfenig showed how deeply he felt Marx's intellectual superiority. The opponents of Marx and Engels may have been justified in calling their party " entirely powerless," but in this conversation they described themselves as the leaders of a party " in the larger historical sense " — a party which would sooner or later number millions of supporters. It is impressive to read how confidently they told Techow that the strength of their party was the " strength of historical necessity," and that for themselves they were content to remain always in opposition. That this was Engels's real belief we can see from the contentment with which he discussed with Marx the schism in the Communist League: he said that, now they were deserted by everyone, they could forswear popularity as they always had done unconfessedly and could renounce any claims to an official position in a party.

Engels's relatives in Barmen were constantly troubled about his future, now that he had ruined his hopes of returning home. His sister Marie (whose advice he was least unwilling to hear) wrote him a letter with his father's knowledge and at his mother's prompting. She said that they thought it was dangerous for him to stay so long in the meeting-place of all the political exiles; it would be better for him to go somewhere else, where the " hobby " to which he had cheerfully devoted so many years might find less to encourage it. She continued: " The thought has come to us that you may perhaps wish to enter business seriously for the time being, in order to ensure yourself an income; you might drop it as soon as your party has a reasonable chance of success and resume your work for the party." When Friedrich got this letter he had already determined to return to his early career in business. In order to make it harder for him to resume revolutionary activities his father tried to find him a post in Calcutta. Engels would rather have gone to New York, for Marx would have gone with him. But, to his great satisfaction, both of these plans fell through. The final solution was the nearest to hand. There was no personal representative of the Engels family in the Manchester mill, which was directed only by the two brothers Ermen; and Friedrich had already learned the business. A secret report of the Prussian police, dated September 1850, said that he consented to go to Manchester because otherwise he " would have no visible means of support." But a man who wrote so fluently as Engels had no need to worry about his future. If he did, nevertheless, return to " filthy business," it was for the sake of Marx; for Engels felt that Marx's great talents were of vital importance to the future of the cause. Marx could not fend for himself and his family; he must not become a victim of *émigré* life. To avoid that, Engels was glad to go back to the office desk.

Engels's father, with his severe principles, had a repugnance for any appearance of dallying with a business into which he himself poured all his energy. But his attitude quickly changed when Friedrich went of his own free will to Manchester in November 1850 and immediately sent him a series of admirable reports on the business. In January 1851 he wrote to his son: " I can imagine that staying in Manchester cannot be very agreeable to you, but in the present peculiar conditions it would be an excellent thing for us in the business." In February the old man confirmed his request. " You please me very much indeed by your proposal to stay in Manchester, where you are in your right place; you are the best possible representative of my interests." Father and son had not met since the tragic Sunday on the Haspeler bridge. They met again in Manchester that June, and Frau Engels awaited the result with anxiety. She was delighted that Ermen had invited her husband to stay, and she wrote to Friedrich: " I think it is probably better that you should not be together all the time, for you can't always be talking business, and it is better to avoid politics, on which you have such different views." Her anxiety was justified.

Young Engels was much upset by the praises which his father lavished on the country which had branded him a traitor. In high dudgeon he wrote to Marx: "A few words and a nasty look were enough to shut him up, but they were also enough to make us as frigid as ever to one another." But he accepted the situation and added: "If there were not a practical side to the matter — namely, my income — I should rather have this cool business relationship than any nonsense about affection."

Father and son soon reached a business arrangement. Friedrich wished to be the Manchester representative of the German firm, without depending on the English firm for his salary. This was the only way of ensuring free time for the work which was his real concern. He achieved his purpose. "On the whole, I am pleased with the result of my interview with the old man," he told Marx; "he needs me here for at least three years, and I have entered into no permanent obligations — I am not even bound for these three years. No conditions about my writing, or about staying here if a revolution breaks out. He seems to have no thought of a revolution — the people are so reliable nowadays! But he agreed to give me from the beginning, as representation and entertainment expenses, about two hundred pounds a year."

Marx had just lost his youngest son — he called him "a victim of bourgeois misery." Frau Marx, in her answer to Engels's letter of sympathy, freely expressed her pleasure that Friedrich was on the way to becoming "a great cotton magnate." She knew that Marx would never find a more sympathetic or self-sacrificing friend, and that there was no one whose help would embarrass him less.

Engels vastly under-estimated the greatness and duration of his sacrifice in returning after eight years to a business career. He hoped, indeed, that the next economic crisis would give him back his liberty, and he still believed that the crisis would soon arrive. His book on the condition of the working

THE MILL IN MANCHESTER

(The section to the right of the photo is the original mill of Ermen and Engels)

class in England had shown that he did not like Manchester. How difficult he found it to acclimatize himself we see from the letters which he wrote during his first months in the great manufacturing city, "which," as he put it, "changes water into stinking slops." In December 1850 Harney replied: " I am not surprised at your strong words about Manchester. It is a damned filthy hole. I would rather be hanged in London than die a natural death in Manchester."

But Lancashire and its smoking chimneys (if judged by the real content of his life) proved to be valuable subject-matter for Engels's analysis. It was the centre of the free-trade movement, and also of the political struggles of the British working class. Engels as yet did not suspect that the failure of Chartism to respond to the call of the Continental revolution was the prelude to its final decline. A short time before, he had discussed the Ten Hours' Bill in Harney's *Democratic Review* and written as optimistically as ever. He said that a judgment of the Privy Council had " in effect " repealed the bill. But the workers who had, with Lord Ashley and Oastler, supported the bill would henceforth ally themselves with the Chartists and with them strive for the political domination of the proletariat. The bill could be revived only through universal suffrage. The approaching commercial crisis would be the signal to move, and it would be accompanied by great upheavals on the Continent.

The Chartist movement had greatly changed during Engels's absence. O'Connor's star was declining, and younger leaders were rising — Harney and Ernest Jones. Engels had for years been working with Harney to establish contacts between the socialists of the more highly developed countries. He could trust Harney as an agitator, but he had not succeeded in converting him to the economic interpretation of history. He considered it to be his special mission to convert the leaders of the English workers' party to the theory of class-warfare. The moment was auspicious.

O'Connor was absorbed in petty-bourgeois schemes of land-settlement; to parry them it was necessary for Harney and Jones to emphasize the class-struggle. Jones, who had been to school in Berlin, knew German and found it easier than the other English labour leaders to understand Engels and Marx. The friends held themselves responsible for his adherence to the idea of class-conflict when most of the workers had long come to terms with the bourgeoisie. Jones had long been striving to transfuse the new blood of class-conflict into the corpse of Chartism. He was as unwilling as Engels to acknowledge that the workers were so vastly benefited by the high development of trade and industry that they must inevitably attribute rising wages and falling prices to the victory of free trade and the growing power of trade unions and co-operatives.

At a conference held at Manchester in 1852 the Chartists attempted to reform the party. At Jones's instigation they repudiated any kind of alliance with O'Brien's National Reform League and demanded that the inborn class-hatred of the workers must continue to be the basis of their propaganda. Engels was so delighted with this resolution that he became a contributor to Jones's *Notes to the People*. The Chartist leaders were much courted by the democratic and socialist *émigrés*. As Engels and Marx became more and more isolated, they became more and more embittered by the way in which Harney accepted contributions from their enemies to the broadsheets which he published. Harney also appeared at the meetings arranged by the exiles and thus got them publicity in the London press. It was natural enough for Marx to tell Engels that Harney had two souls — one his own, and the other made by Engels; one the natural man, the other a sort of strait jacket.

While Engels was in London, the tiny communist group could point to the *Revue* as an earnest that their cause was not abandoned. But when the paper ceased publication, Engels decided that in these inauspicious times more good

would be done if they (or at least Marx) preached their
message " in solid books." In February 1851 he wrote to
Marx: " What happens to all the gibble-gabble of the whole
émigré gang if you answer them with a work on economics ? "
This letter shows with wonderful clarity what Engels felt
when he was forced to retire from active politics. " Now at
last, at long last, we have another opportunity to show that
we do not need the support of any party in any country, and
that our position is entirely independent of any such nonsense. From now on we are responsible for ourselves alone.
When the time comes and our fine friends need us, we can
dictate our own terms. Until then we shall at least enjoy
peace — and, of course, a certain isolation." When his sister
Marie asked what he wanted on his thirty-second birthday,
he replied in a tone of resignation: " *Ma chère sœur,* I've
dispensed with wishes for some time now, for nothing comes
of them. Anyhow, I've really no talent for wishing. If I ever
catch myself in a weak moment wishing for something, it is
always something I cannot have. So it is better for me to
give up the habit altogether. As you see, when I get on to
this subject, I moralize like Solomon the preacher, and so
the less we say about it, the better it will be." Only his
favourite sister caught the gentle melancholy through which
his humour glinted. " For the last six months," he went on,
" I have had no opportunity for exercising my well-known
talent and composing a lobster salad. *Quelle horreur!* It
makes a chap quite sour ! " But Engels was in no danger of
that. As soon as he realized that he might be settled in Manchester for years, he sent for his books and began to " swot "
(as he called it) in his spare time. The communist general
staff should not be unprepared in the coming revolution. In
view of the " colossal importance " he attached to the " military branch " in such an event, he now turned his chief attention to the study of military science.

He was still convinced that the next economic crisis would
bring with it the world revolution. In his office he read a

constant stream of information about the cotton market —
crop estimates and price movements. Chained as he was in
Manchester, he welcomed anything that looked like a storm
signal. At the end of July 1851 he informed Marx that the
bottom was going to fall out of the market. At the same
time there were reports of growing political unrest, and
Engels expressed great delight that the struggles on the
Continent next spring would coincide with an economic crisis.
But neither Marx nor Engels had the same blind faith in
the year 1852 as the other political exiles. To the French,
especially, it was an article of faith that after the election
of the president and deputies on the 2nd of May, they
would be able to return immediately to Paris. Engels had
too low an opinion of Louis Napoleon to be able to foretell
his momentous *coup d'état*. He was more inclined to predict
that General Cavaignac[1] would become President. And he
still expected in the near future a war between the Holy
Alliance and a France in which the revolutionary tradition
was revived. A paper which he wrote in the autumn of
1851 (but discarded after the *coup d'état* in December)
dealt with the military aspects of such a war. We can see here
with what enthusiasm he had tackled those problems which
were to be his own particular preserve in his lifelong partnership with Marx. In July he had asked Weydemeyer for
an exhaustive bibliography of the subject, saying that self-
education was always stupid, " and if one does not study
systematically, one never gets anywhere." With the same
intensity which he had displayed in action during the campaign of 1848–9 he now steeped himself in the wars of the
French Revolution and of Napoleon I. He read every book
which he could find on the subject.

---

[1] Eugène Cavaignac (1802–57), French general, War Minister in May 1848.
As military dictator he ordered the bloody suppression of the June uprising of
the Paris proletariat and afterwards was made head of the Executive Committee.
He was defeated in the presidential elections of December 1848, in which he
was the Republican candidate against Louis Napoleon, later Emperor Napoleon III.

The *coup d'état* carried through by the "most insignifi-
cant man in the world" seemed to Engels to be "only a
travesty of the 18th Brumaire" which could not possibly
last. Still, he admitted to Marx, "it was a desperate business!" A week later he added: "What is clear about the
whole transaction is this — the Reds have ratted, completely
ratted"; and, next day, "the proletariat did not unite and
fight, because it knew its own utter impotence." Engels was
now perfectly clear "that if the revolutionary party in a
revolutionary period begins to let turning-points pass without raising its voice or if it does interfere without winning
its point, you can fairly safely count it out of action for a
considerable time."

We have few details of Engels's daily life in Manchester.
He lived with Mary Burns, but for the sake of respecta-
bility he was forced to have rooms in the city, where he could
entertain business acquaintances and put up his father and
brother when they visited England. In his spare time he
studied military science, also physiology and ethnology and
sometimes languages — especially Russian. He wrote to
Marx that one of them at least should know the language,
history, literature, and social institutions of the nations
which were to be their opponents in the next international
struggle. Occasionally his letters complain about his loneliness and boredom. When his father revisited Manchester in
1852, it was arranged that Friedrich should be general
manager of the office. For this he was to receive a hundred
pounds a year and also five per cent of the profits in the first
four years, seven and a half per cent in the second four, and
ten per cent in the next four. But it was still many years before his income was large enough to ensure Marx a liveli-
hood. Although Jenny Marx was a woman of exceptional
character and intellect, she was a Prussian aristocrat and
never learned to run a household as simply as her husband's
meagre finances demanded. It must have been a welcome
stroke of good luck for Marx when in 1851 the *New York*

Tribune (through its managing editor, C. A. Dana) offered him the post of regular correspondent. But Marx had not sufficient command of English as yet and was therefore forced to depend on Engels to write, or at least translate, his articles. For years, indeed, countless articles which were sent under his name were actually written by his friend. The New York editors never knew that a Manchester industrialist was a contributor to their paper.

When his first articles were due, Marx was deep in his economic studies and asked Engels if he would write a series for him on the German revolution. Accordingly between August 1851 and October 1852 he wrote a group of articles called *Germany, Revolution and Counter-Revolution,* which were issued in book form after his death by Kautsky, with Marx's name on the titlepage.

Weitling and Heinzen were agitating among the German Americans against Marx and Engels. Ever since Willich, and for a time even Kinkel, had begun to associate with them, Engels and Marx felt bound to pay special attention to the activities of the democrats who had emigrated to the U.S.A. They themselves could now publish nothing in German in Europe or America, while their democratic opponents commanded a press of increasing scope and influence. They were therefore only too willing to use Weydemeyer as their agent in America. At that time Engels expected his father to allow him to make a personal visit to the cotton plantations in America. But the "unprecedented time" of prosperity continued, and the people in Barmen thought such a trip unnecessary. Weydemeyer's earnest attempts to convert the German workers in New England to revolutionary communism met with no success. He started a paper called *Die Revolution,* which disappeared after two months; the attempt to keep it going as a monthly miscarried also. Engels had assured him of his co-operation, but his first contributions were lost on the way, and two later articles came too late. One of them discussed the probability of a

French invasion of the British Isles—a common topic in England since the *coup d'état.*

Engels assumed that the danger of war had been increased by Bonaparte's seizure of power. He imagined, like everyone else, that the new Emperor would take as his motto: *"Revenge for Waterloo."* The agitation in England over the inadequacy of the country's armaments Engels took to be a deliberate exaggeration. But he thought it necessary that nothing should be left undone to hinder the success of the detestable Emperor of the French. The English ports, in his opinion, were so poorly fortified that the French could gain temporary victories against single towns, and if fortune favoured them they might even destroy Woolwich. But no more. If there was a real war, it depended entirely on the speed of the French attack and the number of troops which they could land in England. To begin with, the French fleet would be fully occupied in guarding the transports. Later it would have difficulty in keeping the English navy from breaking the lines of communication across the Channel. Time would be the ally of the English. At first England would not have a large force under arms, but the people had plenty of spirit and were excellent military material. Only if the French could transport four hundred thousand men to England would it be at all possible for them to conquer and hold the country as far as the Clyde.

Engels had still better reason for desiring a British victory. He considered it highly important for the development of Europe that the conflict between bourgeoisie and proletariat (most strongly marked in England) should be fought out to the end. Although England had hindered the victorious revolutions on the Continent in 1793 and 1848, he saw in its development more of the stuff of revolution than in that of all the Continental nations put together. The great French Revolution had run aground on the conquest of Europe; but England was revolutionizing society with the steam engine, conquering the markets of the world, and thus preparing the ground for the final battle between industrial capitalists and industrial workers. The undermining of old institutions and the revolutionizing of society through large-scale industry were proceeding here quite undisturbed by the ephemeral victories of revolution or counter-revolution on the Continent. The development of England was not conditioned by political disturbances on the Continent, but by world-wide economic crises. If she were subjugated by Napoleon's cohorts, it would only postpone the decisive conflict between bourgeoisie and industrial proletariat. It was only in England that industry had reached such dimensions that it had become the supreme national interest. All the other sections of the people were grouping themselves round the industrial bourgeoisie and proletariat. That was why England, if anywhere, would be the place where the industrial proletariat could seize political power and where industrial technique was so far advanced that a complete social revolution and the abolition of the class-conflict were real possibilities. Engels reckoned that the scare about national defencelessness would smash the doctrinaire pacifism with which free-trade liberalism had infected not only the bourgeoisie but also whole sections of the workers. " The industrial bourgeoisie will at length break away from all the humbug of peace congresses and peace societies, which has exposed them to such well-deserved contempt and has hindered their political progress as well as the whole development of England. If it did come to a war, the well-known irony of history might bring it about that Mr. Cobden and Mr. Bright (in their double capacity as members of the Peace Society and future ministers of the crown) would have to carry on a stubborn war, perhaps with the whole continent of Europe."

We still possess the manuscript of another article intended for Weydemeyer. It deals with the extension of the suffrage proposed by Russell's liberal ministry. Engels was only interested to know how much of their political power

FRIEDRICH ENGELS, THE MANCHESTER
MILL-OWNER

the landlords would be prepared to sacrifice to the upper bourgeoisie. He still saw the bourgeoisie as the really revolutionary class, the proletariat as a figure like Destiny in the ancient tragedies, which entered the stage only at great turning-points of the action.

At this time the King of Prussia chose to raise the spectre of communism in order to deprive the German bourgeoisie of the last traces of independent initiative. For the job of concocting a conspiracy and having it punished in the courts he found ready to hand a certain Stieber, a "priceless fellow," chief of the Berlin police. In May 1851 the tailor Nothjung (an emissary of the Communist League) was arrested in Leipzig. The papers in his possession disclosed to the authorities the existence of the Central Board in Cologne. Among other things found on Nothjung was a copy of Engels's and Marx's *Plan of Campaign against Democracy,* written in March 1850. The authorities published this in the papers; and Engels regarded their action as "tremendously valuable" propaganda for communism. When the Central Board was arrested in Cologne, Marx advised Engels to hand his papers over for safety to Mary Burns or to a reliable employee of his firm. Engels followed the course of the preliminary trial with the keenest interest. But Marx and he took no really active part until the opportunity came for a duel between their little party and the political police of Prussia. Marx's tireless energy made the stratagems of Stieber and his agents more and more transparent; there was good ground for hoping that the Prussian reactionaries might suffer an open and serious defeat at their hands. Engels procured many "business addresses" and "much commercial correspondence" and thus helped his friends to smuggle in the documents which their lawyers required. He had the best command of English, and so it was that he also wrote the final, and often the first, version of the letters which Marx, Wilhelm Wolff, Freiligrath, and he sent to the papers and sometimes succeeded in getting published. They described it as the duty of the British press to give publicity to every piece of illegality or oppression in those countries where the freedom of the press had been abolished. At the end of 1852 an account published in five London papers focused the public attention on the revelations of forgery and perjury by Prussian police which were to be made at the trial in Cologne by the counsel for the defence.

When Marx had succeeded in proving the forgery of the protocol and the mendacity of some of Stieber's evidence, Engels expected that the Rhenish jury would be forced by public opinion to acquit the prisoners. When they were found guilty, he explained in the *New York Tribune* that the verdict was due to government threats that an acquittal would mean the abolition of the jury system. Marx wrote his *Revelations of the Communist Trial* without waiting for Engels's help, since haste was necessary; and for the same reason the Communist League was dissolved before word had been received from Manchester. The grounds given for the dissolution were (1) that contact with the Continent had ceased since the arrest of the Central Board, and (2) that a propagandist league of that kind was not adapted to the changed conditions.

This was the end, as Engels said, of the first period of the German communist workers' movement. Thenceforth he felt free of all party loyalties. He could now devote to study all the time which he could spare from business, and he knew that by doing so he was best forwarding the work to which his life was devoted.

CHAPTER XIII

THE CRIMEAN WAR AND THE ECONOMIC DEPRESSION

Ever since the establishment of the Second Empire, Engels had been sure that Europe's political apathy could not last much longer. The nations which had not yet secured their independence were about to make a bid for liberty. They would be freed, he expected, not by Napoleon III, the sworn enemy of democracy and socialism, but by a great war which would arouse and encourage the forces of revolution. When the struggle for power in the East began, he viewed it as the mine whose explosion would clear the road. As the conflict grew sharper, he turned to an exhaustive study of the important geographical, ethnological, economic, political, and military problems which were involved. By doing this he was enabled to perform a great service for Marx, for he wrote many of Marx's articles on current affairs in the *New York Tribune* and later in the Breslau *Neue Oder-Zeitung*. International politics, military strategy, and commercial policy are so closely interconnected that Engels could unite his study of these subjects in a comprehensive whole. It is only since the vast mass of his occasional writings has been of recent years collected and sifted that it has become clear that in these spheres Engels was one of the most original thinkers of the latter half of the nineteenth century.

Since 1848 he had devoted constant attention to the future of the Slav peoples. We remember that he had " damned little sympathy " for the western and southern Slav minorities. He still thought that the Czechs were a " vanishing nation." Germany and Hungary should never allow them to become an independent state. Would the United States allow the German farmers of Pennsylvania to make themselves independent? As for the mélange of races and nationalities which inhabited the Balkans, Engels had long felt the Turkish suzerainty less vicious than any other solution. He saw quite clearly the factors which retarded the creation of a great Serbian nation. It was only by slow degrees that he came to see the Balkan peninsula as the natural inheritance of the southern Slavs, and that they were — if not a fully developed nation — at least the powerful and comparatively civilized nucleus of one. The Serbs, the Bulgarians, the Bosnian Christians, and the Slav peasants of Thrace and Macedonia had more points of spiritual contact with Russia, but that would not hinder the appearance of a progressive anti-Russian party among them as soon as they had achieved their independence. Engels differed from the English liberals in thinking that Turkey had lost all its vitality. In March 1853 he wrote in the *New York Tribune* that Turkey was like the corpse of a dead horse, which, despite all congresses and protocols, would perfume its whole neighbourhood as long as the *status quo* was maintained. He prophesied correctly that if Turkey broke up, Egypt would come into the power of England; and he was also right in recognizing Asia Minor to be the focus of any strength which the Turkish nation possessed.

Marx and Engels had at first believed that war would break out between the Holy Alliance and a Jacobin France. If it had, the situation would have been easier for them than what actually happened — a conflict between the Czar and the French usurper, with Britain backing France. Could Engels wish for the victory of a coalition to which Louis Bonaparte belonged? He clung to the hope that the longer the impending war lasted and the more countries it involved, the more certain would it be to release the forces of revolution. The diplomats, as usual, struggled to maintain the *status quo;* and Engels had nothing but contempt for their efforts. In an article for the *New York Tribune* on *The Future of Turkey in Europe,* he said: " Trace the course of history. See how the wheels pass without pity over the ruins of mighty empires, and crush whole generations under their weight. Consider the revolutions of the modern age, an age in which steam and wind, electricity and printing, artillery and gold mines produce more transformations and revolutions in one year than once took place in a century. If you consider these things, you will not shrink from asking ' what is to become of European Turkey? ' simply because the correct answer may involve a European war." In opposition to Cobden, who was fascinated by the great new market provided by Russia, Engels in the *New York Tribune* declared that England was vitally interested in keeping Russia away from the Dardanelles and the Bosporus. There were only two powers left in Europe, he wrote, Russia with its philosophy of absolutism, and Revolution with its philosophy of democracy. A violent clash between these powers had long been threatened. If it came, England would be compelled to ally herself with revolutionary democracy. No English government could allow Russia an outlet from the Black Sea, a concession which would make Russia predominant in the whole of Europe.

In November 1853 Turkey declared war on Russia; two months later an Anglo-French fleet sailed into the Bosporus. Engels now declared that a general European war was inevitable. He was mistakenly convinced that Prussia and Austria would ally themselves with Russia. In October 1854 in the *New York Tribune* he wrote that if " a regular war on the large scale broke out, its battles would only be the prelude to other more decisive battles — the battles of the nations of Europe against the European despots in their temporary security."

At the outbreak of war Engels would have liked to give up his business and to earn a living from his knowledge of military science. It seemed possible that Marx might get him a permanent post on the Liberal *Daily News*. But although his first article, on the fortifications of Kronstadt, was already in press, the negotiations broke down owing to intrigues, which Marx attributed to the Russians Herzen and Golovin. Later *The Times* refused his article on *Napoleon as a Lieutenant of Artillery*. Engels found no outlet for his knowledge except Marx's letters to the *New York Tribune*. His views made a considerable stir in America: Dana, the editor, wrote to Marx that many readers attributed them to General Winfield Scott, who ran for the presidency in 1853. In 1859 his pamphlet *Po and Rhine* was believed in Germany to be the work of a Prussian general.

As is generally known, the decisive factors in the Crimean War were these: the abstention of Prussia and Austria prevented great land-battles; and Austria's mobilization kept considerable numbers of Russian troops away from the front as well as deceiving France and England into postponing the final struggle. Engels described it as an unpardonable error that they let five months pass before coming to grips with Russia. He studied with expert attention the organization and tactical qualities of the various sections of the combatant armies. Even in 1892 he described the Crimean War as a hopeless struggle between a nation with a primitive technique of production and others which were up to date. But he also subjected to devastating criticism the organization of the English army, which allowed the English troops to suffer from the lack of food, clothing, shelter, and medical attention. In England public opinion passionately debated the causes of this scandal; Engels attached the chief blame to the ruling oligarchy.

The war was distinguished by the importance of siegeworks and fortifications. Superficial observers came to the conclusion that the art of war had slipped back from the age of Napoleon to the age of Frederick the Great. " Nothing could be less like the truth," wrote Engels in the *New York*

Tribune after the fall of Sebastopol. Fortifications and rings of forts were, he said, nothing but valuable positions, which it might or might not be prudent to defend to the last. The Russians had been right to consider the safety of their army more important than the abstract value of a fortress. The Entente had a difficult task ahead if their intention was, so long as Prussia and Austria remained neutral, to conquer the Crimea and then attack Russia. He realized that the western powers had good reasons for wishing the war to end. Their *ultima ratio* was to wage a " war of principle " of more or less revolutionary character, in alliance with Germany, the Hungarians, the Poles, and the Italians. The *ultima ratio* of Russia was an appeal to Pan-Slavism. But both Nicholas and Napoleon were prepared only to use such tactics with their revolutionary flavour as a last resort. Engels was absolutely correct in his estimate of the situation. If peace had not come in March 1856, the war could have been continued (as Napoleon III told Queen Victoria) only by calling to arms the peoples who were striving for independence. Engels would have been pleased if affairs had taken that turn, but the monarchs shrank from the dangers it involved.

Engels's sympathy for Pan-Slavism had not been increased when it concentrated the weight of its agitation in Russia. He hated the whole movement, but he had to back it once more when a pro-Russian feeling appeared among the editors of the *Tribune*. This sentiment was fostered by a former Polish revolutionary, Count Adam Gurowski. He chose his arguments carefully, to appeal to the Republican Party, whose chief organ the paper was; he pointed out that Russia and America were two young empires, with common needs which differed from those of western Europe. Their large population and enormous size compelled them to develop their own industry as soon as possible. For this purpose they must raise tariff walls and free the slaves and the serfs. Turkey, where slavery continued, had no chance of continued existence; if it was to develop its commercial and industrial facilities it would be best for it to fall under the control of Russia, which was naturally a democratic nation. Engels and Marx did not at first know the name of the man who was working so successfully against them within the paper whose attitude to European politics they had till then deeply influenced. By September 1853 Engels had declared his willingness to take up the cudgels against him, but the course of the war compelled him to write nothing but military articles. In spring 1855 he wrote his first attack — a series of articles on Pan-Slavism. The first of these articles was printed with large insertions; the others were not printed at all.

A truer picture of Engels's opinions is given by the fragments of a pamphlet called *Germans and Slavs;* he had been working at it since the end of 1854, and Marx had made researches for him in the British Museum reading-room. In it he argued against the " horrible European reactionaries " like his former comrade Bruno Bauer, who vaunted the unity and strength of Russia against the hyper-civilization and disunity of Europe and who praised the obedience of the subjects of the Czar in contrast to the widespread rebelliousness of the European peoples. Engels's remarks on the frontiers and the future of the Russian Empire show that he had a deep conviction of the inferiority of the Russians compared with other countries on an equal or higher stage of development. However, he conceded to the advocates of " Greater Russia " that they, being themselves semi-barbaric, knew how to assimilate barbaric tribes. He believed firmly that Russia had overstepped her natural western frontiers. She must, he thought, either go further and conquer the eastern provinces of Prussia, Galicia, Moldavia, Hungary, and the Balkans, or else sacrifice Poland and Lithuania. For the export of her grain she needed neither Riga nor Odessa, since she had harbours on the Dnieper, the Bug, and the Sea of Azov, as well as at Petersburg and Reval. As her transport, industry, and education developed, Moscow would tend to become more suitable as a capital than Petersburg. The future of Russia lay in Asia. If she did not recognize that fact, she must be taught it by force. Manchuria and Amur would fall into her hands, and in Siberia she had a position on the Pacific, the ocean of the future.

Marx, who found it harder to commit his thoughts to paper, admired the mental agility of his friend and his marvellous and encyclopædic memory. Gratitude was mingled with his admiration, and it was justified. From 1851 till 1859 none of Engels's writings appeared under his own name. His sole purpose was to enable Marx to support his family in the pitiless streets of the world's greatest market and to continue those studies and mature those thoughts which were necessary for the completion of the mighty work he had undertaken — the work which was to demonstrate to the hard world around him the inevitability of its own collapse.

In the summer of 1853 the elder Engels revisited Manchester. Friedrich's supervision of the English branch and his regular reports on its progress had improved his father's opinion of him. His own income had increased as a result, but it was still far from answering the numerous calls which were made upon it. As well as supporting Marx, he was maintaining Mary Burns and her relatives.

In order to help Marx still further, he took, for the time being, cheaper lodgings, and moved to better ones when he had visitors from Barmen. Marx once wrote to Weydemeyer: " I must push towards my goal through thick and thin and not allow bourgeois society to transform me into a moneymaking machine." He succeeded, in spite of terrible sufferings; but Engels was solely responsible for his success. It is impossible to imagine how Marx would have finished his life-work but for Engels's support. But it would be wrong to credit Engels only with the material help he gave Marx and to overlook his assistance in other still more important ways. Marx's meeting with Engels had been the first real confirmation of his own philosophical position. It was through talking to Engels and hearing his friend's voice that he found strength to endure his constant poverty and to oppose his own "bourgeois conscience," which tortured him by asking whether he was justified in leaving his family in poverty while he spent his time in theoretical studies. In spring 1855 Marx lost his only son, whom he loved more than any other human being. He wrote to Engels: "Throughout the agony I have suffered recently, I have been sustained by thinking of you and your friendship and by the hope that we have still a real job to do together." Marx was a hard man, and his enemies infuriated Engels by describing him as "unfeeling"; he gave voice to his true feelings only when real unhappiness touched himself or the friend whom he loved.

Exile dries up the warmer emotions. In foreign countries radical revolutionaries do not willingly speak of their "nation" and their "fatherland": these words refer to objects for which they can no longer feel any sympathy. In Germany during the fifties everything tended to provoke the bitterest criticisms from Engels and Marx. The working-class movement was wiped out. The democratic party had voluntarily dissolved itself. The exiled democrats were their enemies. Their real sympathizers could be counted on the fingers of one hand. The few friends they still had in Germany found it dangerous to correspond with them. Their radical opinions had estranged their own families. Towards England, too, they felt more hatred than love. He who was not with them was against them. Yet who was on their side in the political struggles of those years? They were surrounded by misunderstandings and enmities; all their acts, all their aspirations, all their prophecies were misconstrued. Engels had no illusions on the fact. They were thought to be argumentative fanatics whom it was wisest to leave alone.

If we put ourselves in the place of these two men and realize how, in the conviction that they possessed more correct historical standards than their contemporaries, they strove towards their goal without power and without a party worthy of the name, we can understand that they could retain a belief in themselves only by shutting themselves up in their own faith. It was a desperate enterprise to defend against the whole world the glory of a flag which was then unknown, but which should one day wave on Buckingham Palace, on the Louvre, on the Palace in Berlin, on the Kremlin and the Vatican! No stranger could see what right they had to claim infallibility for their beliefs. If we consider that they had undertaken a task of unparalleled magnitude, how can we condemn them for sometimes transgressing the canons of bourgeois good taste in their private letters and conversations and for yielding (Marx more especially) to a resentment which was fed and fostered by their daily life? Their letters were not meant for a third person to read; if they often slanged their contemporaries, and even their political allies, and if they chose to use the bourgeois *Mr.* to mark distaste (and who was there who did not provoke their distaste?), still all that is little compared with the new, fertile, and important ideas which give their correspondence a universal significance in the history of mankind.

Even a friend like Freiligrath sometimes complained of the " free-and-easy tone " which Engels assumed in his letters; but on another occasion he expressed his admiration for Engels's " noble audacity." Impulsive, self-assured, and energetic, Engels was quite capable of offending his acquaintances unintentionally. But in general society he bowed to the usual conventions, and he was ready to admit himself at fault when he had given offence without meaning to. On the other hand, he had an " almost criminal dislike " for popularity-hunting, and abhorred people who were guilty of it.

Engels was tall and thin, but not heavily built. He had hardened his body, however, by riding, swimming, fencing, and open-air exercise, until it could respond to the demands he made of it. In his rare illnesses he did not rely exclusively on doctors, but attempted to discover the right treatment. He did this by reading medical treatises in the summer of 1857 when he became seriously ill with poisoned glands, followed by relapses and complications. At first he refused to stop work for the sake of his health. Marx had to insist. At last he gave way and spent several months at the seaside, near Liverpool, on the Isle of Wight, and finally in Jersey. Marx wrote to him that Engels's accounts disturbed him at least as much as if he were ill himself, and he took up " meticulous medical studies " in the British Museum. He sent the results to Engels, who replied with long deductions about the health value of cod-liver oil and iodine.

But even in illness he could not quite abandon his pen. Marx's financial position was still shaky, for the *New York Tribune* had cut his honorarium in half. When Dana in the spring of 1857 asked Marx to contribute to a new encyclopædia, the offer was welcomed.

Engels was still in good health at that time, and he would have welcomed the proposal that they should write the whole encyclopædia between them. " We should soon get that done," he cried. Marx could take charge of German philosophy, the biographies of modern English and French statesmen, Chartism, communism, socialism, Aristotle, Epicurus, the Code Napoléon, and some financial subjects. Engels himself would treat Germanic, Old High German, Middle High German, and Romance (especially Provençal) literature. However, the editor in America did not ask Marx to deal with these subjects; he assigned him military affairs. Immediately, with the help of a military handbook and the material which Marx collected for him in the British Museum, Engels began to write many articles on battles, armies, generals, fortifications, army organization, and so on; and he actually enjoyed it. But the work of the friends was interrupted in 1857, not only by Engels's illness, but by the world-wide economic crisis.

In his *Sketch for a Critique of Political Economy* Engels had declared that the law of competition which brought about crises was not a philosophical principle, but simply a law of nature. At that time he had asserted that crises recurred at intervals of from five to seven years, and that each must be more universal and more paralysing than the last. He had added that the English proletariat would put up with only one more. The *Communist Manifesto* declared that the measures used by the bourgeoisie to counteract a crisis only produced greater and more universal crises — a dictum which was only an expansion of the idea already expressed in the *Sketch for a Critique*. As we know, Engels regarded economic crises as one of the most powerful agents of political change. In 1850 he first hazarded the conjecture that the enormous growth in the means of production would bring about crises separated only by short periods of partial recovery. In Harney's *Democratic Review* he spoke of the various reverses which had been luckily compersated by the opening of new markets or by the improved exploitation of old markets through diminution of the costs of production. But that, too, had, he said, " a limit. There are no more new markets to open. When we see that although it is impossible to find new markets, the capitalist system is constantly forced to increase production, it is obvious that the domination of the factory-owners has reached its end. What then? Universal ruin and chaos, say the Free Traders. Social revolution and the dictatorship of the proletariat, say we."

When Engels returned to business, he expected that the next crisis would come in the following year. When it had not come by the end of February 1852, he blamed the opening up of the Dutch colonies, tariff reductions in various countries, and the fall in the price of cotton. Some months later he was puzzled and began to wonder whether the boom, which did not look like coming to an end, should not be credited with a fairly long life. He referred Marx to the unexpected elasticity of the market in the East Indies, the " confusion introduced by California and Australia," the cheapness of most raw products and industrial products, and the absence of speculation. But still he tried to cling to his previous forecast: half a year more or less, he thought, would not make much difference. In August he expected the crisis would come that autumn; he was disturbed only by the question whether it could be intensive enough to provoke a revolution in a few months. The huge markets created out of nothing by the discovery of gold in California and America were factors which the *Communist Manifesto* had not envisaged. In the following months hope and disappointment succeeded each other, and by the end of November his anticipations were cooling. He himself prophesied that only a real failure in the grain crop would make any notable difference in 1853. Engels correctly diagnosed why the boom was so longlived, but his judgment was disturbed by his revolutionary impatience and his belief in the regularity of the trade cycle. In a letter to Weydemeyer in April 1853 he reckoned up the amount of inflammable material stored up for the next European revolution: "Europe is admirably prepared; it needs only the spark of a crisis." This result, he said, could be reached " by the most sober reasoning." But the crisis did not appear. Even the Crimean War did not affect the universal prosperity. From autumn 1853 till spring 1856 his letters to Marx do not mention the hopes of a crisis, which always filled him with dreams of revolution.

At last, in 1857, the event for which he had waited with such impatience occurred. In the second half of that year the first real world crisis shook the foundations of the economic system which had during the last ten years expanded the productive forces of the world at an unparalleled speed. Engels was certain that there would be a terrific crash. All the elements of one were ready to hand: the intensity and universality of the depression and the implication in it of the propertied and ruling classes. He mocked the English for calmly relying on the soundness of their home market and the prosperity of their industry, without noticing that it was their investments on the Continent and in the U.S.A. that had caused the speculative boom.

In September 1856 excessive speculation in Germany had created an alarming shortage of capital. Engels correctly saw this as merely a prelude to the storm. When the slump came he wrote to Marx that it would mean a *Dies Iræ* of un-heard-of severity: " the whole of European industry ruined, all markets glutted, all the propertied classes involved, the bourgeoisie completely bankrupt, terrific wars, and utter chaos." He did not care if this was a little delayed. If the financial crisis grew in intensity throughout the winter, he expected still more deadly effects when it broke out in the spring.

Meanwhile observers on the Continent saw that a dread-ful storm was blowing up. In January 1857 the *Frankfurter Handelszeitung* anxiously asked what would be the result of the struggle between the new economic system and Germany's capital resources. In the United States there had been an influx of English capital, and the German immigrants had brought more; consequently prices and imports had risen while internal production had not slowed down. However rapidly internal markets expanded, demand could not keep pace with supply. The result was that markets became stag-nant and credit very scarce, and so, as soon as it was an-nounced that the European crops promised very well, the crisis broke out on every American exchange. As Engels had prophesied, England was completely taken by surprise; no alarm was felt until the high bank rate in America began to attract English money, with the result that in the second half of October prices started falling rapidly. Engels was not in Manchester when this happened; he was recovering from his illness in Jersey, where letters reached him from his office to protest against his absence. He returned just in time to see the panic which started when several Scottish banks failed. On the 15th of November he began to send Marx regular reports on the crisis. He said that the most noteworthy fact was that America had speculated with foreign capital (as usual), and this time chiefly capital from the Continent. The crisis would soon affect the Continent too; it was delayed by the little preliminary slump which had happened in Germany during September. In the East Indies another crisis was preparing " in case this first blow is not enough to capsize the old tub." Engels was a queer sort of business man — he was delighted to see the panic on the exchange. " People are worrying themselves to death about my sudden and strange good humour," he told Marx, and added that the Exchange was the only place which could transform the weakness which his illness had caused into vigour and gaiety.

Engels's confidence in the " marvellous development " of the crisis increased when " at the first blow " Peel's Bank Act was suspended. At first he even hoped that the Bank of England would be involved through expanding its issue of notes. His optimism was not impaired when he was compelled to foretell a certain degree of recovery for the cotton market during the next few months. He wished that this " improvement " would pass into a chronic crisis before the second and decisive blow fell. Such crises never expended themselves in one shock, and this one would certainly be no exception to the rule; it *must* indeed assume enormous dimensions because of the colossal increase in gold-production and the vast expansion of industry consequent upon that increase.

He now foresaw the revolution with absolute certainty. But he hoped that the masses would have time to be thoroughly roused by the chronic depression. " After such a depression the proletariat strikes with more force and unity, in better *connaissance de cause* — just as a cavalry attack succeeds far better if the horses have to trot for five hundred yards before they come within charging distance of the enemy." Throughout his whole life he was afraid that a proletarian revolution might break out prematurely. Now he wrote to Marx: " I don't want anything to happen too early, before the whole of Europe is under the hammer — if it did, the struggle would be harder and more tedious and less decisive." He was delighted by the thought that he would perhaps soon be able to leave the exchange for the battle-field, and his office stool for a horse. He overflowed with vitality; the man of action revived in him. " Last Saturday," he wrote to Marx in December, " I was out hunting — seven hours in the saddle. That sort of thing makes me hellishly excited for a few days; it is the greatest physical pleasure which I know." He felt that the " bourgeois rubbish " of the past seven years had been a load round his neck and that he was now becoming a new man. He wrote to his friend: " In 1848 we said: ' Now our time is coming,' and in a certain sense it came. But this time it is coming in full measure — a life-and-death struggle. My military studies will at once become more practical. I am throwing myself immediately into the tactics and organization of the Prussian, Austrian, Bavarian, and French armies; and apart from that I do nothing but ride — that is, hunt, for hunting is the real cavalry school." The two friends confessed their joy to each other: Marx said that despite his constant poverty he had not felt so happy since 1849, and Engels that in this general collapse he felt " terrifically confident." Marx was working all night long to pull his researches in economics together. He wished to get the general scheme clear before the deluge came. Engels sent him all the material he could collect about the crisis, in a hurried stream of dismal messages. We hear that he moved at this time a good deal in society, to get information about the course of the crisis.

Until the end of the year Engels's reports to Marx were constantly encouraging. He himself noticed that his illness had made him more excitable than before. He prophesied " terrific results " from the fact that the grain market and the colonial market were now involved. As long as overproduction was confined to industry, he wrote, the story was only half told; but when it affected agriculture also, and agriculture not only in the temperate zones but in the tropics, the thing would be " grand." He thought it was " grand " also when the crisis involved dozens of firms in Hamburg, including some of the first rank. " There has never been such an absolutely first-rate panic as there is now in Hamburg. Everything but silver and gold is worthless, absolutely worthless." This on the 7th of December; on the 9th he wrote to his friend that things looked terribly bad in Liverpool too. " People are absolutely cleaned out and have hardly the courage left to go bankrupt. A man who was there on Monday told me that faces on the Exchange are three times as long as they are here." But in Manchester, too, the storm was growing darker. "The cotton-spinners and manufacturers are paying away in wages and fuel-costs all the money they have got for their goods, and when it disappears they must go sky-high too." He added that people were only now discovering that financial speculation was the least important thing in the crisis. Two days later he said that the form in which over-production concealed itself this time was bill-jobbing. It was a good opportunity to study the growth of over-production through the expansion of credit and false speculation. On the 17th of December he wrote that the crisis was keeping him damned busy; every day prices fell. Even his father had stipulated for an advance of money from Manchester. " I don't think it is serious, but nothing matters now," he said. And later on the same day: " Manchester is getting more and more deeply involved; the constant pressure on the market is having a terrific effect. Sales are impossible. Every day we hear of lower bids, and nobody with any self-respect tries to sell his goods any longer."

But still there was no sign of the second earthquake which Engels had foretold. At the end of December things were generally quieter, and the bank rate sank as fast as it had risen before. Engels was still convinced that the real collapse was impending, but the development of the markets contradicted him: the waves sank, and the " chronic crisis " did not lead to revolution. For a long time he wondered how over-production could be absorbed. He could explain the miracle only by the clamour for imports in India and China. Marx's explanation was that since California and Australia had been colonized and China and Japan opened to trade, a world market and production based upon that market had been at last attained. Bourgeois society had fulfilled its task. But he hesitated to say how quickly it would come to grief. If bourgeois society was on the up-grade throughout such a large part of the world, would it be possible in the near future for a revolution, breaking out on the European continent and immediately assuming a socialist character, to hold its own in this " little corner "? We would fain know Engels's answer to his friend's anxious question, which for the first time in history pointed to the coloured races as an important factor in the historical process.

During the peaceful interval which Marx and Engels greeted with such disappointment, they were enabled to resume their studies. Marx began to make a fair copy of his *Critique of Political Economy* and constantly asked Engels for information about the actual facts of economic life. In April 1858 he sent him a synopsis of the first section. Unfortunately Engels's detailed criticism of the plan has not survived.

CHAPTER XIV

ENGELS AND LASSALLE.
THE WAR OF 1859

Ever since Engels had been driven from Germany by the triumph of the counter-revolution, he had paid little attention to German politics. He was rather ashamed to return to such parochial subjects while all round him in Manchester men were trading with America, India, and China and discussing problems of world-wide interest. And he did not share the extravagant hopes with which the Prussian bourgeoisie greeted the creation of a regency to replace the infirm Friedrich Wilhelm IV. He had learned from the events of 1848 that the liberal upper classes had not the strength to take and keep the mastery of Prussia. In Germany there was now no party or group to which Engels and Marx could belong. Almost the only man who did not allow police interference to keep him from writing to them was Ferdinand Lassalle. During the revolution he had sent contributions from Düsseldorf to the *Neue Rheinische Zeitung*. His respect for Marx had grown into friendship, and he accepted Marx's reserve as natural. Engels recognized Lassalle's talents and his zeal for the cause, but he was repelled by his character. He did not confess this dislike to Marx until 1856, when a Düsseldorf acquaintance of Marx visited him and told him that Lassalle had left the working-class party and was making overtures to the liberals. Thenceforward Engels's descriptions of " the Jew from the Slavonic frontiers " were strongly tinged with anti-Semitism; and even Marx often called Lassalle " Baron Ikey " and " Mr. Ephraim Cute." Lassalle had no discrimination to act as a check on his exuberant conceit. Yet he had a lofty conception of friendship; he revealed himself freely in his letters to Marx, without imagining that every word was weighed and sneered at in Manchester and London. He became a standing joke with Engels and Marx when he moved to Berlin, started to publish books, and "made a dead set at a reputation." But in 1859 they recovered their belief in his political honesty and began to think it might be useful to be his friends, for he found a publisher for Marx's book on economics and for a pamphlet in which Engels discussed the struggle threatened by France's attack on Austria in North Italy.

When this struggle broke out, Engels and Marx found themselves for the first time really opposed to Lassalle. He wanted Prussia to utilize Austria's embarrassment to strengthen her hegemony among the North German states — he regarded Austria as the most dangerous enemy of democracy in Europe. But Engels believed the real enemy was Russia. He supposed that there was a secret military agreement between France and Russia, which would come into force as soon as Russia helped Austria against France. However much he abhorred the Austrian domination of North Italy, he could not wish Austria to abandon her strategic position in Lombardy to Napoleon III. He was convinced also that Austria needed that position for her own safety — only so long as she was independent of Germany. The united Greater Germany of the future would need no troops on the Italian frontier. Inspired by the fear that Germany might have to carry on a war on two fronts (against Russia and France), he wrote to Lassalle: "We Germans must be in the most desperate situation before we can be moved *en masse* by the *furor teutonicus,* and this time our plight seems desperate enough. *Tant mieux.* At such a crisis the powers that be are bound to fall, and the moment will come when only the most determined and relentless party can save the nation."

Engels wrote two excellent pamphlets on the military and political events of that year. The first, *Po and Rhine,* dealt with the situation before the outbreak of war. The other, *Savoy, Nice, and the Rhine,* discussed the situation after the Peace of Villa Franca. Besides this he followed the course of the war in the *New York Tribune* and in an ephemeral little German paper, *Das Volk,* published in London. His remarks on strategy in *Po and Rhine* deserve special mention because they were astonishingly corroborated by the World War. At that time the plea of "natural frontiers" was used to back Austria's claim for North Italy, and France's for the left bank of the Rhine. Engels attempted to show that France could renounce her claim to the military frontier of the Rhine now that she had fortified Paris. Her Belgian frontier was deplorably weak. Belgium was of course neutral—but history had yet to show that in war neutrality "is more than a scrap of paper." "Belgium," he went on, "surrounds the whole of eastern France from Verdun and the upper Marne to the Rhine. Thus an army entering via Belgium could be in Paris before a French army stationed between Verdun or Chaumont and the Rhine could get back to defend it. Therefore the invading army could — if its offensive were successful — drive a wedge between Paris and the French army of the Rhine or the Moselle." France must defend itself by delivering an offensive on the Belgian frontier, based on Paris and its forts. " If this offensive is repulsed, the army must make a final stand on the Oise-Aisne line; it would be useless for the enemy to advance farther, since the army invading from Belgium would be too weak to act against Paris alone. Behind the Aisne, in unchallengeable communication with Paris — or, at the worst, behind the Marne, with its left wing on Paris — the French northern army could take the offensive and wait for the arrival of the other forces." Thus Engels prophesied the miracle of the Marne.

But, for all his military interests, he did not abandon his

FERDINAND LASSALLE

hopes of revolution. He was, like everyone else, interested in the Peace of Villa Franca. He wrote in *Das Volk* that, apart from a continued war which would have involved all Europe, a peace like this was the best, because only the Russians and the revolutionaries gained by it.

In the second pamphlet he expressed his fear that Napoleon, after the pale glories of Magenta and Solferino, would seek new laurels on the Rhine with the help of Russia. Russia needed this alliance to checkmate Austria, for the Austrians were being more and more provoked by Russian encroachment on the Vistula and Danube. It was lucky for the Czar that the French Emperor had to make war to keep his throne and could nowhere else find the necessary ally. But France was a danger for Germany only if she was supported by Russia, while Russia was a constant menace —she could incite France by an offer of the left bank of the Rhine whenever she wished. Once again we see that Engels considered Czarism the most dangerous enemy of European liberty and of the victory of the revolution. When Alexander II was considering the abolition of serfdom, Marx and Engels thought that " Russia's internal history was beginning." And when the nobles were called together in the autumn of 1858, they believed it to be a symptom "that the revolution had begun in Russia." When the peasant revolts and the constitutional agitation among the nobility grew in strength, Marx as commander-in-chief of the world revolution issued Napoleonic commands from his wretched home in London: "At the next revolution," he wrote, " Russia will kindly join the rebels." In his second pamphlet, then, Engels explained to the German public the conclusions which he and Marx had reached in common. " The whole system of Russian foreign policy will now be undermined by the war which has broken out in Russia between the ruling class and the oppressed peasants. The system was possible only while Russia had no internal political history. But that time is now over. The industrial and agricultural developments

which have been encouraged by the government and the nobility have reached a stage which makes the present social
system impossible. On the one hand it is necessary to abolish
it, and on the other its abolition is impossible without a violent change." Until then Engels had never believed that
Russia might have a revolution. Thenceforth such a revolution became a permanent factor in his political speculations.

In midsummer 1859 Engels's father revisited Manchester. Friedrich spent September with both his parents in
Scotland. It was the last time he was to see his father. In
March 1860 the news of his death reached Engels. The
amnesty allowed him to return to Germany — it was his
first visit since the revolution. His brothers took it for
granted that they would inherit the German factory and
that Friedrich would be content with the Manchester
branch. They had not imagined that he could be a partner
in the German business even when he was living abroad. But
the English law did not allow the heir of the head of a firm
to become a partner automatically on his father's death.
Friedrich was embittered by the attitude of his brothers.
However, he signed the agreement they proposed, to save
his mother's feelings. He wrote to her: "I'll make any
sacrifice to save you from being annoyed by this business any
longer. I won't hold it against my brothers, and I'll never
bring it up against them unless they drive me to it. It is all
over now, and I don't want to make much of the fact that I
have given up a good deal to them." His mother's answer
has not survived. But there is a letter which Friedrich wrote
to her a fortnight later to assure her once more that he
would harbour no grudge. " I can get a hundred other busi-
nesses, but never another mother." Engels was a good
fighter: if he thought he was in the right, he stuck to his
point; but here it seems as if he were almost happy to show
his mother (who was so pained by his political opinions)

that his break.with family tradition could not diminish his love for her.

His brothers said they were willing to leave ten thousand pounds in the Manchester business. Friedrich was assured of a larger percentage of the net profits than before. He also inherited some money from his father, so that his income was considerably increased. He became a partner in 1864, but all this only confirmed his decision to abandon commercial life as soon as the interest on his capital was enough to support both himself and the Marx family.

CHAPTER XV

THE AMERICAN CIVIL WAR

ᔪ

Although Lassalle, with his more rigid Hegelianism, described all American events as uninteresting (because the Americans had no "Ideas"), Marx and Engels always realized that they possessed a "world-transforming significance." Both the abolition of slavery in the U.S.A. and the abolition of serfdom in Russia seemed to them to be decisive stages in the process of the development of freedom, for with Hegel they held that all history consisted in that process. In 1850 Engels had surmised that the future abolition of Negro slavery would ruin the existing productive system. His excitement was great in the spring of 1861 when, after the breach between the Northern and Southern states, the Civil War began, to end, after four years of struggle, with the victory of the opponents of slavery. Throughout that time his political and military interest was fixed on America; and since the war affected the cotton market, he was interested in it also from a business point of view.

Politically Engels viewed the war as a war of conquest carried on by the South in order to spread and perpetuate slavery. The oligarchy which set the tone of the South knew that if (as Lincoln demanded) no new slave territories were to be created, the slave system would perish even in the districts where it still flourished. The rulers of Britain saw in the rapid growth of the U.S.A. a threat to their world monopoly. The North possessed industries and protected them by tariff barriers; the South produced the raw material for the most important of England's industries. The British feared that if the superior navy of the North could block the harbours of the South, the Lancashire looms would be forced to cease production. It seemed to be in the British interest that the breach within the great North American republic should not be healed; accordingly Britain hastened to recognize the Confederate States of the South as a belligerent power. Gladstone, who was Chancellor of the Exchequer, stated publicly in October 1862 that the victory of the South was certain and that it had become not only a new state, but a new nation. But in liberal England it would have been hardly decent for the press to take up the cause of slavery. They therefore concealed the real object of the war and pretended that the North, in its desire for ascendancy, was endeavouring by force of arms to hold the South to a union which the South had a right to reject. Many in Britain did not realize that the issue was the abolition or continuance of slavery until the great demonstrations which were held by the workers in London, Manchester, and Sheffield in and after December 1862 to oppose a declaration of war on the Northern states. War was then imminent, for the English shipbuilders were supporting the privateers of the South; the North, goaded into reprisals, had arrested some Confederate diplomats on an English mail-steamer. Engels disapproved of the Yankees' tomfooleries; he wrote to Marx: " To arrest travellers on a foreign ship upon a political charge is the clearest *casus belli* in the world."

Contemporary events kept Engels busy writing continuous articles on military science. Between the Italian war and the American Civil War, he wrote in the *New York Tribune* on the recent general changes in infantry and artillery armaments, the army reforms in the German states, England's war in China, Garibaldi's Sicilian expedition, the prospects of a French invasion of England, and the defences of the British Isles. He wrote (under the pseudonym of a foreign officer) an article on the outbreak of the Civil War, but it was not printed in the *New York Tribune*. His articles were published in two specialist papers — the *Allgemeine Militär-Zeitung* of Darmstadt and the *Volunteer Journal for Lancashire and Cheshire*. (Isaac Hale, the editor of the *Journal*, constantly tried to induce Engels to accept a post on his staff.) Engels assembled some of these articles in a pamphlet, published in 1861 under the title *Essays Addressed to Volunteers*. In a short preface he observed that he claimed no originality for the facts discussed, but only for the opinions he expressed and the inferences which he drew. He viewed the Riflemen with some sympathy, because they were subject to a less rigid system of drill than the regular army. But his sympathy did not blind him to the weakness of these formations which had been organized when France increased her army immediately after the Italian war and laid down new war-ships.

The confidence of the English in the safety of their island was shaken when France increased the proportion of steamships in her fleet. Not public opinion alone, but even the government, headed by the Francophile Palmerston, was inclined to distrust a policy which had begun to put the principle of "the natural frontiers" into practice by annexing Savoy and Nice. People were anxiously asking whom Napoleon would choose to attack next. In the *Allgemeine Militär-Zeitung* for September 1860 Engels stressed the point that the origin and principles of the volunteer Riflemen made them enemies of Bonapartism. In 1861 he added, in the *Volunteer Journal*, that if they ever exchanged bullets with an enemy, that enemy would be the French light infantry. In the open field he did not consider that the English volunteers were a match for the "best military organization in Europe"; he therefore opposed the plan of the Commission of National Defence, which was determined to fortify a number of great military harbours, but not the capital itself. He feared that if new fortifications were established they would have to be guarded by too many of the regular army, while one lost battle would mean the loss of London and of the whole country.

In the American Civil War Engels expected that the Northern democracy, superior in men and materials, would bring their superiority increasingly into play as the war continued, and would at last be victorious. For a time this view was proved wrong, when the improvised armies and inexperienced generals of the North suffered defeat after defeat. It was difficult in Europe to obtain facts on which to base a judgment of the war. The news-service by cable was very limited; the American papers and the reports of the European press correspondents did not arrive for weeks, and then they did not often give a full answer to the questions which a military expert wished to ask. Also, there were no good maps of the most important areas of operation. The nature of the war was very different from any which Engels had seen or studied. He considered it to be a " drama without parallel in the annals of military history," because of the huge area at stake in the war, the vast extent over which military operations were carried on, the size of the opposing armies, the fabulous expense involved, the types of strategy and the generalship employed. As we know, this was the first war where any important strategic use was made of railways and armoured ships; at first neither side had a real army; there was an appalling lack of trained officers; and (as Engels pointed out) had it not been for the experienced soldiers who had entered America after the European revolution — especially from Germany — the organization of the Union army would have taken still longer than it did. Most of the trained officers in America belonged to the aristocratic South, so that the Confederates could develop their resources quicker than the North; the soldiers of the North entered the war " sleepily " and " reluctantly." But as Engels told his friend Weydemeyer towards the end of the war, he had never realized what discipline the Northern army possessed, what morale under fire, what ability to withstand fatigue — in short, what demands could be made on it without causing demoralization.

Engels was disturbed by the constant defeats of the North, but even more by the fact that the North did not seem to press towards their goal with " revolutionary energy." He was perplexed that they should depend so much on the results of great battles and be so little inclined to take up arms themselves. He thought that their war-cry: " War to the knife ! " was empty boasting, and was forced to recognize, like everybody else, that Lee had more military ability than McClellan — who, as Engels bitterly said, was less concerned to strike the enemy than to avoid being struck. Engels confessed to Marx that he would not have been disheartened by the defeat of McClellan in Virginia and the other failures of the North if he had not feared that the North now intended to parade nothing but a skeleton army " to demonstrate during the negotiations for peace." He contrasted this " slack management " with the deadly earnestness of the South. At the end of July 1862 he declared to Marx that until the North put on revolutionary colours it would be soundly beaten. And Marx also blamed the North for trying to carry on constitutionally a war which should be waged in a revolutionary manner. But he repeatedly warned Engels not to be prejudiced by one-sided attention to the military aspect, and actually it was Marx who proved to be the true prophet : " The North-West and New England wish to and will force the government to stop waging the war with only diplomatic weapons. . . . If Lincoln does not give in (but he will), there will be a revolution." Lincoln, as we know, gave way, and on New Year's Day 1863 guaranteed freedom for all the Negroes. That was at last the really revolutionary act !

But it was some time before Engels ceased to fear that the war might lead, not to a clear-cut decision of the slave question, but to a hollow peace. Even in the succeeding months, when he came to realize that there would be no premature peace and that the Northern states were at last preparing armaments on the grand scale, he still had not an unqualified confidence in their determination to win and in their chance of winning. His doubts lasted until General Grant became more prominent. Then at last he saw that the Confederate forces were flagging. He was still ready to acknowledge the superiority of Lee's strategy. In the summer of 1864 after Lee's masterly defence of the fortified camp at Richmond, Engels wrote to Marx that the Prussians (if they were not far too stuck-up) could learn from Lee exactly how to conduct a campaign round the fortified camp of Coblenz. When Lee was surrounded by the Northern armies next spring and had to lay down his arms, Engels saw the strategical position as an exact repetition of Jena. Like Napoleon, Grant had captured the whole of the enemy's army.

After the war was over, Engels bitterly condemned the race-hatred which broke out in America, and the hesitation of its statesmen to give the Negroes a vote. He correctly prophesied the future of the great new country: slavery, he said, had been the greatest hindrance to the political and social development of the U.S.A., and when it once was removed, the country would receive an impetus which would soon give it an entirely different position in history and in the world. He also conjectured that the Union would sooner or later adopt an imperialist policy and thus employ the army and navy which had been created by the Civil War.

The war had lasted so long that the English cotton industry ran short of raw material, despite its careful precautions in buying up reserve stores. Production had to be limited or even discontinued; workers were paid off, and those who were still employed suffered terribly from poverty. Engels in his office followed the daily progress of the cotton famine. It was indeed thrust on his attention by the pressure of extra work and the diminution in his income which it caused. In *Capital* Marx has left an admirable account of the cotton famine. Engels was too busy to have time to write a close description of it in his correspondence with Marx or elsewhere. The few remarks on it which we possess show that he was far less sanguine about the results of this crisis than about that of 1857, which had sprung from other causes. The disappointment he had felt in 1857 had left lasting effects. In particular, he was more reserved in his judgments about the immediate political effects of crises, even when they were caused by over-production. In November 1864, when the worst of the famine was over, he complained to Marx " that a thing like this seldom nowadays comes to a head." Marx replied that crises nowadays made up in frequency what they lacked in intensity.

In 1857 a little legacy had enabled Marx to take a small house and furnish it, but just then the economic crisis made a considerable diminution in his literary market in America. Engels had imagined that everything was going " on splendid lines " for his friend and therefore had got a horse from his father as a present for Christmas 1856. When he saw that Marx was once more " in the soup," he was much embarrassed by his little luxury. All the help he could give was not enough to keep his friend permanently above water. Marx hated having constantly to " squeeze " Engels; but if he complained that he had to do it, Engels simply answered that he wished he had more " that could be squeezed out." Marx's household suffered a specially severe crisis when in February 1861 the *New York Tribune* cut down their staff of correspondents in Europe and Dana suspended the appearance of the encyclopædia. This time Marx determined to look for a fundamental remedy for his troubles. He went to see his mother in Trier and his uncle in Holland, and he determined to make a trip to Berlin, because he had recently been asked by Lassalle to help him to publish a great radical journal. In Prussia at that time the conflict between the monarchy and the Chamber of Deputies was growing more and more acute. But Marx did not think it was sharp enough to justify his accepting the offer; it was only his desperate position that made him think of sacrificing his scruples. He stayed with Lassalle in Berlin and avoided giving a direct decision — he said that he could make no decision without Engels and that his friend must become a co-editor with himself. But Engels refused. He did not see his way to give up his independent position in England (at a moment when revolution was not imminent) in order to make himself more or less dependent on Lassalle. Marx replied to Lassalle accordingly. Engels's determination made it easier for him to refuse a proposal which had been repugnant to him also.

Marx brought home some money, but it was not enough to enable him to dispense with the " Manchester supply " for current expenses, or even to clear off his load of debt. In December his debts had again mounted to a hundred pounds. It gave him such agony to confess to his friend that he was once more in difficulties that for some time he kept silent. But at last he revealed himself : " You make such great efforts for me — greater than even you can cope with; and it is loathsome for me to plague you constantly with dismal messages." Six months later he was again compelled to write: " It is loathsome for me to speak to you of my wretched poverty once more — but *que faire?* Every day my wife tells me she wishes she and the children were dead and buried; and I really cannot blame her, for the humiliations, tortures, and fears which we must face in this situation are literally indescribable." It was very painful to Engels to hear his comrade complain of being a burden on him. He attempted to make Marx feel less dependent by saying that it was in fact a matter of no importance who was " squeezing " and who was " squeezed." But Marx replied: " Dear boy, you can say what you like, but it really is very painful for me to cause you so much bother by my poverty. If I could only start some sort of business! " In September 1862 he did actually apply for a post as a railway clerk. But he was refused because of his handwriting.

Just when Marx's affairs were in their most desperate condition, in the summer of 1862, Lassalle turned up in London,
to see the Exhibition. He imagined that Marx's visit had
completely re-established their old friendship. But in fact
Marx had been diplomatic. He continued to be so; he made
use of Lassalle, but he acknowledged to himself the hollow-
ness of their relations. Owing to pressure of business Engels
did not see Lassalle again, and the final meeting of Marx and
Lassalle in London was decisive for the future. Marx tacitly
renounced Lassalle when Lassalle told him that he intended
to restart the German working-class movement, to put himself at its head, and to make his chief plank the old Chartist
cry of universal suffrage. What he said on this plan was
enough to show Marx that he and Engels had now neither
principles nor tactics nor aims in common with Lassalle. It is
true that Lassalle asked Marx to help him in this also. But
could he have shared the presidency of a party based on the
leadership of one man? Marx told him to his face that
Engels and he could no longer agree with him. But that did
not make Lassalle falter in his determination.

Engels was delighted that after a longish interval Germany was once more awaking to an interest in social questions
and thus creating a " basis for anti-bourgeois action." Alas,
that it should be Lassalle who was " getting himself a position " through it and taking over their stock! Engels had always held to the belief that Lassalle was Marx's pupil — a
belief which contained only a small proportion of truth. Both
the friends always criticized his work as an agitator because
he neglected the doctrines they had expounded in their writings. They had applied the acid of the theory of class-conflict
to the state and had seen it dissolve under the test. Lassalle
had not; he could still reverence the state, and therefore he
could still juggle with the idea of the *Volksstaat*. Engels disapproved of him for opposing the liberals who were then at
war with Bismarck; he did not know that Lassalle and Bismarck had struck up a sort of alliance. In June 1863 Engels

wrote to Marx: "The fellow is now serving Bismarck, out and out; one day it may happen Monsieur Bismarck will change his mind about him, and he'll be whipped off into the jug." For the time being, Marx and Engels did not want to declare themselves either for or against Lassalle's agitation.

Marx's position was momentarily eased by a loan which he had obtained from Lassalle (on Engels's security) before Lassalle left London. But before the end of the year everything movable in his house was in the pawnshop once more. Once again the shopkeepers became pressing, and the children had to stay at home because their school-fees could not be paid. Marx felt that this time ruin could not be averted. He was on the point of writing to his friend when he received the unexpected news that Mary Burns was dead. For nearly twenty years she had been Engels's faithful comrade, with whom he could relax after his detested labours in the city and collect his forces for his real work. She was very dear to him. "I cannot tell you how I feel," he wrote, in the letter telling Marx the news; "the poor girl loved me with her whole heart." But at that moment Marx's mind was so occupied by his own impending ruin that instead of expressing true sympathy for his bereaved friend, he replied baldly that he was both surprised and grieved by the news. Then, after adding that Mary had been very kind and very witty, and that she had been deeply attached to Engels, he proceeded immediately to describe his own difficulties at great length. He did mention that it was "frightfully egoistic" of him to tell Engels all this at such a moment, but he consoled himself (and Engels, too, he thought) by calling his conduct a homœopathic remedy, on the principle that one evil drives away another. "And *au bout du compte*," he added to appease his friend, "what am I to do? There is nobody in all London to whom I can speak freely"; under these conditions, he said, it was impossible for him to work. In a postscript he asked where and how Engels intended to live now that he had lost the home in which he had been able to spend his time when-

ever he liked, " free and out of reach of this filthy world."
We know of no other occasion on which Engels felt himself wounded by Marx. But this time he was deeply hurt.
When he got this letter, he could not help feeling that Marx
(whose wife was socially and intellectually his equal) did not
understand what Mary's death meant to him — Mary, who
was not yet in her grave. He let a week pass without answering. When he eventually answered, he was so afraid that he
might give full vent to his feelings that he wrote a draft of
the letter first. " You will of course realize," he said in it,
" that in this case my own misfortune and the frigid way you
took it have made it absolutely impossible for me to answer
you earlier. All my friends, even my philistine acquaintances,
have shown me on this occasion, which, heaven knows, has hit
me pretty hard, more sympathy and friendship than I could
expect. You found it a suitable time to drive home the superiority of your cool philosophical attitude. Enjoy your triumph; I shall not challenge it." But when he came to copying
out the letter, he felt worried by its sharpness. He therefore
cancelled the last sentence and toned down the one before it.
Then he turned at once to discuss his friend's necessities; he
explained what he could and could not at the moment do, and
concluded with the assurance: " I will do my share."

Marx decided that it was better to wait some time before
he answered, since, as things stood, it was difficult for both
of them " to get a ' cool ' idea of the position." Then he assured his friend candidly that he had regretted his letter as
soon as he had sent it, and entreated him not to accuse him
of heartlessness. " My wife and children will testify that
when I got your letter early in the morning I was as shaken
as if my nearest and dearest had passed away. But I wrote
you in the evening, when things looked desperate for me."
The landlord had put the bailiffs in, the butcher had sent in
a demand for immediate payment, there was no coal or food
in the house, one of the children was ill in bed. In such hopeless situations he usually had recourse " to cynicism." He

had been especially maddened by his wife's constant reproaches for not telling the whole truth about their plight to
Engels. Now she had at last agreed to his proposal that the
two eldest daughters should look for posts as governesses;
and Marx and his wife were going to move into a tenement-
house with the youngest.

In Engels's answer we can still see how deeply he had been
affected by the incident, but his anger had cooled. " I thank
you," he wrote, " for your candour. You understand yourself
what sort of an impression your letter made on me. No one
can live so long with a woman without being terribly moved
by her death. I feel that with her I buried the last of my youth.
. . . I tell you, your letter stuck in my head for a whole week,
I couldn't forget it. Never mind, your last letter made it
quits; and I am glad that when I lost Mary I did not also lose
my oldest and best friend. Now, to turn to your affairs. . . ."

Engels wrote that he could not allow Marx to carry out
these plans, and that he had got hold of a hundred pounds
by " a very daring stroke." Marx answered with deep gratitude for this self-sacrificing act of friendship, and went on
with obvious sincerity to say: " I may tell you without evasion
that, in spite of the pressure under which I have been living
for these last weeks, nothing worried me nearly so much as
the fear of a break in our friendship. I told my wife again
and again that I cared nothing about the whole filthy business, compared with the fact that all this bourgeois meanness
and her hysterical behaviour had made me capable of thrust-
ing my private needs on you, instead of consoling you at such
a time. . . ." Engels was more silent than usual during the
succeeding weeks, and Marx was afraid that he had given
him new ground for offence. But Engels explained his silence
by the " very dreary state " he had been in. He had tried to
work himself out of it by learning the Slav languages, but he
had found the loneliness unbearable. " I had to distract myself. That helped. I am my old self again."

Engels's recovery was chiefly due to the fact that his relations with Mary Burns's sister Lizzy became more intimate. But the military interest and revolutionary hopes aroused in him by the rising in Russian Poland also helped to cheer him. He believed that if the rising continued long enough it would infect Russia proper and lead to a general European revolution. In June 1863 he told Marx that he expected even the bourgeoisie, having lost all fear of the communists, to join them at a pinch. The argument of Proudhon and his group, that Russia was freeing her slaves while the Polish nobles and priests had always refused to do so, seemed to him to be threadbare. He firmly believed that an independent Poland would drive Czarist Russia, the most dangerous enemy of the European revolution, further back towards the East.

Marx and Engels were forced to watch their rival Lassalle closely. It was therefore most welcome to them that their most dependable adherent should move to Berlin in 1862 under the amnesty. Liebknecht became a member of the General Association of German Workers, came into contact with Lassalle, and kept a sharp eye on his activities. As a political exile Liebknecht had seemed to Engels to be a sound party comrade, but not a man capable of playing an important part in politics. Engels and Marx knew that his hot-headedness made him an easy prey to illusions, and they thought it necessary to examine with a critical eye all the information he sent. But Liebknecht (they called him their " governor-general in Germany ") never told them as long as Lassalle lived of the latter's intrigues with Bismarck. He thought that his policy was dangerous, but not that he was a traitor to the workers' cause. He wished to check his influence, if he could not abolish it, and put Marx in his place. Without the consent of his friends in England, he arranged a conference for the following September between them and Lassalle, at which they could finally determine whether or not they could work together in future. Under the influence of a gross misconception of the real balance of power within the little party, he wrote to Marx shortly before Lassalle's death saying that he need only say so if he wished to take over the leadership of the Association.

Although Engels spoke spitefully of Lassalle while he was alive, the unexpected news of his death inspired him to a characterization of his old enemy which was really historical in its objectivity. He wrote to Marx: " Let Lassalle's character, literary and scientific talents be what they may, from a political point of view he was one of the most important people in Germany. He was for us today a very uncertain friend, and in future he would have been a pretty certain enemy — but it's all one now. . . ." And of course Engels could not understand how " a politician like him could go and fight a duel with a Wallachian adventurer. That could only happen to Lassalle, with his singular mixture of frivolity and sentimentality, Jewishness and pseudo-chivalry — a mixture peculiar to himself." During Lassalle's life Engels had often been offended by his " Jewish respect for ephemeral success "; and now he asked seriously " whether his agitation was only a flash in the pan, or was there really something in it? " However modest the immediate results of his agitation were, we now know that there was something in it — something with enough vitality to keep Marx and Engels or their confederates from taking over the young movement and leading it where they wished it to go. As soon as Engels had recognized this fact, he came to see that the dead Lassalle was a far more dangerous enemy of Marx and himself than he had been when alive, and that he must lose all his influence — not only physically, but historically — before the German proletariat could rally to the banner of the *Communist Manifesto*.

As things were, neither Marx nor Engels was attracted by the prospect of carrying on a petty warfare with the Prussian police, as Liebknecht was doing and as he expected them to do. They held it to be their obvious duty to take up their positions in any revolutionary crisis, but until then they preferred to leave agitation to others who were less qualified for the theoretical side. Besides, even Liebknecht held that the moment had not yet come when anyone could make an open break away from " Lassalleanism " with any chance of success. The two friends were compelled to admit that it was the really proletarian elements in the movement who were among the most devout worshippers of the " one man who put swords into our hands," and that their own influence on the members of the Association was non-existent. The truth was almost exactly as their old enemy Hess (lately allied with Lassalle) described it: the Marxian party consisted only of the " master " himself, his " secretary " Engels, and his " agent " Liebknecht. The most important elements in the General Association did not care to emphasize the connexion of the new movement with the old one which had been focused on the *Neue Rheinische Zeitung* in 1848.

Marx and Engels knew the weakness of their position, and for this reason they could not out of hand reject the proposal when in November 1864 the publisher of the new party-organ offered them a chance to remind the German proletariat of their existence and their point of view. Johann Baptist von Schweitzer, a *déclassé* aristocrat, ambitious and clever, a product of the Jesuit schools, addressed them with much respect as the " founders of the German working-class movement " and invited them to collaborate with him on the *Sozialdemokrat*. Although they held fast to their belief that the Association must later be "broken up," they agreed with as good a grace as they could. They had hardly done so before they heard from Liebknecht (who was editing the paper along with Schweitzer) the truth about Lassalle's connexion with Bismarck.

In violation of the express promise which Schweitzer had given to both Liebknecht and Marx, the *Sozialdemokrat* soon resumed Lassalle's tactics, concentrating its attacks on the Progressive Party and showing an appreciation of Bismarck's policy which almost passed into active sympathy.

At first Liebknecht wrote to tell Engels and Marx that he hoped gradually to give " a correct attitude " to the paper, and that his task would be easier if they " worked with a will " as collaborators. Engels wanted to test this. He declared himself ready to deliver the article on the Prussian army reforms which the editorial board had asked him to write. Marx was afraid that his friend in handling this subject might fall into a one-sided dispute with the Progressives. But Engels pledged himself to attack the government as much as the bourgeois opposition. He was delighted by addressing the German public on the reorganization of the army as a military specialist, and as a revolutionary politician on the struggle for the constitution: and he enjoyed using the organ of the Association to employ against the tactics of Lassalle and Schweitzer the tactics prescribed for similar situations by the *Communist Manifesto.*

Engels had carefully followed the army reforms from their beginning. But, living abroad, he could not make a proper estimate of the fighting capacities of the reorganized army. Still less could he realize the good luck which the Hohenzollerns had in being served by von Moltke and Bismarck. He was in the Wuppertal visiting his family when Bismarck was made Prime Minister, and he described to Marx the roars of laughter with which the bourgeoisie greeted the news.

Engels was delighted that " the liberal bourgeoisie, fourteen years after 1848, was forced into the most extreme revolutionary dilemma." But he had " no trust " in " feeble progressive democracy " and he expected that the " inevitable row " would start rather among the " common soldiers, who will think twice before accepting three years' service instead of two." His Rhenish distrust of all things Prussian was so deep-rooted that he would not even put his confidence in a revolution if it started in Berlin.

When the diplomatic negotiations about Schleswig-Holstein began, he meditated writing a pamphlet to show

that the only chance its inhabitants had of being freed by
Germany was a war by Germany against Russia in defence
of Poland. The collapse of the Polish revolution turned him
against the idea. He followed the events of the Danish war
with attention. In mid-February 1864 he laid down, in an
article in the *Manchester Guardian,* that the numerical
superiority of the German infantry over the Danes was just
enough to conquer the Dannewerk, Düppel, and Fridericia.
He was astounded by the speed with which the Prussians
took Düppel: it was "more than one could have given the
lads credit for." He reminded Marx that he had always said
"the Prussian firearms, both rifles and artillery, were the
best in the whole world." He spent his yearly holiday in
Schleswig-Holstein just after the Prussians had conquered
it, and wandered up and down the country with an attentive
eye on its language and the problems of its nationality, which
especially interested him as he was at this time spending
his leisure hours in studying Frisian, Anglian, Jutish, and
Scandinavian philology.

Engels's writings on the army reforms grew into a pamphlet instead of an article. It was published at the end of
February 1865 in Hamburg, under the title *The Prussian
Military Question and the German Working-Class Party.*
Its premises were that the struggle between the government
and the conservatives on one side and the liberal and radical
bourgeoisie on the other was now approaching a crisis, and
that it was time for the working-class party to speak out.
How many soldiers the Prussian state needed might be a
matter of indifference to them, but not how many workers
were trained to arms. The more, the better. For the German working class the conflict between the government and
the parliament was more important than the army reforms.
In countries where the industrial revolution was complete,
the only opponents of the working class were the bourgeoisie.
But in Germany there were still feudal lords, squires, guilds,
privy-councillors, state-councillors, and so on. In a conflict

like this, the moment must come when both parties would ask for the support of the proletariat. Neither of them would be prepared to grant its wishes, but both would be ready to make concessions if an independent working-class party were in existence as a political factor to be reckoned with.

From which side could the workers expect greater concessions? In his answer to this question Engels took the chance of writing a damning criticism of Schweitzer's policy, without mentioning his name. Every victory of the forces of reaction, he explained, postponed the date when the workers could reach power. But every victory of the bourgeoisie was a victory for the workers: it would help to clarify the class-conflict and would hasten the moment when the proletariat would conquer the bourgeoisie. Lately a new type of reaction had become fashionable with certain people (an allusion to Bismarck). This was Bonapartism. In a Bonapartist state every vestige of political power was withdrawn from both workers and capitalists alike, the freedom of the press and the right of combination was forbidden, and universal suffrage was cramped in a way that made it almost impossible to elect opposition candidates. In such a system neither side could hope for more than a rest from battle, in which industry could develop fast and far and create the elements for a new and more violent struggle.

In the present conflict in Prussia, the question was whether the government wished to retain all real power or share it with the parliament. A parliament was good for nothing unless it would keep " a hand on the purse-strings." If parliament could do so, it was not in the interest of the proletariat to deprive it of all power. But if the government imposed universal suffrage from above (as Lassalle had pressed Bismarck to do), and the working class consented to this, they would thereby be recognizing the government's right to abolish universal suffrage again by a new decree. The feudal landlords were still exploiting twice as many workers in Germany as the bourgeoisie. Through the paternalism of the squires, through bad education, through systematic brutalization and remoteness from the world, the agricultural proletariat had become that part of the working class which would be slowest to realize its own social position. In a country where there were two agricultural workers to one industrial, what would be the result of universal suffrage? As long as the land-workers were not drawn into the proletarian movement, universal suffrage was for the proletariat of the towns not a weapon, but a trap. The inevitable battle between the working-class party and the bourgeois opposition could not be fought out until they stood face to face, alone. The bourgeoisie could not achieve political power without demanding universal suffrage, freedom of the press, and freedom of combination. But these things were what the workers' party needed in their own struggle for emancipation. Therefore it was to their interest to support the bourgeois against the forces of reaction, as long as the bourgeois remained true to the interests and the principles of their own class.

Before he sent off the manuscript, Engels wrote to Marx: " Ikey has given the movement a Tory-Chartist character which it will be hard to eliminate, and set a course previously unknown among the workers. This disgusting truckling to reaction is always cropping up. We shall have some trouble with that." And, speaking of the probable effect of his pamphlet on the German proletarians, he added: " Mark my words, the chaps will say: ' What does this Engels mean? What has he done all this time? How can he speak in our name and say what we are to do? The fellow sits in Manchester and exploits the workers,' etc. It's all the same to me, of course, but it will be said without a doubt, and for that we have to thank Baron Ikey." In this we hear a new motif which was bound to increase Engels's wish to be free of business life as soon as he could.

As they read the *Sozialdemokrat,* Marx and Engels grew

more and more indignant with Schweitzer's " cowardly co-
quetting with Bismarck and his constant hero-worship of
Lassalle." But they did not break with the paper for good
until Liebknecht gave notice of his resignation from it, and
Schweitzer wrote to Marx denying his competence to interfere in questions of " day-to-day tactics." In a letter to Weydemeyer, Engels emphasized the obtrusive Lassalle-worship
of the *Sozialdemokrat,* which was all the less justifiable because Schweitzer must know that there had been a formal
alliance between Bismarck and Lassalle.

Schweitzer risked nothing in pouring scorn upon the
" antiquated coterie of Marx " for its lack of influence. He
felt the wind in his favour. The problem of German unity
was just coming to a head in the war of 1866, and it was
becoming increasingly likely that Bismarck would grant
Germany universal suffrage and by so doing execute Lassalle's last will and testament. Engels and Marx were not
attracted by a working-class agitation which was only permitted as long as it took a " form which Bismarck could approve." They preferred " a hundred times rather an agitation in London through the International Workingmen's
Association." This Association was founded while Engels
was touring Schleswig-Holstein. Marx helped in its foundation, because " real forces " in both England and France
were taking part. The young party's early years are of no
importance in the biography of Engels. He had recently
become one of the proprietors of the mill in Manchester and
was therefore unable to do more for the party than contribute money. He prophesied that the new Association would
split up " as soon as the problems at issue were more accurately defined "; and he was afraid that Marx's activities in
the International might keep him from completing *Capital.*
But he agreed that Marx should exert himself for this new
task, which opened such wide prospects. The friends were
fascinated by this thought above all — that at last a means

had been found to inspire the English working-class movement with the spirit of revolution. If this "fresh charge of electricity" succeeded, Engels told Marx on May 1st, 1865, the International would have already done more for the European working-class movement than could have been accomplished in any other way.

CHAPTER XVI

THE RISE OF PRUSSIA.
THE IRISH PROBLEM

⨯

Engels had nothing but contempt for Prussia and the Prussian dynasty. He relied almost entirely on the English papers for news of events in Germany and therefore was slower than Lassalle and Schweitzer to recognize the added political importance which Prussia gained from the character and direction of Bismarck. As in 1863, so too at the beginning of 1866 he considered that a revolution was possible in Berlin when the troops were mobilized and withdrawn from the capital. Once more he believed that there was a league between Prussia and Russia. If there were a war with Austria, he feared that Napoleon would be able to establish himself on the left bank of the Rhine. A Prussian success would involve the interference of France; therefore Engels hoped that his countrymen would " get a frightful beating." To all responsible for this war of German against German he could wish no better fate than the gallows.

Like most democrats, he at first held Bismarck's proposal to the Bundestag to summon a German popular assembly to be nothing but hocus-pocus. But after two days he was convinced that the German liberals would, after a short resistance, allow the Prussian monarchy to carry out their own program. He now saw that Bismarck's Bonapartism was " the real religion of the modern bourgeoisie." In a letter to Marx on the 13th of April he emphasized the incapacity of the bourgeoisie for independent political action. " It is becoming more and more clear to me that the bourgeois has not got it in him to take real control; therefore the normal form of government is Bonapartism, unless, as in England, an oligarchy can take over the task of guiding state and society in the bourgeois interests — for a rich reward. A semi-dictatorship on the Bonapartist plan maintains the chief material interests of the bourgeoisie even in opposition to the bourgeoisie, but leaves it no share in the control of affairs. On the other hand, the dictatorship is itself forced against its will to adopt the material interests of the bourgeoisie."

At this time of uncertainty in Germany, Engels cherished far-reaching hopes. If there was war, he told Marx in mid-May, Bismarck would have to " move hell itself," and hell would swallow him up. But even a direct victory for the Progressive Party would have in those circumstances a revolutionary character and must lead to further developments. " Despite everything," he said, " I still cannot think that in the middle of the nineteenth century North and South Germany are going to come to blows simply because Bismarck wants them to do so in the interest of Bonaparte and Russia." In the event of war Engels prophesied the defeat of Prussia. On this occasion his military judgment was more mistaken than ever before or after, owing to his erroneous belief that the discipline of the Prussian army had been undermined by the constitutional struggle. He foretold to Marx that a military revolution would break out at the end of June: " If this chance passes without being used, and if people let it pass, then we can pack up our revolutionary bags and turn to studying pure theory." It was a correct description of the huge importance of the impending decision for the future of the German revolutionary party. At Sadowa the decision was made — for the rest of his life Engels could pack his revolutionary bags and, at least as far as military matters went, stick to pure theory.

Marx's wish that Engels should become military correspondent of a great English paper was now fulfilled. The *Manchester Guardian* printed five articles by him on the resources and prospects of the belligerent states and on the course of the campaign. These essays show us the enormous surprise which the Austro-Prussian War had in store for Engels. With astonishing shortsightedness he prophesied the defeat of Prussia. And on the day of the great Prussian victory he subjected von Moltke's plan of campaign to a sharp criticism. Next day he was forced to admit that the Prussian generals, despite their sins against the " higher laws of warfare," had not done badly. And in the same place where shortly before he had spoken so contemptuously of the Prussian army, he expressed his unconditional admiration for it on the 6th of July.

Engels immediately saw the political consequences of the Prussian victory. On the 4th of July he wrote to Marx: " In any case Bismarck will now try to bring into being his German Empire." Bismarck, he said, had grown too big for his master Napoleon III and had shown the whole of Europe the insignificance of this " umpire of Europe." On the 9th of July he went on: " The simple fact is this: Prussia has five hundred thousand needle-guns, and the rest of the world has not five hundred. No army can be equipped with breech-loaders under two or three or perhaps five years. Until then Prussia is on top. Do you suppose Bismarck will not use his moment? Of course he will! " Engels's eyes had suddenly been opened. Now he saw who was the most dangerous enemy he had to fight. It was no longer Bonaparte, but Bismarck, who embodied the forces which must be overthrown before the European proletariat could be victorious.

Engels was warned by the disappointments he suffered that summer. Never again did he allow disgust so to blind him to the truth. While Liebknecht refused to believe that the decision made at Sadowa was final, Engels saw at once that he must accept the fact and reckon with it. He deplored " the inevitable result, that Germany would be flooded with Prussianism," and he lamented " the temporary separation of German Austria," which would immediately lead to an increase of Slavism in Bohemia, Moravia, and Carinthia. But he hoped that German Austria would soon be united once more with the rest of Germany.

During these great political changes in Germany, Marx was busy putting the finishing touches to the first volume of *Capital,* in whose fate Engels was so deeply involved. Tortured with illness and poverty, Marx acknowledged to his friend that it was all one to him whether he " croaked " today or tomorrow, so long as the book was ready and his family was provided for. Engels replied: " You know that I am ready to do what I can, and, in this extreme case, to do more that I could risk in other circumstances. But be reasonable and do me and your family the favour of seeing a doctor. What would happen to the whole movement if anything went wrong with you? " When Engels heard, in November 1866, that the first batch of manuscript had gone to the printer, he drank " a special glass " to the " particular health " of its author. Like Marx, Engels was convinced that the book would make a very " great impression," and also that it would add something to Marx's future income. And with this expectation went the hope that he himself could in the not too distant future abandon that business life which he feared was breaking him. He now confessed as much to Marx, adding that if he gave up commerce, his income would be very much more scanty; " and this has always been on my mind — what are we to do with you then? But if things turn out now as they promise, that will soon settle itself, even if the revolution does not come meanwhile and do away with all this financial planning." There is a significant sentence in Marx's answer: " Without you I could not have completed the book, and I assure you that it has always been a load upon my conscience to think that you, chiefly for my sake, were wasting your brilliant powers in business routine, and had perforce to share all my *petites misères* into the bargain."

Marx and Engels intended that *Capital* should have its

merits recognized as soon as possible, that it should be sold out and translated into other languages without delay. Engels thought it permissible to ensure this by " little manœuvres." He wrote a great number of anonymous notices of the book, and adherents of his in Germany saw that they were inserted in bourgeois papers. Liebknecht put his *Demokratisches Wochenblatt* at Engels's disposal. But a scientific work of that kind is never a best-seller. And in England it was still longer than in Germany before it received any notice. The historian Edward Spencer Beesly was a friend of Marx; as sub-editor of the *Fortnightly Review* he had promised to accept a review by Engels. But the editor, John Morley, sent it back with the remark that the subject was too dry for a magazine. All these notices were written with the intention of giving a first idea of Marx's economic doctrines to a public which had yet to be educated to receive their message. But they also allow us to see what Engels admired most in his friend's scientific work. One of them says that *Capital* contains a criticism of all previous systems of political economy and at last furnishes socialist aspirations with the scientific basis " which neither Fourier nor Proudhon nor even Lassalle has been able to give them heretofore." In these words Engels stated the most profound reason for the material and spiritual sacrifices which he made in order to allow *Capital* to be completed — sacrifices so great that he could not justify them to himself on the grounds of personal friendship alone. We can see that Marx realized this, from a letter he wrote to his friend on the 22nd of June 1867 : " That you are satisfied so far is more important to me than anything the whole of the rest of the world may say about the book."

What was the significance of the rise of Prussia for the future of the working-class movement in Germany ? Engels and Marx both saw clearly that the creation of the North German League offered a new opportunity to unite and organize the proletariat throughout the country — an opportunity which they must use to the best of their ability. But it was hard for them to do all that was needful, since their only trustworthy ally in Germany seemed to have no other aim during the next few years than the destruction of Prussia's hegemony. On the other hand, Schweitzer considered that the national problem was really solved, and he could therefore devote his energy to emphasizing the social and economic interests of the proletariat. It should have been a real pleasure to Marx and Engels when Liebknecht began to produce a paper of his own in January 1868. Only Liebknecht made it so difficult for them to collaborate with him! Engels was a business man and had been at considerable pains to make himself careful and prudent in business matters; he was offended by the negligence of this bohemian journalist and agitator. Engels was a well-read man and a sound politician; he was brought to despair by Liebknecht's refusal to "look at the facts." Engels was, lastly, a trained philosopher, and he could not excuse Liebknecht for doubting the importance of theory in practical politics. In fact, he did not think that Liebknecht's achievements justified him in assuming as a matter of course that Marx and Engels would help him intellectually, morally, and materially in his political undertakings. He made repeated and unsuccessful attempts to explain to Liebknecht how mistaken it was to regard the whole political situation solely from the point of view of his anti-Prussianism and to choose his friends only to fit in with that. When Engels pointed this out, Liebknecht assured him that he could not yet ask his supporters to break with the petty-bourgeois South German People's Party. "Here I have not highly trained communists to deal with, but communist recruits; and they still have some prejudices which must be spared." And he urged them: " Do not blame me only; I have got myself a certain position here; it is my task now to hold it and consolidate it; to use it for the interests of our party is your job. So fall to! " He alluded to the influence which he had acquired, through Bebel, on the

Saxon Popular Party, which consisted chiefly of factory-workers.

Between the Austro-Prussian and the Franco-German wars, the German working-class movement was torn by internal conflicts. Since Bismarck had granted universal suffrage throughout the North German League and had made peace with the liberals it had become necessary to redefine the aims of the working-class movement. On one point Engels and Liebknecht were agreed — that it was necessary to break the influence of the dead Lassalle and to destroy the rigid organization of the General Association of German Workers. But Engels could not reconcile himself to Liebknecht's tactics. He was pursued by the thought that the proletariat might once more become a mere appendage of petty-bourgeois democracy. Meanwhile a dangerous rival to Schweitzer's party had arisen in the League of German Workers' Education Association; these associations had gradually grown into a radical democratic party, and Liebknecht's diplomacy had brought them into sympathy with the International Workingmen's Association. Lassalle's party was mostly Prussian, but this new working-class party was principally composed of Germans from outside Prussia. Its heart and soul was the master-turner August Bebel — a fiery but dependable young man, with conscientiousness and a thirst for knowledge. In Bebel Liebknecht found the ally he needed to bring the working classes under his influence, for he himself was only a writer, with no roots in his native country. In their deadly struggle against Schweitzer they passionately upheld the principle of democratic organization against the principle of dictatorial leadership in the German working-class movement.

In the summer of 1868 the German trade-union movement got into full swing for the first time, and Schweitzer immediately attempted to dominate it. Engels considered it a grave error that he should centralize the trade unions as he had centralized the party. During his first stay in England he had made up his mind as to the importance of the trade unions for improving the living-conditions of the working class. Even then he described them as powerless against " all major causes " which affected the labour market and as powerful only " against smaller causes with narrow individual effects." When the trade unions began to gain ground in Germany, he declared to Marx: " Trade-union business is a money matter, and there dictatorship stops automatically." Schweitzer and Co. would soon discover that in this sphere their " tricks, and their attempts to impose their will upon the real movement, were no longer effective." Engels had no doubt that the working-class movement in Germany had outgrown the age when it could be led by one person alone. He was confirmed in this opinion by the meeting at Nuremberg in autumn 1868, where Bebel and Liebknecht won their first great victory over Schweitzer and enticed away some of his lieutenants. Next summer the Social Democratic Workers' Party was founded in Eisenach, and a little later it finally broke away from the relics of bourgeois democracy. Liebknecht might therefore hope that his old dispute with Engels was at an end. He tried again, accordingly, to make Engels see the justification for his tactics during the previous years. " I had the choice of plunging into the stream which was rushing past or of standing still on the bank making philosophical observations. I chose the former, and although I know I made many false steps, yet I think that in general I was absolutely right and that I acted in the interests of our party. I merely used other parties, without letting myself be used by them — which, I should think, might be clear enough from the outcome of it all." Liebknecht in those years of his hardest struggles and most obvious victories was approaching his goal, and he cared little whether his political action at one minute or another had been in accordance with the prescriptions of the *Communist Manifesto*. If he had been more squeamish in that respect, he would have spared himself many reproaches from

Marx and Engels, but he would hardly have managed, in a country which was still very little industrialized, to recruit so many of the proletarians who had been impervious to, or had outgrown, the influence of Lassalle and Schweitzer.

Engels's partner Ermen knew that he disliked business and wished to give it up. Their contract ran out in the summer of 1869. Ermen accordingly in the autumn of 1868 offered to let him withdraw his capital and to compensate him for his goodwill in the firm. Engels was only too pleased. Throughout the negotiations about the sum to be paid as compensation, he was ruled by the thought that the interest on his capital must be enough to satisfy Marx's needs year by year as well as his own. Although he drew £7,500 out of the firm in May 1869, the negotiations continued for some time after that. But in July he was able to write to Marx: " Hurrah! From today no more of the *doux commerce*. I am a free man." At that time (as often) Marx's youngest daughter, Eleanor, was staying in Engels's house. " I shall never forget the triumphant ' For the last time! ' which he shouted as he drew on his top-boots in the morning to make his last journey to business," she said after his death. " Some hours later, when we were standing at the door waiting for him, we saw him coming across the little field opposite his home. He was flourishing his stick in the air and singing, and laughing all over his face." Engels wrote to his mother : " Since yesterday I have been a different chap, and ten years younger. This morning, instead of going into the gloomy city, I walked for some hours in the fields in beautiful weather; and at my writing-table in a comfortably furnished room, where one can open the windows without blackening everything with smoke, with flowers in the window and a few trees in front of the house, work is very different from work in my gloomy room in the warehouse looking out on the yard of a public-house."

It was eighteen years since Engels had returned to the office, in the belief that when the next economic crisis broke

out, the renewed revolution would call him back to full
activity in the task of his lifetime. He had not allowed others
to see much of the disappointment he felt when again and
again he was cheated of his hopes. But he well knew the
danger to which every gifted man is exposed if he is too long
chained to a job in which his real nature cannot fulfil itself.
Since he had become a partner, he felt even more confined
than before, and his anxiety that his talents might rust and
his fertility perish grew into the fear that the hour of liberation might be too late in striking. But it had come at last,
and not too late! True, he was forty-nine years old now, and
he was no longer the impetuous youth who had known many
men in Paris, and many women a little better; a fall from his
horse when out hunting had caused a fracture, and he was
no longer the same reckless horseman for whose sake Marx
had so often been anxious. But he still felt himself to be in
the prime of life — a man whose brown beard had some grey
hairs, but who did not yet possess " the *dignitas* which should
come with them," as he himself acknowledged. Eager for
life, active and cheerful, and a good drinker — that was
Engels, and he remained so until an advanced old age; he
knew marvellously well how to use his time, and he was not
given to fits of depression. Even now he did not need to wait
to consider which task to embark on in his retirement. He
was one of those fortunate mortals who choose their vocation in early youth and never doubt its importance and even
its holiness.

In September he undertook a trip to Ireland, with Lizzy
Burns (whom he always thenceforth described as his wife)
and with Eleanor Marx. Ireland became lastingly important
in his thought. Lizzy had much mother-wit, though she could
neither write nor read properly. Her whole soul was filled
with love of her people, and she passionately sympathized
with the revolutionary Fenians. More than one of them
found shelter in her house, and she was always *au courant*
with conspiracies which had been planned. Engels himself

was not unaffected by the atmosphere of a house in which the colours of the movement, black and green, were always revered. He felt that the character of the movement ("in the first place violent and in the second place anti-English ") was something "unheard-of in English conditions, and really amazing." His revolutionary expectations were increased by the sympathy which was manifested for the Fenians by a considerable number of the London proletariat. But he viewed with fundamental disapproval the "Bakuninistic, braggart, aimless propaganda through action," and he insisted that communism should not be made answerable for such "donkey-tricks." Still, he was convinced that the agrarian murders in Ireland could not be stopped as long as they were "the only real means of defending the people from extermination by the landlords."

For years Marx and Engels had been concerned to discover the economic causes of the constant unrest in Ireland and the political results of the increasing estrangement between the English and the Irish. When the conflict grew sharper after the end of the American Civil War, the friends imagined that in due course it might prompt the outbreak of the general social revolution for which they had waited so long. They still saw in the English bourgeoisie the enemy who must be overcome before communism could triumph in any part of the world; and only the English working class could break the power of the English bourgeoisie. Engels had long hoped that the flame of Chartism might be blown up into a fresh glow. But towards the end of the fifties he realized "that the English proletarian movement in the traditional Chartist form" must "be quite destroyed" before it could revive with some chance of living. He could not imagine, however, what new form it was to assume. When he remembered the condition in which he had found the British working class at his first arrival in Manchester, he was forced to recognize that they had benefited from the increase in British trade, and began to fear that in this, "the most bourgeois of all nations," " a bourgeois aristocracy and a bourgeois proletariat " might one day arise alongside the present bourgeoisie. He even thought that this would be " to a certain extent justified " in a " nation which was exploiting the whole world."

In the International, Engels believed he had found the instrument which would rouse the English working class. But its early success in converting some of the workers to radicalism ended, if not with the establishment of the Reform League, at least when the suffrage reforms were carried out. It was Disraeli who was responsible, in Engels's view, for getting under way a movement which could not now be stopped. He was disappointed that John Bright should be regarded as the political leader of the working class; but he looked forward once more to the rise of a really revolutionary workers' party and expected that revolutionary conditions would soon appear. His hopes were far in advance of reality, however, as was shown by the elections of November 1868, when the workers voted *en masse* for the first time. He called it " a desperate proof of the incapacity of the English proletariat " that not a single workers' candidate was elected, while, as he complained to Marx, " any parvenu swell " got " the votes of the workers and was welcomed by them." He was furious at this disappointment; like a true Rhinelander, he made the son-in-law of his doctor (who had duly done his best for the liberals) " royally drunk " on the evening of the elections. Since the extension of the suffrage did not move the English workers to independent action, the Irish question gained a new significance for him, and Marx's hypothesis seemed more and more attractive — that the fall of the landed oligarchy and the revival of revolutionary spirit in England must start in and be prompted by Ireland.

During his travels in Ireland with Lizzy, he determined to write a social history of the country. When he visited it in 1856 with Mary, his eyes had been opened to the fact " that the so-called freedom of the English bourgeoisie depends on the oppression of the colonies." Since then, he had held frequent discussions with Marx about the oppression of Ireland. Engels was inclined to believe that Ireland would not obtain justice until the English working class had seized power. The elections had shown him how deep-rooted in the heart of the English industrial workers was their distaste for their Irish competitors, with their lower standards of life. He met this distaste later, even on the Council of the International. There he opposed the proposal that the Irish sections should be subject to a British federal council, but it was only in the teeth of violent opposition that he could make the Council regard Ireland as an independent nation. Engels now studied the Irish Home Rule movement on the spot. He told Marx of the difficulties which arose from the fact that most of the leaders of that nation of peasants came from the bourgeoisie of the towns; the peasants therefore could not grasp " that the socialist working men are their only comrades in Europe." He was especially struck by the fact that the Irish agricultural population was still living among the ideas of the age of gentility and had no comprehension of " a property which had rights, but no duties."

On his return to Manchester he began to assemble all the material dealing with Irish history which he could collect from Manchester libraries and London booksellers. He was delighted to find that hunting for sources was a pleasure far superior to hunting for customers on the " confounded " exchange. His work was planned in four sections. The two first, " Natural Conditions " and " Ancient Ireland," were found among his papers after his death. The third, on the English conquest, and the fourth, on the English domination, do not exist. The fourth section was intended to be in three subsections: " Penal Code," " Rebellion and Union, 1780–1801," and " Ireland in the United Kingdom." Engels agreed with Marx in dividing the last subsection into two periods: the age of the small farmers, 1801–46, and the age of extermination, 1846–70.

The book was intended, first, to explain the destiny of Ireland by her " natural conditions " — by showing that the English, as soon as they became a united nation themselves, aspired to assimilate the Irish. " If they succeeded in assimilating them, the whole course of Irish history belonged to England. It might be criticized, but it could never be undone. But if after seven hundred years of struggling they had not succeeded in assimilating the Irish? If, instead, every new wave of invaders was assimilated by the Irish? If the Irish today are not the West Britons any more than the Poles after a century of oppression are West Russians? If the struggle is not yet ended, and there is no prospect that it will end otherwise than through the extermination of the oppressed race? *Then* all the geographical excuses in the world are not enough to prove that England has a mission to conquer Ireland." Engels considered that Ireland's "ill luck " began millions of years ago, when the island's coal deposits were washed away and she was condemned ("as if by Nature's decree ") to be a farming country neighbouring a great industrial land.

Was Ireland destined by its climate for agriculture or cattle-breeding or both? An answer to this question would (as Engels tried to show) involve a judgment on England's attitude to the oppressed island. " Compared with England, Ireland is more suitable for cattle-breeding — but compared with France, England is the more suitable. Are we to conclude that the whole of England should be changed into cattle-ranches, and the whole of the agricultural population sent into the factory towns or shipped to America (except for a few cattle-ranchers) to make room for cattle which are to be sent to France in exchange for silks and wines? " Thus Engels opposes the idea that the Irish people could be doomed by fate to be shipped overseas, so that their country might supply England with meat and butter. " The Irish landed proprietors put up their rents, and the English bourgeoisie decrease their wages — thus inducing a social revolution in a land devoted chiefly to agriculture on a small scale; and that social revolution means the transplantation of four million people, the extermination of the Irish people." " To- day England needs grain quickly and dependably — Ireland seems to have been made for wheat-growing. Tomorrow England needs meat — and Ireland is fitted only for cattle- ranching. The very existence of the five million Irish is a direct insult to all the laws of political economy." Thus the very nature of the Irish soil becomes a ground for quarrels between the two nations. The social condition of the Irish had, according to Engels, suffered no appreciable set-back in the four hundred years since the first English invasion. But that first invasion " cheated Ireland out of her whole de- velopment and threw her back hundreds of years." We can have no doubt about the train of thought which Engels would have pursued in the two missing chapters. Like Marx, he thought Ireland was the bulwark of the English landed aris- tocracy. If the landed aristocracy fell from power in Ire- land, it would fall in England. And then the preliminary condition for the proletarian revolution in England would be fulfilled.

Thus the Irish question gave both Marx and Engels im- portant arguments to back their theoretical and practical deductions. But it affected Engels personally as well. On a page of notes among his papers we find this remark: " The English have attempted to reconcile to their domination people of very different races. The Welsh set great store by their nationality and speech, but they have been assimilated to the British Empire. The Scottish Celts, although they were rebellious until 1745 and since then have been almost exterminated, first by the government and then by their own aristocracy, have now no thought of rebellion. The French of the Channel Islands fought hard against France during the great revolution. Only the Irish are too much for the English, and the reason is the terrific recuperative powers of their race. After the cruellest oppression, after every attempt to exterminate them, the Irish soon lifted up their heads once more, stronger than ever." With his whole heart Engels loved the unhappy nation which had given him Mary and Lizzy. He was thinking of them when he described the Irish climate: " The weather, like the inhabitants, is full of violent contrasts: the sky is like an Irishwoman's face, rain and sunshine succeed each other suddenly and unexpectedly, and there is none of the humdrum greyness of England."

CHAPTER XVII

THE FRANCO–PRUSSIAN WAR

In the autumn of 1870 Engels and Lizzy moved to London and took a house in Regent's Park Road, scarcely a quarter of an hour from the home of Marx. As a factory-owner Engels had been unable to take an active part in politics, but as an independent writer he was immediately elected to the General Council of the International, which had just then reached the height of its prestige and influence in the European working-class movement. After a long interval Engels now came into contact once more with leading personalities of the British workers' movement. In all other countries there were special federal councils, but in England the functions of a federal council were performed by the General Council. This increased the personal influence of Marx (and now of Engels also) on the English. Liebknecht would have been glad to see Engels return to Germany and be elected to the Reichstag. But Engels believed that he could do more lasting work by keeping out of reach of Bismarck's police and following developments on the Continent from England, raising his voice only when there was something of real importance to say. He always took this latter task very seriously, and for its sake he would interrupt his own studies, although he grumbled at leaving the work which gave him so much personal satisfaction.

When he left Manchester the war between France and the Prussian king's German troops was in full swing. He had never doubted that the whole of France, including the proletariat and the socialists, would answer the call to con-

quer the left bank of the Rhine. He himself was a Rhinelander and a revolutionary, and he had always despised the
Jacobin fable about liberating oppressed peoples. Now once
again (as his correspondence with Marx shows) he claimed
that the French socialists should not believe " Bismarck-
ism " to be " something natural to Germany," to destroy
which they must intervene in German affairs. " I think it
extremely important," he wrote, " particularly in the event
of a revolution, that these gentlemen should get used to
treating with us *d'égal à égal.*"

The Second Empire had suppressed the socialist working-
class movement in France, but in Germany it had awakened
to new life. Indeed, it was the German movement on which
Marx and Engels now set all their hopes. There was still
much in it which they wished to alter, but they had begun,
not without success, to inspire it with their conception of history and with its application to practical politics. When
war broke out, Liebknecht (now editor of the *Volksstaat*)
and the committee of the Social-Democratic Workers' Party
found themselves at variance on several points — their differences being very like those which split social democracy
during the World War. Marx was called in to settle
the dispute, but would not say anything before consulting
Engels.

Engels's response (on the 15th of August) started with
the assertion that Napoleon had " involved Germany in a
war for her existence as a nation." If she were defeated, she
would be ruined for years, perhaps for generations. " Then
there will be no more talk of an independent German working-class movement. All energies will be absorbed in the
struggle to restore Germany's existence as a nation, and
at best the German working class will become a mere appendage of the French. If Germany conquers France, Bonapartism will be destroyed, the never ending row about the
unification of Germany will be ended, the German workers
can organize themselves on a larger national scale than

before, and the French workers (whatever kind of government they get) will certainly have more free play than they
have under Bonapartism." Engels advised, then (and Marx
agreed with him), that the German working classes should
back up the national movement so far as and so long as it
was confined to the defence of their country. If as a result of
a German victory a non-chauvinist republican government
were set up in Paris, the party should work for an honourable peace. Stress must be laid on the community of interest
between the working classes of both countries; they had not
approved of the war and were in no sense enemies of one
another.

Wilhelm Liebknecht's attempts to oppose the national
movement provoked Engels's scornful laughter. He said to
Marx: "If that was the general feeling in Germany, we
should soon have the Rhenish Confederation again, and the
noble Wilhelm would see what kind of part he played in
that, and where the working-class movement would be left.
A people which gets nothing but hard knocks is the right
one to make a social revolution!" Engels wished for the fall
of Bonapartism in France and the unification of Germany
and therefore at first welcomed the victories of Germany.

Throughout the campaign Engels discussed the fighting
in the liberal *Pall Mall Gazette*. He published about sixty
Notes on the War between July 29th, 1870 and February
18th, 1871; they were reprinted as a book during the World
War. Engels enjoyed working at military science and was
pleased by the favourable attention which his articles received. The *Spectator* described them as the only important
articles which had appeared in the English press. Frau Marx
and her daughters were constantly irritated by the "pla-
giarisms" from them in *The Times* and other great papers.
Their admiration was unbounded when Engels accurately
foretold, a week before the event, the capitulation of General MacMahon's army at Sedan. Marx wrote to him on
the 2nd of September: "It is now time, after the brilliant

confirmation of your first article on MacMahon, for you to begin the next article with a résumé of your own *Notes on the War*. You know that you must shove anything under the nose of an Englishman before he notices it, and that too much matter-of-fact modesty will not do with full-mouthed John Bull."

The most powerful man in Europe was a prisoner of the Germans, and a bourgeois republic had been proclaimed in France. Now that it was clear that there was nothing in the way of Germany's unification, Engels's attitude to events changed. He now saw the danger, not in the chauvinism of the French, but in the chauvinist German demands for extension of their territory. He agreed with Marx that the annexation of Alsace-Lorraine was the greatest danger Europe could run. He thought it to be ridiculous for Germany to attach to her western frontier " a German-speaking Venice," and he did not believe that France " could be muzzled by the loss of a strip of land with about a million and a quarter inhabitants." Even if Metz was annexed as well as Strasbourg, that would not keep the French from creating a new fighting line at Nancy or Verdun. In the famous address of the 12th of September in which the International foretold the danger of a forcible annexation of Alsace-Lorraine, the military points are clearly inspired by Engels.

In the second phase of the war Engels's attitude was determined by his fears for the future of the European working-class movement if the struggle ended with a complete triumph for Prussian militarism. He thought that if the popular armies which Gambetta was raising in the conquered country managed to thrust the armies of the German princes out of France, both France and Germany would have proved to each other that they were invincible. His sympathies for the belligerent nations changed so much that towards the end of 1870 he drafted a plan of campaign which might enable the French to raise the siege of

Paris and liberate France. (It is asserted without proof that he sent this plan to the French government through Paul Lafargue, French revolutionary who married Laura, second daughter of Karl Marx, in 1848.) He had not much opinion of the value of the demonstrations held in Hyde Park from September onwards, at which radicals, proletarians, and Irish demanded England's intervention on the French side. But when on October 31st Russia repudiated the provisions of the Peace of Paris made in 1856, by which her sovereignty in the Black Sea was limited — an act which caused much excitement in government and bourgeois circles in England — he made cautious allusions in the *Pall Mall Gazette* to the possibility of such British intervention. On the 21st of November he added that, now that Russia had broached the Eastern question, it was possible that the fate of Paris might be decided, not in the trenches, but in the Cabinet of a power not yet at war. But it was a long way from Lord Granville's strong words, the excitement of the press, and the partisanship of the London mobs and the radical intelligentsia, to armed intervention. The Premier, Mr. Gladstone, was not inclined to take that road.

Engels now had no scruples in asserting in the *Pall Mall Gazette* that Prussian complicity in the Russian breach of contract was highly probable. He said that if Prussia could not clear herself of that suspicion and if Europe decided to oppose Russia, it might all happen before France was beaten to the ground. If Prussia did not give a categorical explanation of her conduct, steps must be taken immediately to raise the hopes of the beleaguered city. Thirty thousand British soldiers landed in Cherbourg or Brest and added to the Loire army would stiffen it enormously; the influence of an army corps of that kind would be far greater than its numerical strength. In Spain and in India the English infantry had proved that its merits and its defects alike made it particularly suitable to stiffen up newly levied troops. In the

Gazette he also surmised that Austrian, Danish, and especially Italian troops might be brought in to draw the German armies away from Paris.

Even after it was too late, he was still patently earnest in his idea of setting limits to the advance of Germany by a European coalition. On the last day of January 1871 the General Council of the International opened a discussion, which lasted for several meetings, on the subject of the past, present, and future attitude of the British proletariat to the developments on the Continent. The discussion dealt with three theses, proposed and worked out by Engels. The first asserted that the English working-class movement must direct all its efforts to induce the British government to recognize the French Republic. The second laid down that military intervention on the French side could have succeeded only at one particular moment, which was then past. The third declared that England would be incapable of playing a part in Continental affairs and of defending herself against the absolutist military states of Europe until she had won back her liberty to make use of her real strength — namely, her naval power. But she could recover such liberty only if she repudiated the declaration made by Lord Clarendon at the Congress of Paris. On the 27th of September Marx had demanded in the General Council that England should repudiate the Declaration against Privateering made at Paris on April 16th, 1856.

Engels's speech on this occasion is one of the longest which he ever delivered, for he preferred usually to present his opinions in writing. He spoke with disapproval of the split in the movement caused by certain British working-class leaders (he alluded especially to George Odger and Robert Applegarth) who had attempted to force Gladstone into armed intervention. Agitators who had not succeeded in getting the Republic recognized would hardly induce Britain to declare war. The antiquated military organization of Britain was scarcely suitable to furnish a great expeditionary force. The only real help England could have given France was to answer Gorchakov's note with a declaration of war. Engels added that he had no doubt that there was a secret arrangement between Prussia and Russia. If both states had acted in concert in the autumn, they would have found the whole of Europe against them, and France would have been saved. Since then Jules Favre had openly admitted France's defeat, and there was no longer any doubt that the bourgeois Republic must soon make peace. Then Russia's intentions must be revealed. Russia and Prussia needed wars, as Napoleon III had needed them, in order to stop the popular movements at home and to maintain their position abroad. Although England's whole power depended on her fleet, she had helped in the Declaration of 1856 to create a new maritime law by which privateers were abolished. She abandoned the right to search foreign ships, so that enemy goods on neutral ships, and neutral goods on enemy ships, were now inviolate. It had never been known who was Lord Clarendon's authority for his pronouncement in Paris, by which he deprived England of the possibility of injuring Russia by sea. If it was wished to put Russia out of action, her foreign trade must be crippled. Therefore England must recover the sinews of her power, which her bourgeoisie had renounced with the declaration that private property must be as safe at sea as it was on land. The working class had no private property to lose and had no interest, therefore, in securing its safety. But it had an interest in England's recovery of the instruments of power which were indispensable to her and in her preservation of them until the dissolution of the Russian Empire. All states whose basis was force must one day be destroyed, the British Empire among them. But that was not an immediate question, and it could perhaps be solved in a peaceful way. No country but England could so effectively counter the impending Russian war of conquest, for which extensive preparations had already been made. Therefore England must retain her right to use privateers at least until Poland was again an independent state.

In his closing speech on March 14th Engels emphasized that the agreement to which he referred had never been ratified by Parliament and was therefore not binding on England. He quoted Lord Derby, who had declared that the necessity of self-defence overrode all treaties. He withdrew his first two theses after they had been clarified by discussion. The third was unanimously accepted.

We see, then, that Engels wished to see England's naval supremacy once more restored because he held it important that, now France had collapsed, one strong military power should remain in western Europe to counterbalance the Russo-German hegemony. He and Marx always wished those states to be humbled or broken which seemed to them to be the strongest bulwark against the near or remote attack of the revolutionary proletariat. If the domination of the Hohenzollerns, the Junkers, and the military caste were established over Germany, the new German Empire would become paramount in Europe. And that was not in the interests of communism.

CHAPTER XVIII

THE STRUGGLE AGAINST BAKUNIN

✍

For the authors of the *Communist Manifesto* Bakunin was to the international working-class movement what Lassalle was to the German. It was necessary for them to counteract his influence if the movement was to develop in the only way which they could accept as correct. Both temperamentally and politically they were poles apart. Between them lay fundamental differences in their objectives, their scale of values, and their outlook; and these differences had their roots in social, national, and cultural differences, impossible to overcome. Their political disputes were embittered by temperamental incompatibility. In the heat of the struggle each side accused the other of causing all the trouble by greed for power, whereas in fact their personal quarrels sprang from infinitely deeper differences. Even a revolutionary cannot erase all traces of the nation and the social class to which he belongs. Engels and Marx were sons of German bourgeois families; their revolutionary attitude was founded on deep and systematic thought; they were ready to wait long for the fulfilment of their ideals, and their primary impulse to revolution was not emotion, but the pressure of objective factors. But revolution for the Russian aristocrat, Bakunin, was really emotional intoxication. Some men have an intellectual superiority to which those who know them must bow — and such was Marx. Others have a superabundant vitality which puts a spell on other men — and such was Bakunin. But the erratic aristocrat differed still more widely from Engels than from Marx. His business training had made it a spiritual necessity for Engels to conduct his life in an orderly way. But Bakunin had no taste for systematic study — his passion was not books, but men, and he spent his life in making them the instruments of his will. For him a gulf was fixed between science and life — and science seemed to him a barren pursuit. Engels, on the other hand, believed that science could map out the way which he as a revolutionary must follow. Again, Engels had been familiar with large-scale industry from childhood. In the land where Bakunin grew up there were no factories; the whole world seemed to be made of large estates and small farms. And in later life he never believed that large-scale industry could affect the Slavs and Latin peoples as deeply as it had affected England. Engels, again, was a man of order — his finances, his clothes, his papers, his thoughts, were systematized. Bakunin's life was chaos. He himself was chaos — but a chaos of heat and fire, constantly shooting forth burning thoughts and blazing emotions. Those sparks were meant to kindle Europe into a blaze, but in the end they died away like rockets in mist.

Bakunin demanded for the liberation of mankind the utter self-sacrifice of the individual. Engels looked for that liberation to the slow development of supra-personal forces and not, as Bakunin did, to the efforts of small groups of devoted conspirators whose task it was to set in motion the masses with whom the consummation lay. Bakunin had a deep-rooted trust in the forces rising " from below " — he detested all authority, whether of state or church, of a conception of history or a dominant personality. A man who puts such faith in individual efforts must needs trust the individual, and Bakunin had a genius for friendship. He could be generous even to his opponents. Engels, on the other hand, was easily led to excessive admiration of those whom he

MICHAEL BAKUNIN

loved, but he never felt drawn to do justice to indifferent or hostile characters. He felt himself a fighter, who had not come to bring peace. *A la guerre, comme à la guerre.* And supra-personal motives kept him from being gentle to those who opposed his policy. There is no more place for isolated personalities in his conception of history than in Hegel's. When Marx and he met quacks with some social panacea, or hotheaded revolutionaries who wanted to lay the world in ruins, they treated them as dangerous vermin. And they viewed Bakunin as one of those vermin, for he boasted that the abolition of the state would enable him to heal all the evils of society.

After his escape from a long imprisonment in Siberia, he had begun by resuming his old efforts to revolutionize the Slavs. Then, at a congress of the democratic League of Peace and Freedom in 1868, he demanded the abolition of all states and the institution of a world federation of free productive societies. When that proposal was ridiculed by the conference, he turned his attention for the first time to the International Workingmen's Association. Marx and Engels had known him in youth; they did not really distrust him until they began to suspect him as a general without an army who intended to make the forces of the proletariat (represented by the International) into the instrument of his ambition and his anarchism. It was no easy task even for them — in an association containing so many differences of social standing and political maturity — to show the necessary restraint in putting forward their own ideas. Were they to allow "antiquated doctrines" which could only injure the "real working-class movement" to implant themselves in the International and there create "a state within a state"? For that was really Bakunin's aim. The power of the International was sufficient only to organize the working class; therefore he considered it indispensable that there should be an invisible organization within it, aiming at "collective action." He believed it to be his task to organize and to lead this invisible organization within the working-class movement.

Thus Bakunin brought the germ into the Association which was to be fatal to its continued existence. Previously he had founded an anarchistic Alliance of Socialist Democracy, which he had to dissolve in order to introduce its members into the International. But Marx and Engels always suspected that it was dissolved only in name. We need describe the details of the great struggle which broke out in the summer of 1870 only in so far as they immediately affected Engels's life.

At an early date Engels had told Marx that he feared the Parisian working class might rise against the Government of National Defence even before the end of the war. When they did rise, in March 1871, he was more passionately interested in Paris than he had been since June 1848. As long as the war was carried on by the central committee of the National Guard, he was still hopeful. It was he who gave the advice which Marx transmitted to Paris, to fortify the northern slopes of Montmartre. But the Commune let the right moment for the offensive slip past. While thousands of proletarians were butchered in the streets of Paris, Marx declared to the General Council that the Commune might fall, but its principles would never die until the working class was liberated. It was in the General Council that he read the famous address in which he explained the historical significance of those bloody days. When Engels republished that address twenty years later, the historical facts of the Commune had changed, under their influence, into a proletarian myth, which had its own existence and did not always correspond with the facts which had occurred. Engels was well aware of the origin and existence of that myth. On New Year's Day 1884 he admitted to Bernstein that Marx "had improved the unconscious tendencies of the Commune into more or less conscious projects," and he added that that improvement had been "justified, even necessary, in the circumstances."

Forthwith began a hue and cry after all persons and parties who had been partisans of the Commune. The Continental governments and the press of almost all Europe joined the hunt with zest. In England, too, liberal and conservative journals vied with one another in their ferocity. Engels therefore severed his relations with the *Pall Mall Gazette*. Although he did not personally approve of all the acts of the Commune, the unanimous fury of the bourgeoisie drove him to espouse its actions and its aims without reserve. Even his mother heard of this. In a letter, which we do not possess, she lamented that her eldest son should belong to the dirty gang from whom the whole world turned away in horror, and hinted that his political opinions would be different if his evil genius Marx were not with him. Friedrich answered: "You know that my views have not changed for nearly thirty years, and it cannot have come as a surprise to you that, when events compelled me, I should not only maintain them, but also do my duty in other ways. You would have reason to be ashamed of me if I did not do so. If Marx was not here, if he did not exist at all, it would make no difference to that." Later letters to his mother have not been preserved, but it cannot be doubted that this last outburst of the old dispute with Engels's family tradition made no serious alteration in the charming relationship with his mother which Engels maintained throughout his life.

The bourgeois hatred which raged round the International after the Commune, and the universal enthusiasm which it awoke among the working classes of the Continent, led Engels and Marx to identify themselves with it as fully as possible. On the other hand, the two English trade-union leaders Odger and Benjamin Lucraft (who were co-founders of the International) took Marx's address as a pretext for resigning from such a revolutionary association. Engels reproached them with allowing the International to support the Reform League as long as they were agitating for the extension of the suffrage, only to desert it now because they did not care to fall out with the liberals, who were to get them seats in Parliament. After the Commune a stream of refugees flowed into England and sought assistance from the International. Those were anxious days for Engels, who was among the moving spirits of the relief work. At a meeting of the General Council he deplored the reluctance of the English workers to assist the refugees; " They have no political life," he complained.

While the members of the International were being hunted out and prosecuted in France, the internal conflicts in the Association increased in violence. Was it prudent to bring them to a head at a public congress? Engels held it wiser "to have a public palaver and do the business in secret." In agreement with Marx he moved that the disputed points of organization and policy should be settled at a private conference in London. They both considered that it was indispensable, for the survival of the International, to preserve the full ascendancy of the General Council. They were convinced that the Association must perish if the connexions between the centre and the branches were loosened. Therefore Engels (with Marx, and often even before him) became the motive force of the defensive struggle against the constantly increasing attacks on the predominance of the General Council.

At the private conference in September there were scarcely any representatives of the opposition present. It consisted, as Bakunin later declared, almost "entirely of the intimates of Herr Marx—carefully chosen by himself —and a few dupes." A committee working entirely under the influence of Engels and Marx formulated the resolutions which were adopted. One of these deprecated every effort at decentralization which might impair the influence of the General Council. Another declared that economic successes could not be won apart from political action, and described it as essential that the working class should everywhere constitute itself as an independent political party. This was the signal for open warfare, for Bakunin considered these resolutions to be a *coup d'état* designed to transform the International into a centralized machine in which the General Council would be dictator, while making the Marxist program obligatory on the whole Association.

Would the next public congress sanction these resolutions? It was now all-important for both the opposing parties to make sure of their majority at the congress. Engels had been elected corresponding secretary of the International for Italy and Spain. These countries were the strongholds of his opponents, and during the succeeding months he multiplied his efforts to capture them. In Spain he relied on Lafargue, a refugee from the Commune. In Italy he placed his trust in young Carlo Cafiero, who had been a close ally of his in London. But on his return to Italy Cafiero had soon gone over to the anti-authoritarian and anti-political party which predominated there, and become the leader of the movement against the General Council in Italy. He was in the chair at the conference in Rimini in August 1872 which dissociated itself from the General Council and even declined to participate in the coming public congress in Holland.

At first, most of the General Council held that the opposition would not appear at all at The Hague. A subcommittee under Engels's presidency had charge of the preparations for the congress. On the 2nd of July, at a plenary meeting, Engels maintained that the Council should be strengthened, not weakened. The only concession he would make was that all the powers granted to the executive should be duly safeguarded. He made especial efforts to secure for the General Council the right to suspend individual branches or entire federal councils until the next annual congress. But the discussion aroused by this proposal showed him and Marx that the General Council was no longer merely the instrument of their wishes. At this preliminary discussion Engels remained staunch to the principle that the creation of special political working-class parties was indispensable for the seizure of power, and the seizure of power was indispensable for every social revolution. Accordingly he opposed the tactics of the English trade unions, which did not preach the class-war.

Even those English working-class leaders who were still on the General Council and endorsed political action became less friendly with Marx and Engels now that opposition to them was increasing so rapidly on the Continent. An English Federal Council had existed since the previous year, and it held its first congress in July 1872. At this congress John Hales (secretary both of the General Council and of the Federal Council) moved that the English Federation should have the right to enter into direct relations with the federations of all other countries, thus eliminating the General Council. He publicly admitted that this was an attack on the irksome surveillance of Marx and Engels. On August 6th, when Engels, in the name of the subcommittee, made an official complaint at the General Council against Bakunin and his "secret alliance," Hales championed Bakunin's claim that there were really two secret societies fighting for power within the International. It was therefore not surprising that in the congress at The Hague almost the whole English delegation supported the anarchist opposition, whose decentralizing tendency they approved in this case.

When he arrived in Holland, Engels found that he could count on a safe majority. He knew that the real decision would be over once the credentials of the delegates had been examined. The hall in which the meeting opened (on the 2nd of September) was called Concordia — but the proceedings were far from harmonious! Bakunin did not attend. The opposition was led by the Swiss. James Guillaume.

Engels's tactics worked perfectly. Marx proposed that a subcommittee should sit in judgment on the evidence Engels had collected against the " secret alliance." The two friends made their depositions in person and managed to have Bakunin and Guillaume expelled. The verdict charged Bakunin not only with irregular conduct, but also with common blackmail. It would be unfair to blame Bakunin for calling the congress a " sorry product of lies and intrigue " after his unjust condemnation. Marx deserves censure for extending the war against his political opponent into private life, and Engels for not dissuading him from this course.

But there was another sensation to come. To everyone's astonishment, Engels proposed that the offices of the central committee should be moved to the United States. Apart from London, the cause of the international proletariat was nowhere so alive as in New York, and scarcely anywhere else was there so little risk that the police might interfere with the archives of the International. He said that the meetings of the General Council (whose proper functions were general supervision and administration) had become more and more like heated parliamentary debates since the arrival of refugees from the Commune. This was not in the interests of the International. Engels recommended that the move should be provisional and for one year. The proposal was accepted. He and Marx believed that they could not get much done in a General Council sitting in London, now that the leaders of the English working-class movement had deserted them. The hope of influencing them had drawn Marx eight years before out of his scholarly retirement. But now that the disputes within the International were growing ever more violent, he grudged the interruption of his scientific studies by practical work. While they had been living together in London, Engels had taken over most of the burden, but it became too heavy even for him when he saw that the International had fulfilled its mission.

It was the International that first aroused the working-class movement in many countries from its slumbers and made it class-conscious. But as the strength of the movement increased, it became increasingly clear that it differed in essential features from country to country. They all had a common point of departure, but it seemed inevitable that the rest of the journey must be made independently by the proletariat of each country, and that the course to be taken would depend in each case on the special historical and economic conditions there prevailing. Engels had at first seriously under-estimated the problems presented by the differences in degree of development between the various nations, but now that rifts and schisms were splitting the International into radically opposing factions, he began to see that it was vain and fruitless labour to try to impose the same tactics on Englishmen and Italians, Spaniards and Germans.

But if Engels realized this, why did he fight on to the bitter end, as though the International could be saved if only Bakunin was put out of action? The answer is more obvious than may at first sight appear. However personal a struggle Engels made of it, his motives were at bottom purely disinterested. His real aim was not to preserve unity and continued life for the existing organization, but to give the greatest possible unity and compactness to the European working-class movement in its future development. He was fighting for the victory of communism against anarchism.

The Controlling Commission at The Hague was instructed to prepare a memorandum on Bakunin's "conspiracy" and the "secret alliance." It was intended chiefly for the Latin countries and was therefore written in French — Lafargue assisted Engels to compose it. *L'Alliance de la Démocratie Socialiste et l'Association Internationale des Travailleurs* is the passionate speech of a public prosecutor who is convinced of the justice of his cause and omits no argument which can lead to the condemnation of the accused. It does not aspire to be an objective or unbiased history. Even before 1870 the fanatical anarchist Nechayev had induced Bakunin to write pamphlets which were far wilder than anything else he ever wrote in any European language. Engels declared that only an *agent provocateur* would (as in these pamphlets) glorify bandits as the real Russian revolutionaries, preach the cult of ignorance to the young, and identify the revolution with acts of individual and collective murder.

Bakunin never attempted to publish a reply to these charges. He was broken by heart-trouble and compelled to rest. Ever since the centre of gravity in European politics had moved to Berlin, he had lost faith in the imminence of the social revolution. In his declining health his last hope was a world war in which the enormous military states would sooner or later devour one another.

Engels had expected that his pamphlet would have a great effect: he claimed it to be the political death-sentence of Bakunin. But the events which had occurred before and during the Hague Congress had shaken the prestige of the International beyond repair. The strands which had been joined in London could not hold together in New York. Engels and Marx were compelled to acknowledge that the Association, in its old form, could not survive. Two years after The Hague, Engels (writing to the general secretary, Sorge,[1] in Hoboken) said that the proletarian world had become too big for a new International in the likeness of the old, an alliance of all proletarian parties in all countries. But he was hopeful even in defeat. " I believe," he proceeded in the same letter, " that after the influence of Marx's writings has been felt for some years, the next International will be purely communist and actually disseminate our principles."

If the future International was to be founded on the *Communist Manifesto,* all the other competing doctrines must be deprived of their influence on the working-class

---

[1] Friedrich Albert Sorge (1828–1906), German communist who emigrated to the United States after the revolution of 1848 and became the representative there of Engels, with whom he remained in regular correspondence.

movement. For this purpose Engels saw that the first necessity was the completion and publication of *Capital*. In order to give Marx leisure for this purpose, he himself took over more and more exclusively the task of combating the views of their opponents in the press.

CHAPTER XIX

THE GERMAN EMPIRE AND THE UNIFICATION OF GERMAN SOCIAL DEMOCRACY

Although Engels had now lived in England for more than twenty years, he was not at home there. He was German by nature and by sentiment. But he had no kindly feelings for the united Germany which had been created by the victory over France. His Pan-German sympathies resented the severance of German Austria, and, as a Rhinelander, he disliked the shift of political predominance to the east of Germany. But his keenest disappointment was the fact that the bourgeoisie, so long after 1848, were still not the chief power in the country; and he earnestly desired the fall of the military monarchy, which backed up all the forces of authority and counter-revolution in Europe. Still, he did not believe (like the bourgeois democrats) that it would be brought low by the inevitable triumph of the idea of Law, or (like Bakunin) by the revolutionary instincts of the peasants or the desperation of students without careers. His hopes were built on the progressive development of the forces of production — a development which not even Bismarck was strong enough to arrest. So he saw the new Empire simply as a historical phenomenon like any other, which it was the task of the class-conscious proletariat to suppress. He did not under-estimate the terrific military equipment possessed by the Empire — he considered it impossible for any coalition of its enemies to overcome it at any time in the near future. Therefore he looked forward, all the more confidently, to its collapse under the steadily developing class-consciousness of the workers who composed its fighting forces.

Engels was the most important German political thinker who lived abroad during the Bismarck period. Through his economic conception of history he was enabled to look through German political phenomena to the more important economic and social facts below. He believed that (despite many differences) it was the same empire which had ended so ingloriously in France that was now transplanted to the land of its conqueror. The German elections were conducted on a basis of universal suffrage, but the police were all-powerful. The people had no voice in the conduct of the country; all was done by the Emperor, with the advice of the Chancellor and the General Staff. But, according to the theory expounded in the *Communist Manifesto,* the proletariat could not expect to seize power until the bourgeoisie had secured political supremacy and brought a democracy and a republic into being. Granted that the inclusion of South Germany in the Empire had given a numerical majority to those sections of the population which had long outgrown Junker feudalism, it was still unlikely that any united democratic front would be built up in the near future. In Liebknecht's *Volksstaat* for January 1873 Engels drew a comparison between the old Prussian monarchy and the new " Bonapartist " monarchy which he said was then rapidly coming into being. The basic principle of the former, he pointed out, had been the balance of power between the bourgeois and the landed aristocracy; that of the latter was the balance between bourgeois and proletariat. In both, the real power lay with a special caste of officers and bureaucrats which seemed to be superior to the rest of the people and independent of them, and hence the state itself appeared to be independent of the people. The contradictions in this social system were bound to lead to a sham constitutionalism.

Much as Engels hated the Junker class, he could not deny that they had the will to rule; and he deplored the absence

of such a will in the German bourgeoisie, who had bought
their social emancipation from the government at the cost of
immediately sacrificing their claim to political power. Nevertheless they justified themselves industrially and commer-
cially, and therefore (he believed) their claims must be
granted even if a thousand Bismarcks refused them. He
watched with much satisfaction the astonishing burst of industrial expansion which followed upon the unification of
Germany. "We have at last," he wrote in 1874, "created
a world commerce for ourselves, really large industries, and
a really modern bourgeoisie. Accordingly we have also had a
real slump and have now got a really powerful proletariat.
The historian of the future will consider the battle-thunders
of Spicheren, Mars-la-Tour, and Sedan, with all that depended on them, far less important events in the history of
Germany between 1869 and 1874 than the quiet, unosten-
tatious, but unbroken development of the German proletariat." During the seventies and the early eighties Engels
would not allow that Germany had any large-scale industries
except ironworking. Even in 1884 he asserted that German
industries ("although it was at last large-scale") only made
articles "which were too paltry for the English and too
vulgar for the French."

Engels and Marx no longer thought it important to preserve their neutrality towards the two warring factions
within the German socialist workers' movement. For Liebknecht had now severed his alliance with bourgeois democracy and joined Bebel and several distinguished former
disciples of Lassalle in founding what the two friends could
agree was a real *class*-party, although certain points of
theory in the Eisenach program failed to satisfy them completely. Engels, who detested the dictatorial spirit of the
General Association, considered its destruction and the elimination of Lassalle's ideals to be the most important mission
which he had in German politics. But these aims were beyond
his reach as long as the General Association of German

Workers commanded a more efficient organization, a larger membership, stronger finances, and a more influential press than the Socialist Workers' Party. After the war Schweitzer had retired from politics. That fact, as well as the foundation of the Empire and the necessity of frequent co-operation in election-work and in the Reichstag, had done much to ease relations between the two factions. The need for reconciliation became really urgent in the beginning of 1874, when Bismarck enlisted the law, the police, and soon the legislature as well in a fierce attack on both social-democratic parties. But every time the bridge was built between them, it was swept away by the flood of hate and distrust which had grown and gathered for years. Engels and Marx were against any fusion while the socialism with which the masses were familiar was based on Lassalle's pamphlets — that is, while they anticipated that the united party would be ruled by Lassalle's principles instead of theirs. Engels was particularly opposed to any compromise which left room for such co-operation with the existing state as Lassalle and Schweitzer had attempted. He therefore endeavoured in Marx's name and his own to persuade Bebel and Liebknecht not to pay " too much attention to their competitors." But, as we know, Liebknecht claimed to have more practical experience than Engels, who, he implied, under-estimated the difference between " a purely theoretical and a militant party."

It became absolutely necessary for the two parties to negotiate a coalition when in June 1874 Lassalle's Association was dissolved by the police. Engels and Marx wished the Socialist Workers' Party to wait a few months, till the " disorganized mob " of Lassalleans sought refuge with them. They did not wish the German party leaders to think that they were simply doctrinaires, trying to satisfy theoretical scruples by impeding a necessary practical step. Yet they attached far more importance than their practical colleagues to the form which the program of the new party would take. Liebknecht knew that fusion was impossible without concessions to Lassalle's old political demands; he feared the objections of Marx and Engels and therefore told them nothing about the details of the negotiations during the next few months. Bebel was still in prison, so that Liebknecht held all the threads in his own hands. It was not until the beginning of March 1875 that Engels and Marx were shown the draft of the program which the negotiators on both sides intended to lay before the meeting in Gotha where the fusion was to be ratified. They were both absolutely horrified.

The proposed program seemed to them to be an unparalleled " prostration of the sound socialist proletariat before the idol of Lassalle." They hoped that Bebel (who was about to be released) would oppose it, and therefore sent him the theoretical arguments against it in a letter written by Engels on the 18th of March. Its contents and its point of view were the same as those of the *Critical Comments* which Marx sent on the 5th of May to the leaders of the Socialist Workers' Party.

In this " flabby and flavourless program," as he called it, Engels complained of the " historically false Lassallean phrase " about " one reactionary mass, composed of all non-proletarian classes in opposition to the proletariat." He said that this was true only in certain exceptional cases — for example, in a country where the bourgeoisie had formed the state and society in its own image, and also where the petty-bourgeois democracy had carried that transformation to its final conclusions. Next Engels criticized the program for denying that the principle of the internationalism of the working-class movement was immediately applicable, for not mentioning the trade unions, and for naming the Lassallean plan of public assistance as the only starting-point for solving the social problem. These great concessions to Lassalle's party, he declared, were balanced only by a string of purely democratic demands, some of which could well be planks in any bourgeois liberal platform. Outside Germany, said Engels, he and Marx were held responsible for the words and acts of the German Socialist Workers' Party; but if a program of that kind were adopted, Marx and he could not belong to any new party based on such principles.

Did Bebel really receive Engels's letter? He did not answer it, at least. And we now know that Liebknecht did not send him Marx's *Critical Comments*.

Indeed, Liebknecht did not send an answer to the " row " raised by his unkind critic until a month had passed. He did not gloss over the faults of the program, but explained that he and his friends had agreed to it because the Lassalle party had faced them with the two alternatives: either to accept the program or to break off negotiations. He assured Engels, a little prematurely, that the unification of the parties meant not only the death of Lassalle's ideas, but the complete victory of Marxist communism over Lassallean sectarianism, and said that he would have been ready to make further concessions to secure that victory. After his release Bebel was forced to the conviction that the masses, who were clamouring for a coalition, had pressed the negotiations too far to allow anyone to raise further difficulties about the program, at least with any hope of getting a hearing.

Engels and Marx thus suffered a twofold disappointment. The opposition which they had tried to foster among the leaders of the party had fallen flat, and their own criticisms (which very few people had seen) were quite neglected by the congress. They felt their defeat particularly keenly since they had just lost their control of the International. And now they had threatened to sever all connexion with their German allies — only to find that, under the pressure of circumstances, those allies would allow them to fulfil their threats! Practice had shown itself stronger than theory. Liebknecht had successfully flouted their wishes in an important matter, although he was very faithful to them and — conscious of his own inadequacy in the sphere of theory — had an unqualified respect for their superiority in it. As time passed, Engels came to place more implicit confidence in Bebel than in him. Bebel was a trained man of business; he was accurate; he was no flibbertigibbet like the restless journalist Lieb-knecht. Engels found him more and more indispensable as a correspondent in the German Workers' Party. A fine speaker and a great organizer, he was more of a proletarian by origins and instinct than the other, and he was a sharper critic of the intellectuals who thrust themselves into the party. Although his optimism led him to expect too rapid progress, in concrete political situations he seemed to Engels to have a sober judgment. In the sphere of theory he was at the time of the Gotha congress still an inquirer, and he fre-quently disappointed Engels, before the latter managed to make him into a sound disciple.

As it became plain that the working-class movement had increased its recruiting power by the new united front, Engels became more disposed to accept it as an " educational ex-periment." But Liebknecht had greatly anticipated the real process of development when he declared that the elimina-tion of Lassalle's organization meant the final victory of Marxist communism. As a matter of fact, hardly any in-fluential person in the party (far less the mass of ordinary members) understood the basis of Marx's and Engels's theory or the political deductions which they drew from it. The leaders had no time to plunge into a book like *Capital.* At most they knew the *Communist Manifesto* and realized that it developed the doctrine of the class-conflict more thoroughly than Lassalle's *Workers' Program,* which was the usual introduction to socialist education in Germany at that time. Most of the party members believed in a common-place socialism which laid much more emphasis on the politi-cal end to be achieved than on economic causation. There was so far no simple presentation of the materialist conception of history; no one comprehended Marxist doctrine as a con-nected whole. Marx and Engels were spoken of with much respect, but such of their views as were understood were often criticized for appealing to the workers' heads more than to their hearts. Even in the domain of class-conflict German sentiment had to be satisfied. Again, Engels despised " utopian pictures of the future society." But Marx and he saw how popular such fantasies were, when Bebel's book *Woman and Socialism* found a more enthusiastic market than any of their own works.

During the negotiations for the coalition a young man from Berlin, called Eduard Bernstein, had come to the fore for the first time. He was a bank clerk and the son of a Jewish engine-driver. He knew the views of Marx and Engels only by hearsay; but he was struck by the fact that, since Lassalle's particular ideas had faded into oblivion, the political leaders had found no theoretical substitute. At that time he had a great admiration for the work of the positivist philosopher Eugen Dühring, the blind tutor at Berlin University — who lost his post there because of his vicious attacks on persons of recognized standing in the university. He therefore attempted to fill the gap by extolling Dühring's books, which he even sent to the two most powerful agitators in the Social-Democratic Party, Bebel and Johann Most,[1] who were both at that time in prison.

In one respect Dühring had a slight resemblance to Marx and Engels: he differed from most German university teachers by attempting to relate political science to actual problems of society. But in other ways Marx and Engels were poles apart from his " Philosophy of Reality," — which was really an optimistic positivism on the American model. His *Critical History of Political Economy* had nothing good to say of *Capital*. He described Marx as a " scientific figure of fun " in the tone of coarse arrogance which he used against Helmholtz the physicist and others whom he imagined to be his rivals. His own economic ideas were borrowed from the American economist H. C. Carey. To Marx's dialectical communism he opposed an " Anticratic " socialism of his

---

[1] Most later became an anarchist. In 1882 he came to America, continuing his anarchist activities.

own, whose solid practical proposals suited the mentality of the politicians and agitators who attended his lectures. They were delighted that Dühring should deny that the economic process is governed by immutable laws, and should leave great scope for individual action. They were enraptured when he spoke in his lectures of the labour problem as the real problem of the century and — with spiteful asides against all who differed from him — demanded a complete reconstruction of industry after a " socialitarian " recipe of his own. Their human sympathy was won by his physical infirmity, their confidence by his determined espousal of socialist aims, their respect by his malicious attacks upon great scholars and scientists.

Neither Bernstein nor the socialist intellectuals who (in ever increasing numbers) were attracted by Dühring realized that to admire him was to oppose Marx. " If the matter is good," wrote Bebel to Bernstein, " I don't care a straw for the method." And Most, even more earnestly, cried that they " must take the best " where they found it. In prison Bebel wrote an article (published in the *Volksstaat* without his signature) which was full of admiration for the " new communist." In a letter to the editor Engels attacked this article as " cringing " to Dühring. How furious he was later when he learned that it was Bebel who called the *Course in Political Economy* the best modern work on economics after Marx's *Capital*! At first even Liebknecht did not mistrust Dühring. " Have you two any grounds for assuming that he is a scoundrel, or a disguised enemy? " he asked Engels on the 13th of June, 1874. But his tolerance gave way when he became personally convinced that Dühring was a megalomaniac, and also learned that the second edition of his *Critical History of Political Economy* repeated all his " envious tomfooleries " against Marx. He immediately asked Engels to write a " sharp snub," and added that the man had ingratiated himself with many party members, especially in Berlin. During 1875 he repeated his attempts to get Engels to dispose of Dühring. Engels and Marx were unwilling to interrupt their studies, but they began to listen when Liebknecht sent them letters from German workers which proved to them that the " danger of a campaign for watering-down the program " (as Marx now called it) was really threatening the party. And their minds were made up finally when in May 1876 they received from Liebknecht a manuscript article extolling Dühring's philosophical attainments and his fight in the cause of knowledge. Most had sent this to *Vorwärts,* but Liebknecht refused to print it. When he was reproached (at the party congress in August) with a conspiracy of silence about Dühring, he replied that he had already commissioned Engels to write an article on him.

Engels firmly believed that not only Marx but he himself was bound in the interest of the movement to carry on certain definite scientific studies, and that the uneventful times which they were living in should be used to complete them. But as soon as he had read Most's glorification of Dühring, he agreed with Marx that immediate and ruthless measures must be taken against this " muddler." No more confusion must be introduced into the minds of the party leaders, or else there would be even longer to wait before the German working class could accustom themselves to Marx's and Engels's point of view. Marx must not interrupt his work on *Capital,* that was certain. But Engels, too, was reluctant to tear himself away from his studies to perform what he at first thought to be a thankless task. He did not suspect that he was about to strike the decisive blow for the conversion of Continental social democracy to Marxism.

The name of his book was *Herr Eugen Dühring's Revolution in Science* — an allusion to Dühring's own work, *Carey's Revolution in Economics.* We recall that *German Ideology,* the joint work of Marx and Engels, was never printed. The *Communist Manifesto,* with its specific appeal to the proletariat, gave them no opportunity to develop their philosophical point of view. In Marx's *Critique of Political*

Economy and in the first volume of *Capital* there was little room for a discussion of this phase of the question. That explains why the so-called materialistic conception of history which we today call, more correctly, the economic conception of history, remained a book of seven seals to most of their friends and all of their enemies until the moment when Engels struck out against Dühring. Now Engels felt himself compelled to give the public an explanation of the foundations upon which he and Marx had based their communist credo and their revolutionary program.

On the intellectual development of the young Engels, in the early forties of the nineteenth century, Hegel's philosophy had exerted an overwhelming influence. In the interim a generation had passed. The triumphant progress of natural science and technical development had overshadowed interest in speculative philosophy, even in Germany. The German public of that period knew of Hegel little more than his name. Dühring consigned the dialectic of Hegel to the rubbish-heap and in so doing he expressed the viewpoint inherent in the strong positive tendency of the times. Marx and Engels were ridiculed by professionals and misunderstood by that part of the population which was interested in philosophical problems, when they declared that it was wrong to dismiss Hegel so unceremoniously. They tried to transfer the doctrine of " conscious dialectic " over into the realm of a " materialistic conception " of history. It was Engels who undertook the difficult task of elucidating these associations in his *Anti-Dühring*.

This work falls into three divisions: philosophy, political economy, and history. In the division on philosophy Engels ridicules Dühring as a mere imitator of the tenets of the eighteenth century who, like the thinkers of that earlier period, believed in the " eternal verities " and showed no understanding for the fact that morals, justice, and other abstractions also change under the influence of economic development in the course of history. " The principles," he said, " are not the starting-point of the investigation, but its final result; they are not applied to nature and human history but abstracted from them; it is not nature and the realm of humanity that conforms to these principles, but the principles are valid in so far as they are in conformity with nature and history. . . . Herr Dühring's contrary conception makes things stand completely on their heads and fashions the real world out of ideas, out of schemata, schemes, or categories existing somewhere outside the world, from eternity." It is impossible in the brief space of this work, to explain the essence of dialectics. We would only remind the reader that this word springs from the same root as the word " dialogue." As in a dialogue, two persons present their arguments to each other, which move forward as the conversation proceeds and in so doing produce new thoughts which nevertheless conserve what has been said before in some form or other. So nature and history move in a dialectic process. " Dialectics," says Engels, " is nothing more than the science of the general laws of motion and development of nature, human society, and thought." What he meant when he spoke of dialectics in history, Engels described more minutely in his small booklet on Feuerbach and the decline of the era of classic German philosophy (1886). " Just as little as knowledge can history find a conclusion, complete in one completed ideal condition of humanity; a completed society, a perfect state, are things which can exist only as fantasies. On the contrary, all successive historical conditions are only places of pilgrimage in the endless evolutionary progress of human society from the lower to the higher. Every step is necessary and useful for the time and circumstances to which it owes its origin, but it becomes weak and without justification under the newer and higher conditions which develop little by little in its own womb. It must give way to the higher form, which in turn comes to decay and defeat."

In Engels's opinion this was the driving force — in human thought, the natural sciences, and history. He had tried to describe its bearing on the natural sciences in a lengthy volume on which he worked for many years until Marx's death caused him to drop his own work. Above all else he wanted to finish the last part of *Capital*. On his belief in historic dialectics Engels based his firm conviction of the inevitability of communism. It differentiated his " historical materialism " from the " metaphysical, mechanical materialism " of those who applied their theories to nature only and refused to recognize their social and political implications, those theories which had become immensely popular in the last decades of his life.

It was characteristic of Engels that he sought to illustrate the dialectic method in history by applying it to the development of military institutions. He was emphatic in his condemnation of what he called Dühring's " lamentations," with its conviction that force is in all circumstances an unmitigated evil. He showed that violence has had not only a negative but a positive function as well. He called it the tool with which new social movement attained influence and power and finally broke down atrophied social institutions. Force, in order to accomplish these ends, he showed, required certain prerequisites and to make the point clearer traced the development of armaments from the introduction of gunpowder to the flint-lock musket. Each technical change, he maintained, has had a direct effect on relations between the ruling and exploiting classes, just as each change in the character of the nation's soldiery produces new methods of warfare. To a certain extent he premised his expectation of the overthrow of capitalist régimes on the deeper dialectics of the nature of militarism. " Militarism dominates and is swallowing Europe. But this militarism," he wrote, " also carries in itself the seed of its own destruction. Competition of the individual states with each other forces them, on the one hand, to spend more money on the army and navy, artillery, etc., thus more and more hastening towards financial catastrophe; and on the other hand to take universal compulsory

military service more and more seriously, thus in the long
run making the whole people familiar with the use of arms;
and therefore making the people more and more able at a
given moment to make its will prevail in opposition to the
commanding military lords. And this moment comes as soon
as the mass of the people — town and country workers and
peasants — *has* a will — at this point the armies of princes
become transformed into armies of the people; the machine
refuses to work and militarism collapses by the dialectic of
its own evolution."

In the second part of *Anti-Dühring,* Engels, with the active assistance of Marx, presented to the public an authentic
and popular compilation of the most important economic
theories of *Capital.* To the deep regret of its author, this
learned and costly work had, up to that time, not penetrated the masses, for whom it was primarily intended.
Engels's intelligent popularization paved the way, pains-
takingly and slowly, for its penetration into wider and
wider proletarian circles, both on the European continent
and in other parts of the world.

The third and final part of the book gives a graphic account of the growth of the socialist idea in connection with
economic development after the French Revolution. It shows
how the "utopian socialism" of Saint-Simon, Fourier, and
Robert Owen reflected the undeveloped conditions governing production in the early nineteenth century while the
"scientific socialism" promulgated by himself and Marx was
conceivable only as the product of the capitalist system. The
genesis of capitalism Engels described by reviewing the development and increasing complexity of commodity production since the Middle Ages, with special emphasis on the
contradiction between social production and capitalist appro-
priation which, in a capitalist era, finds concrete expression in
the antagonism between proletariat and bourgeoisie. Finally,
he describes in detail how the historical dialectic will force
capitalist methods of production to yield to communist

forms. " The seizure of the means of production by society,"
says Engels, " puts an end to commodity production and
therewith to the domination of the product of the producer.
Anarchy in social production will be replaced by conscious
organization on a planned basis. The struggle for individual
existence comes to an end. At this point, in a certain sense,
man finally cuts himself off from the animal world. Now for
the first time in history the social causes set in motion by men
will have the effects willed by men. It is humanity's leap from
the realm of necessity into the realm of freedom."

Anti-Dühring was the first book to reveal the content and
viewpoint of Marxism to the leaders of German social democracy. And, more, it won thousands upon thousands of
workers — in fact, whole generations — for Marxism. In it,
for the first time, the real attitude of Marx and Engels was
revealed to the clearest minds of the younger generation of
social democrats — Bebel, Bernstein, Kautsky, Plekhanov,
Axelrod, Victor Adler, Labriola, Turati — men who did
most to hammer Marxist doctrines into the proletariat of
the Continent. Now for the first time a real Marxist school,
a real Marxist tradition, was created on the Continent. Today the lengthy polemics against an almost unread author
may seem tedious, but the book introduced to the public of
the seventies a difficult and hitherto unintelligible system in
lucid and simple language. It was now that others first came
to understand how Marx and Engels interpreted the course
of history and the problems of their own day, and what
political inferences they drew from their interpretation. The
book was immediately banned in Germany; therefore its influence was not fully felt until the introduction and the concluding chapter on socialism were printed in Switzerland as
a pamphlet — much revised and simplified, with most of the
polemic omitted. Next to the *Manifesto*, *The Development
of Socialism from Utopianism to Science* is the most challenging product of the workshop of Marx and Engels. It was
soon translated into almost all European languages, and

everywhere it paved the way for the acceptance of their economic and dialectical conception of history and for the revolutionary policy which was a consequence of it.

In the preface to *Anti-Dühring* Engels voiced his sorrow that Germany had gained her empire and industrial prosperity at the cost of her intellectual pre-eminence. The spiritual life of the country had been blasted, and Dühring was only a typical specimen of the new vulgar " pseudo-science." Engels was one of the first to observe how material wealth brought with it the spiritual impoverishment of the bourgeoisie. Dühring's attempt to turn German socialism into " superior nonsense " was bound to wreck itself upon the essential soundness of the German worker. Ten years later the same thought recurs in his *Feuerbach.* " Only among the workers do we still find the German tradition of scientific integrity. For there no one is worrying about his career, about profits, or about patronage. On the contrary, the more freely science develops, the more it harmonizes with the interests and objectives of the workers. . . . The mantle of classical German philosophy has fallen upon the German working-class movement."

CHAPTER XX

THE ANTISOCIALIST LAW.
DEATH OF MARX

Even in January 1877 Frau Marx could write to Sorge in Hoboken: "Our friend Engels is as well as ever. He is always hale and hearty, gay and happy." Next year a Prussian police agent thought that some letters of Engels which were intercepted in Paris proved the opposite. But Engels's sufferings were not physical. Lizzy's health had given him cause for anxiety since September 1877, and in September 1878 he stood for the second time beside the deathbed of a comrade and lover. Fourteen years later he wrote of her to Julie Bebel: "She came of real Irish proletarian stock, and the passionate feeling for her class, which was instinctive in her, was worth more to me than all the blue-stockinged elegances of 'educated' and 'sensitive' bourgeois girls could have been." Engels's views on marriage were later expounded in *The Origin of the Family*. Neither his convictions nor his sentiments would allow the claim of state and church to legitimize his closest human relationship. But to give one last pleasure to Lizzy he married her on her deathbed. We cannot know his feelings when she was torn from him in his fifty-ninth year. He was still in the prime of life; and his life gained richness and meaning from the countless tasks and plans with which he filled it. The world of strife was too much with him to allow him to give way to enduring melancholy at the loss of his companion. Yet Lizzy's death was a turning-point in his private life. It meant a change which he must often have felt without betraying it. The noontide of his life was over, and sunset was approaching.

The death of Lizzy may have helped to keep Engels from offering his immediate and unconditional help to the German party in October 1878, when the special decree against their " dangerous activities " was passed. But there were other, more important reasons for his reluctance. He and Marx were still depressed by the neglect of their criticisms of the Gotha program and indignant at the censure of Engels's attack on Dühring which had been expressed at a party congress.

Even before the Antisocialist Law came into force, Engels took it for granted that by this measure Bismarck would only benefit the party which he intended to crush. " If we were paying the old boy, he couldn't do better work for us," he said in a private letter to Germany. And in the same tone he wrote to Peter Lavrov, Russian philosopher and sociologist: " Herr Bismarck has been working for us for the last seven years, as if we had been paying him for it, and now he seems to be unable to moderate his efforts to hasten the advent of socialism. ' After me the deluge ' is not enough for him; he insists on having the deluge during his lifetime." As long as the special decree remained in force, Engels avoided entering Germany. But he followed all the events there with eager attention. Marx and he always considered it their chief duty to the German movement to ensure that its guiding principle in all circumstances should be the class-war. This meant that, in the new situation, the party should make no essential concessions to the government, despite its precarious position, but should hold fast to its revolutionary aims. The parliamentary faction were now their only public representatives, and it was only a minority of these (although an important minority, since it contained Liebknecht and Bebel) who were unalterably devoted to the class-war. The majority (who were for the most part without theoretical training) held that the proper policy for the party in the new situation would be to abandon its class-outlook and seek support from the democratic wing of the bourgeoisie. This " spineless " attitude of the majority drove Engels to distrust the whole party-leadership. His letters to Bebel, Liebknecht, Bernstein, and Johann Philipp Becker are filled with expressions of contempt for those " petty-bourgeois social democrats." He believed that bourgeois converts to social democracy were noticeably the most prone to ally themselves with the bourgeoisie. His distrust of the " educated " members of the party was in sharp contrast to his unshaken faith in the class-instincts of the workers. As a general encourages good troops, Engels constantly extolled these " splendid fellows." " Say what you like," he wrote to " the only German revolutionary general " (as he called old Becker), " we have never seen a proletariat which has learned so quickly how to act collectively and to maintain an unbroken front."

At that time Bebel and Liebknecht had to defend themselves not only against strong opposition from the Right, but also against some small attacks from the Left. The Left reproached the party leaders with a determination to keep within the law in order to preserve the existence and effectiveness of the party. But Liebknecht and Bebel declared it senseless to attack without hope of victory, or at least of moral effect; and all the more senseless because they knew that the government wanted a putsch in order to obliterate the party for years to come. If anyone could not accept their decision not to act and wished to give full vent to his exasperation at the decree, he was obliged to go abroad and do so. Johann Most, the greatest demagogue of the party, decided on this course. Without making any previous arrangement with the other leaders, he emigrated to London and started a paper demanding that illegal propaganda should be carried on within Germany. Its name was *Die Freiheit*. It relentlessly exposed the internal disputes which were troubling social democracy. At first Engels did not dislike its revolutionary tone, although he met Most's advances with reserve. But as soon as it espoused the cause of anarchism and began to compromise the working-class movement by its bloodthirsty tirades, he turned his back on it. When Most was expelled from the Social-Democratic Party, Engels did not oppose the decision.

Since the party was not allowed to publish a paper in Germany, a new party-organ was founded in Zürich. But for years Engels refused to contribute to the *Sozialdemokrat,* in the fear that the petty-bourgeois elements in the party might gain control of the paper. It was difficult to conquer his distrust when it had once been awakened. Bebel experienced this now, although he constantly represented to Engels that his fluent pen would be the most valuable instrument to inspire the new party-organ with the outlook which he desired it to have. Engels once sent him this testy answer: " You and Liebknecht know that the only thing I have always asked of the party is to leave me in peace to finish my scientific work. You know that for sixteen years, despite that, I have been constantly approached to write for the party papers — and that I have done so, and written whole series of articles, and whole pamphlets, at the special request of Liebknecht. You know also that Marx and I will voluntarily carry on the defence of the party against its opponents outside Germany as long as the party exists, and that the only thing we ask in return is that the party should remain faithful to itself." It was self-evident, he went on, that Marx and he were delighted at every victory the party won in Germany, because it had always had a certain dependence upon Marxian theory. But for that reason it was specially important in their eyes that the practical conduct of the party, and especially the public utterances of its leaders, should continue to harmonize with the general theory of Marxism. It was long before Engels began to feel reassured. A visit of Liebknecht to London cleared up the worst misunderstandings. And Engels's distrust was even more fully appeased when the first party-congress held under the Antisocialist Law (which took place in Switzerland) passed resolutions full of determination and warlike spirit.

At Christmas 1880 Bebel came to London with Bernstein to see if they could compel Engels to reconcile himself to the party. This was the first time Engels and Bebel had met in person, and they found themselves in complete agreement on questions of principle and tactics. Engels was charmed by Bebel's trustworthy nature, his " just sense of tact," and his clear intelligence. He put complete trust in his new friend and kept it as long as he lived. But Bernstein too, the one-time champion of Dühring, had been converted by Engels's *Anti-Dühring* into such an out-and-out supporter of historical materialism that his host was bound to be delighted with him. Engels actually approved Bernstein's provisional appointment to the responsible post of editor in Zürich and, when he filled the post successfully, demanded that it be made permanent. He considered it an advantage that Bernstein was " not a university man " like Kautsky, who was better fitted to be the editor of a periodical.

One of the most important points in Bebel's conversation with Marx and Engels was the severe economic crisis which was raging in most countries in Europe, and especially in Germany. Bebel had come to the conviction that the crisis would drag on like a lingering illness until the impending " general explosion " which would usher in the revolution. Marx and Engels were more experienced in matters of theory, and felt that Bebel's judgment was based on insufficient facts. They now held that, since England had been compelled to share her industrial monopoly with America, Germany, and France, while protective tariffs had been raised in America and Europe, the character and rhythm of crises had altered. However damning might be their long-term auguries for the capitalist economic and social system, they saw the immediate prospect to be a new period of prosperity, whether of long or short duration. But they expected that there would in future be no more fully developed booms.

The decennial slumps in which Engels had once believed were now, he held, a thing of the past, but intermediate crises would occur at shorter periods — a " proof of the complete exhaustion of capitalist methods of production." He was in greater agreement with Bebel about the political effects of the crisis in Germany. They were both convinced that it would hasten the inevitable advance of social democracy. Their correspondence on this point is overflowing with optimism.

The first Reichstag elections under the Antisocialist Law brought the party a loss of votes in the country and the smaller towns, but an increase in the larger towns. This proof of the party's " unimpaired vitality " was one of the last pleasures which Jenny Marx was to enjoy, as Engels said in the obituary of her which he wrote for the *Sozialdemokrat* after her death, on the 2nd of December 1881. Marx himself was now constantly ill and survived his courageous wife by only fifteen months. During that time his broken health kept him almost always away from London, and he and Engels could converse only in letters. In the autumn of 1882 Marx returned once more to spend some weeks in his bereaved home, and several times climbed with Engels the heights of Hampstead, as they had so often done together — the heights from which, as the " general " used to declare, London could be so nicely bombarded. Engels knew that doctors could have made it possible for Marx to live a vegetable life for some years longer. But (he wrote to Sorge the day after his friend died) Marx would never have borne that. " To live with the vast uncompleted work before him, with the Tantalus-thirst to finish it, and without the power to do so — that would have been a thousand times more bitter to him than the gentle death which overtook him. He used to say, with Epicurus, that ' death is not a misfortune for him who dies, but for him who survives.' To see that colossal genius surviving as a half-dead ruin, on which the doctors could congratulate themselves, and the philistines heap their scorn — those philistines whom he in his full strength had so often dashed to the ground — no! It is a thousand times better as it is . . . a thousand times better that we should, two days from now, lay him in the grave where his wife is sleeping."

For years Engels had been forced to see that his great comrade's energy was beginning to flag. He feared that the statistics of *Capital* might become out of date before publication and thus impair the huge influence which he expected of it. Accordingly he often pressed Marx to hurry on, to continue and complete his work. But Marx was growing old. He felt that he no longer had the strength to master the endless mass of new material which was daily mounting up. He may have been annoyed by Engels's impetuous enthusiasm. After his death Bebel expressed surprise that he had kept Engels in ignorance of the stage of completeness which the work had reached. " It was simply because if I had known," Engels answered, " I would have given him no peace night or day until it was finished and printed." Marx knew that, and he told his daughter that if the worst came to the worst, Engels could publish the manuscript in any way he chose.

It was Engels also who wrote to two other old friends, Becker and Liebknecht, as well as to Bernstein, the editor of the *Sozialdemokrat,* to tell them of Marx's death. To Becker he wrote: " The greatest mind in our party has ceased to think, the strongest heart I have ever known has ceased to beat." And to Bernstein: " Unless one were continuously with Marx, one could have no conception of his value to us in the sphere of theory, and in practice, too, when great decisions had to be taken. His mighty vision will be buried with him, for years to come." Liebknecht during his exile had become specially attached to Marx and his family. To him Engels wrote: " Although I saw him last night lying in his bed with his face fixed in death, I cannot believe that this brilliant spirit has now ceased to enrich the proletarian movement of both worlds with its powerful thoughts. We are what we are because of him, and the movement is what it is today because of his theoretical and practical activities. Without him we should still be sunk in a slough of confusion."

Engels delivered the funeral address in English. He tried to express what Marx had done for humanity in general and for the world proletariat in particular. " Just as Darwin," he said, " discovered the law of evolution in organic nature, so Marx discovered the law of evolution in human history. . . . Marx also discovered the special law of motion governing the present-day capitalist method of production and the bourgeois society that this method of production has created. . . . However great the joy with which he welcomed a new discovery in some theoretical science whose practical application perhaps it was as yet quite impossible to envisage, he experienced a quite other kind of joy when the discovery involved immediate revolutionary changes in industry and in the general course of history. . . . His real mission in life was to contribute in one way or another to the overthrow of capitalist society and of the forms of government which it had brought into being, to contribute to the liberation of the present-day proletariat, which he was the first to make conscious of its own position and its needs, of the conditions under which it could win its freedom. Fighting was his element. And he fought with a passion, a tenacity, and a success such as few could rival. . . . And consequently Marx was the best-hated and most calumniated man of his times. Governments, both absolutist and republican, deported him from their territories. The bourgeoisie, whether conservative or extreme democrat, vied with one another in heaping slanders upon him. All this he brushed aside, as though it were a cobweb, ignoring them, answering only when necessity compelled him. And now he has died — beloved, revered, and mourned by millions of revolutionary fellow-workers — from the mines of Siberia to California, in all points of Europe and America. . . . His name and his work will endure throughout the ages."

Engels vowed to preserve and continue his friend's scientific and political work as long as his own strength held out. In view of this mighty task he silently abandoned the work on which he himself had been engaged. Thenceforward he gave most of his time to the task, for he was certain that he alone could edit Marx's manuscript. Marx had left the second book of *Capital* so far completed that Engels could write an introduction to it on its author's birthday in 1885. But he now discovered that only an "extremely incomplete first draft" of the third book had been written. Although his political and journalistic duties became heavier with the growth of the movement, and although he now began to feel physical infirmity, he was able to publish the third book also in the last year of his life. When he first approached it, he considered it to be better than the first. But as he advanced in the work of editing it, he saw how the energy of its author had flagged and what a burden of his responsibility he would himself have to bear. He often told his friends that the work depended on a conception of the eighteen-sixties and was based on data which did not go beyond the first half of the seventies.

After Marx's death Engels's intimate friends advised him to move to Zürich. They did not believe that he was held to England by any unbreakable ties. But Engels valued London as an environment in which the researcher could feel himself completely neutral. His relations with the English working-class movement were now severed; he could no longer hope to resume any real influence over it. When Germans visited him with letters of introduction, he warned them not to mention his name as a recommendation to English working-class leaders, because he was "in their bad books." The circle of his friends in England had grown much smaller. The only real friends he had in old age were his fellow-countryman Karl Schorlemmer, of Owens College, in Manchester, one of the founders of the science of organic chemistry, and the ex-manufacturer Samuel Moore, who had been a senior judge in Nigeria after the failure of his mill in Manchester and who translated *Capital*.

The leaders in the struggle of German social democracy against Bismarck believed that the adviser whom they honoured so highly would be delighted to live near them. But Engels did not think it would help him in his most important tasks if he were to change his surroundings. Nor did he wish to go to a country from which he might be exiled. He told Bebel that England offered him the greatest advantage — peace to continue his theoretical studies. Anywhere else he would be driven to take a practical part in agitation, although he had no special merit as an agitator. But he could not see anyone to replace him and Marx in the sphere of theory. " And now when I am sixty-two, with as much of my own work as I can manage and the prospect of one year's work at the second volume of *Capital* and a second at Marx's biography, as well as a history of the German socialist movement from 1843 to 1863 and a history of the International from 1864 to 1872, I should be mad to give up my peaceful retreat here for places where I should have to attend meetings, take part in newspaper controversies, and, of necessity, disturb my clear outlook on things. If it was like 1848 and 1849 again, I would mount my horse once more if need were. But as it is — a severe division of work. I must even withdraw as much as possible from the *Sozialdemokrat*. Only think of the terrific correspondence which I once shared with Marx, but have had to carry on alone for the last year. I want, as far as possible, to keep the threads which came from all countries to Marx's study still unbroken in the future." This passage shows us how many obligations Engels felt on his shoulders when Marx was taken from his side. It is sad that he was able to carry out only a fragment of the program he mapped out for himself.

It was not without timidity that Engels took the place of Marx in the sphere of theory; his scruples are betrayed in the letter to Becker in which he calls himself Marx's second

FRIEDRICH ENGELS

fiddle. He looked forward to future revolutions with some anxiety, because he felt himself a less sure observer, a less unerring judge, than his dead friend. At a revolutionary crisis Engels would have felt more at home in a high military post than as a political leader. And he was nothing of a diplomat.

The day after Marx died, Engels wrote to his comrade in the rising long ago in Baden: " We still hold the breach. The bullets are whistling, and our friends are falling, but we have gone through all that before. And if a bullet finds one of us, even that is good, provided it goes right home and does not keep us struggling long." And so it was. His good comrade had fallen — the man who had been nearest to him, the only man whom he had looked up to, was no more. But the world-wide struggle continued, the struggle whose future course the two friends thought they had been the first to reveal — the struggle which now demanded a double portion of alertness and effort and responsibility from the one who was left behind.

Engels was able to pass a cooler judgment on the conflicts within the German party when he was once sure that its most important organizer and parliamentarian and the editor of its paper would oppose any attempt to deny the principle of determined class-conflict. The internal conflicts became sharper as a result of the state insurance system introduced by Bismarck in order to make the proletariat masses (whose rights as citizens he abused) forget " hatred for the state " in their delight at the material benefits he offered them. Bismarck consoled the bourgeois for the financial sacrifices he demanded, by telling them that the system was really an insurance against revolution. The German professors of political economy extolled the new state insurance as a turning-point in the history of the world. Many social-democratic deputies even took it as a hopeful sign and played with the thought that Bismarck might take his promises to Lassalle seriously and create a " popular Hohenzollern monarchy."

Engels was horrified that the new wave of state socialism (which was really a resurrected Lassalleanism) should be a menace even within the party. He immediately induced the *Sozialdemokrat* to publish several articles explaining to the workers that this so-called socialism on the part of the government was simply a pretext to enable them to organize a disciplined army of workers alongside the armies of soldiers and officials which they already commanded. Bernstein would have preferred Engels himself to write against the resurrection of Lassalleanism, but when Engels heard more favourable reports of the situation he refused to do so.

The second party congress under the Antisocialist Law was held in 1883 at Copenhagen, and at it, once more, resolutions were passed which had Engels's full approval. He was pleased "that the half-baked socialists were defeated out and out." He did not wish the party to split as long as the socialist laws remained in force. But he took it amiss that Liebknecht had succeeded in his efforts at Copenhagen "to conciliate and gloss over, to postpone the crisis." Behind all the conflicts which disturbed the party in those years, there was one ultimate question — whether or not a revolution in Germany could be expected in the near future. Bebel affirmed that it could, and, among others, Bloss and Auer, Social-Democratic Reichstag deputies, denied it with equal conviction. Bebel hit the real point when he wrote to Engels: "A man who believes that we must wait at least a century for the social revolution will act differently from a man who thinks it will come in the near future."

Did Engels count on a revolution in Germany during the eighties? We can answer that question only by deciding what were his views of Bismarck and of the developments which must follow if the omnipotent Chancellor lost his power. Since Bismarck's first successes Engels's admiration for this "creature whose ideas were so irrational and whose conduct so changeable" had not grown. A comparison with the Cæsarism of Napoleon III was useful to enable him to judge what position Bismarck's system would occupy in history. He considered that if Bismarck had the stronger will, he had narrower views. The Frenchman at least had his "Napoleonic ideas," while the Prussian "never managed to produce anything like an original political idea." The bourgeoisie showed him the goal, and Louis Napoleon showed him the way to it; all he did was to travel along that way. When he had completed, in his own way, the mission which others had prescribed for him, he showed himself "an ignoramus about theory," incapable of "understanding the historical situation which he himself had created." His strength of will made him the tyrant of the German bourgeoisie, and, against their better judgment, they never failed to perform their tricks for him. But the German working classes showed the Chancellor more clearly at each election that their will could not be mastered by his, however strong it was. Engels embodied these views in an essay shortly before Bismarck's fall. It was not completed, but a sketch of it has survived, which shows us the conclusion to which it was to lead. We find in it these rough headings: "Complete transformation of Bismarck into a Junker"; "Social policy *à la* Bonaparte," "bogus social reforms," and a lapidary expression of Engels's gloomy forebodings for Germany's empire: "Result: (a) a situation which collapses with the death of some characters — no Empire without an Emperor! the proletariat pressed towards revolution, and unheard-of boom in social democracy after the repeal of the socialist decree — chaos; (b) a peace, worse than war, the net result of the whole thing, if things turn out well, or else a world war."

If, as Engels hoped during the eighties, the Russian revolution was soon to break out, its sparks were bound to fly over central Europe also. He often spoke to Bebel of the character and course of the future German revolution. Bebel could not imagine that in such a revolution bourgeois democracy might still have a task to fulfil, even a temporary one.

Engels knew that it had. "At such a time," he told his friend on December 1st, 1884, "the whole mass of reaction retreats behind bourgeois democracy and strengthens it; everything which has been reactionary disguises itself as democratic then." He did not wish the German bourgeoisie to be nothing but "the one reactionary mass." He explained to Bernstein in June 1883: "We cannot advance until at least part of the bourgeoisie is pushed over on to the side of the real movement, through a change of internal or external events. Therefore we have now had enough of Bismarck's régime; he can now help us only by a conflict or by his resignation." And two months later he expanded this point: "In Germany the first immediate result of the revolution must take the form of a bourgeois republic. But that will be only a brief transitional stage, since we have fortunately no purely republican bourgeois party. The bourgeois republic — perhaps headed by the Progressive Party — will give us the chance of winning the masses of the working class for revolutionary socialism (which will take one or two years), and will give the middle parties the chance of proving their futility or committing suicide. Only after that has been done shall we be able to move."

The impulse to a revolution in Germany (he saw quite clearly) could only come from the army, if it did not come from a Russian revolution. "An unarmed populace," he wrote to Bebel in December 1884, "against a modern army is in the military sense only a negative quantity. Suppose, however, that our reserves (men of twenty to twenty-five who do not vote but are trained soldiers) side with the revolution, the period of pure democracy might be skipped." A month before, he had explained to Bebel: "As the military situation is at present, we must not open the attack as long as we have an armed force against us. We can wait until that armed force ceases to be a force against us. Before that any revolution, even a successful one, would give the power, not to us, but to the most radical of the bourgeois, namely, the petty bourgeois."

Always a keen observer of the military balance of power, he had early noticed that the absolute loyalty of the army to the Kaiser was being sapped by the spread of social-democratic agitation. But with a strategic eye for every possibility, he reflected that German social democracy might be " swept in on a European flood " and come to power too soon, before " the bourgeois and petty-bourgeois parties had shown palpably and obviously their incapacity for government." He himself preferred " the slow but certain pace of history " to any such precipitate development, by which the party might be called to take responsibility too soon.

Engels believed implicitly that Bismarck feared a Russian revolution more than anything else. As soon as the government would be taken over by the Crown Prince (the husband of the Princess Royal), Engels looked for an end of the stagnation in internal politics which had marked Bismarck's later years. " The bourgeoisie will be driven at last to knock another knob off the old régime, and to play a role in politics, as they damned well should. Only a little fresh life in the place, that's all we need." In autumn 1886 Bebel repeated his doubts whether they could expect the German bourgeoisie to take the initiative again. Engels replied that he, too, had no doubt that the bourgeois were ready to drop their liberal phrases; the only question was whether they would be able to do it, when there was no Bismarck to govern for them. " Large-scale industry does not allow the cowardice of industrial magnates to dictate laws to it; economic development causes constant collisions; it increases and aggravates them, and does not allow semi-feudal Junkers with feudal tastes to dominate it for ever."

If the situation demanded it, Engels was ready for an alliance with a really radical bourgeois party in order to obtain the repeal of the Antisocialist Law, the abolition of

the protective tariffs, and of entail and other feudal prescriptions. In 1889 he told a Danish party member named
Trier: "I am revolutionary enough to adopt even this
policy as a means to my end, in a situation where it is the
most advantageous or the least injurious." "Questions of
morality apart," he added, "in my opinion any means are
justified by which you achieve your end — the most violent
and also the gentlest." All this, of course, on the assumption
that the proletarian class-conscious character of the Social-
Democratic Party was not called in question; for that always
remained the basic principle of his judgments. He rightly
considered Bismarck's last great victory at the polls, in
February 1887, to be only an episode. The social democrats
might have lost seats, but they had gained voters. Everything was going excellently, he wrote to Sorge on January
7th, 1888. If Wilhelm I died soon and the hopelessly infirm Crown Prince took over the government for only six
months, everything would be in confusion. On the next day
he wrote in the same tone to Liebknecht and concluded:
"Now I want neither war nor putsch; everything is going
too well for that." In August 1888 he told Sorge that the
conflict between Wilhelm II and Bismarck was imminent.
In February 1889 he added: "The old reactionary gang,
clergy and Junkers at the court, are doing all they can
to provoke the Kaiser against Bismarck and to start a conflict." In February 1890 he declared to Bebel that Wilhelm II had always seemed to him to have been specially
created in order to shatter the apparently stable system in
Germany. "But I could not expect that he would have managed to do it so quickly and brilliantly as he has. The man
is worth twice his weight in gold to us. He doesn't need to
fear attempts at assassination; it would be not only a crime
to shoot him, but a gigantic blunder. If necessary we ought
to give him a bodyguard against anarchist tomfooleries."

   In February 1890 the social-democrat gains at the Reichstag elections surpassed Engels's brightest hopes. He wrote

exultantly to Liebknecht: "In three years we can win the agricultural labourers, and then we shall have the cream of the Prussian army. And to prevent that, there is only one means, and it must be used relentlessly; that is the only point on which Willie and Bismarck still agree — a regular massacre and a reign of terror. They would use any pretext to bring that about." Engels was fascinated by the thought that social democracy was about to flood the greatest reservoir of recruits for the Prussian army. In April he told Sorge also that there was a good chance of bringing into the movement the agricultural proletariat of the eastern provinces of Prussia, and with them the soldiers of the crack regiments; "then the whole caboodle would be burst up, and we would be masters." But he did not believe that the victory was within the grasp of his party yet, or that it would come without a struggle. "The Prussian generals," he went on, "must be bigger asses than I can believe, if they don't know all this as well as we do; and so they must be burning with eagerness to put us out of action for a time by a massacre. Hence a double reason to keep outwardly quiet." Engels's estimate of the generals was just. Today we know that the chief of the General Staff, Count Waldersee, thought that only a *coup d'état* would save the situation, and was "very willing to help." If the struggle was really inevitable, the monarchy could gain nothing from postponing it. Waldersee entirely agreed with Engels when he wrote in his diary: "The second generation of a Social-Democratic family brings ready-made subversive ideas into the army." But Engels was sure that time was the ally of social democracy; only the party must give the government no chance for violent interference.

In April 1888 the organ of militant social democracy had been expelled from Switzerland (under pressure from Berlin) and had been forced to move to London. It was now edited by Bernstein under the superintendence of Engels, and especially in matters of international politics directly under his influence. In February it brought out a special number in celebration of the victory at the polls. In it Engels asked: *What now?* and gave the answer that the 20th of February meant the beginning of the end of the Bismarck epoch. Nothing could help Bismarck now except a rising provoked by his brutality and repressed with redoubled brutality. " That is the only means he has — and we know that Bismarck is one of those people who think any means to their end is right." Therefore the party must not be drawn into any ill-advised action. " It must never come to that again. The Antisocialist Law has drilled our workers too well, and we have far too many old soldiers in our ranks for that — among them many who have learned to stand at attention in a rain of bullets until the moment has come to attack." These military analogies flowed spontaneously from the old " general's " pen when he appealed to the discipline of the German workers, whom he loved so dearly and so much admired for that very discipline.

The fall of Bismarck followed more quickly than the most far-sighted of his enemies had foretold. The young Kaiser thought that the Antisocialist Law could be dispensed with, and it disappeared on the 1st of October 1890. This was the beginning of a new historical period for Germany and for the German working-class movement. Engels saw more clearly than most of the politicians of his time that the new age would not bring " glorious days " to the German people, as the Kaiser had boastfully prophesied. Instead, he uttered the gloomy oracle: " If Crœsus crosses the Halys, or Wilhelm the Rhine, he will destroy a great Empire."

CHAPTER XXI

FROM THE FIRST TO THE SECOND INTERNATIONAL

৵

Between the Franco-Prussian War and the World War, working-class parties in other countries looked up to German social democracy with admiration and often turned to it for help. Even in the days of the First International it had always directed its effort along the lines of political democracy, so that it had been immune from the quarrels which split the International Workingmen's Association. And as its tactics proved successful, working-class leaders in other countries became convinced that the surest way to success was to carry on a legal agitation, in the press, in meetings and associations, in elections and in parliaments. The German example won many converts even in those countries which had been induced by Bakunin to distrust all political action.

Engels was delighted by every fresh proof of the decreasing influence of anarchism in the European working-class movement. More and more anarchist papers failed, and the Bakunist Counter-International broke up. But Sorge, too, grew tired of the First International, which was lingering weakly on after its move to the U.S.A., and in 1876 he prorogued it "till an indefinite date." Engels believed that its time had come to die, for it had fulfilled its mission. But its tradition was to be maintained by a paper published in New York. This was the *Labor Standard*, edited by MacDonnell, who had represented Ireland on the

General Council in London. For this paper Engels wrote a series of articles called *The European Working Class in 1877*, in which he described the movement as making "not only favourable but rapid progress." Recalling the recent disputes between the various factions, he said it was especially remarkable that a single spirit now pervaded the whole movement; but he was a little premature in his prophecy: "We have now once more reached complete harmony, and with it has arisen a constant and regular intercourse between the workers of various countries"; and in his declaration that "the men who founded the International Workingmen's Association in 1864, who upheld its banner during the struggles against enemies without and within, until they were driven even more by political pressure than by their own mistakes to defeat and seeming retirement — these men can now proudly affirm that the International has completed its work; it has attained its great aim, the unity of the proletariat throughout the world against its oppressors."

By now the most important part of the proletarian struggle was the battles which were being waged in the individual countries, and political interest was chiefly focused on those internal problems which differed according to the special conditions in each country. Lassalle had always known that the rise of national working-class parties was a necessary stage in the movement; while Marx and Engels, who had rather neglected that point of view, had learned from their mistakes. Towards the end of 1876 Johann Philipp Becker at Geneva proposed to revive the International as a federation of the individual national parties. Engels strongly opposed this and he did the same in 1882 when Becker repeated his proposal. One of Engels's points was that in a new International the *émigrés* would still play too large a part. Only when there was a prospect of great events of European importance would the movement gain strength from grouping its national units around a main centre. In

that case the International would be no longer an organization for propaganda, but an organization for action.

The personal significance of Engels for the development
of the European working-class movement since the fall of
the First International can be best understood if we grasp
his connexion with the origin and development of the socialist parties in the different countries. Marx and Engels
considered it to be their special task to watch the development of the movement in connexion with the course of
international politics and the expansion of production
throughout the world. They were political exiles and belonged to no national party. Without holding any official
position, it was their purpose to direct and influence the
socialist movements of the several countries. But their experience had taught them that this must be done with extreme tact and prudence. Not long before Marx's death
Engels elaborated this point to Eduard Bernstein. " Marx,"
he wrote in 1881, " has such achievements to his credit in
the spheres of theory and practice that the best people in
all the various working-class movements have complete
confidence in him. At critical moments they turn to him for
advice, and they usually find that his advice is the best. That
is the position he holds in Germany, France, and Russia,
not to speak of the smaller countries." He added: "We
have constant contact with them, as far as it is worth the
trouble and as far as there is opportunity. But any attempt
to influence people against their will would only hurt us and
destroy the old confidence, which dates back to the International. We have too much experience *in revolutionaribus
rebus* for that."

On practical questions, therefore, Engels maintained his
reserve towards the working-class movements in the various
countries; he never forced his opinion on them, but gave it
if it was asked for. He held it to be his special task to preserve the purity of Marxist theory where it had adherents
and to attempt to disseminate it where that was possible.

His mission, he thought, was to follow the course of the movement throughout the world and when he was asked questions (especially by the leaders of the Continental parties) to furnish information and advice from the wide experience which he and Marx possessed. In all this he had the same ultimate end in view which he had tried to achieve too directly and mechanically during the struggle with Bakunin: to win over the working-class movement of the world to the ideas, aims, and methods which Marx and he held to be the only possible means of abolishing the proletariat. Class-antagonism, he believed, could be conquered only if the workers of all countries were resolved to shape their own destiny and organized themselves as independent political parties based on the class-struggle. That was the principle which underlay all the advice which Engels gave the various parties.

There was increasing agreement on this final objective during the seventies and eighties; but even so, the European working-class movement of those years was far from homogeneous. Each time that Engels was asked for advice, he found that he had to deal with an entirely different problem; he could not have hoped to produce harmonious solutions for them all without the clear guiding principles which his great conception of history gave him. We have already seen his attitude to the movement in Germany. Here at least there was a party which expressed the intention of working on the principles of the *Communist Manifesto*. The situation in France was much more difficult. There Marx and Engels had to cast their seed on ground which had already been ploughed and planted by others. Engels was too optimistic in thinking that the Commune had killed the old "eclectic man-in-the-street socialism," and that the future belonged to international communism. During the next decades things did not run so smoothly as he hoped, and there were many impediments which proved too stubborn for his revolutionary impatience.

The most zealous and successful champion of Marxism in France was the former Bakunist, Jules Guesde. Marx and Engels did not exchange letters with him, since they could influence him indirectly through his closest coadjutor, Lafargue, who was Marx's son-in-law. But Guesde personally came to them for advice when it was time to draft a program for the first French working-class party on the Marxist model. The meeting took place in Engels's study. It was an important one, for it was the first opportunity the friends had had of exercising any direct influence on the ideas of the French proletariat. The new party (the *Parti Ouvrier*) found its chief support in the industrial areas. In Paris the *Possibilistes* still held the field.

After Marx died, Engels attempted to influence the French movement on two main lines. On the one hand, he endeavoured (as we shall see) to reconcile the social democrats in France and in Germany, in order to combat the danger of a war. On the other, he encouraged all efforts to create in France a Social-Democratic Party as strong and as united as the German party. In 1893, for the first time, a considerable number of socialists was elected to the Chamber. But only a minority of them endorsed the program which had been drawn up in Regent's Park Road. The majority belonged to a group of independent socialists, who declared it impossible to reduce their principles to one formula. Engels said that they had not got further than a Platonic love for socialism. He considered Millerand one of their shrewdest men, but he feared (with justice) that he retained " many bourgeois juristic prejudices " more ineradicable than he himself knew. Engels at first described Jaurès as a professor who liked to hear himself making speeches and whom the Chamber would rather hear than Guesde or Vaillant, the Blanquist, because he was more bourgeois-minded. But he gave him credit for the honest intention of " developing into a regular socialist." In the year of his death he wrote to Plekhanov, the great Marxist theoretician: "Jaurès is on the right road, he is learning Marxism. We must not hurry him too much. He has already made excellent progress — far better than I hoped. Anyhow, we must not demand too much orthodoxy! The party is too large, and Marx's theories are too widespread, for a few more or less isolated cranks in the western countries to do much harm." Engels was convinced right down to the last that the doctrines of Marx and himself would eventually mould the working-class movement even in the land of Proudhon.

Living in England, Engels had watched with deep attention the development of the English proletariat for more than half a century. But he was in close touch with the movement only during the Chartist period and while distinguished British working-class leaders still belonged to the International. We know that its course from year to year had brought him only disappointments. In 1879 he wrote to Bernstein: "It must be acknowledged that at this moment there does not exist in Britain a real working-class movement in the Continental sense."

Some years previously Harney (who had long since moved to America) had offered financial help to enable Engels or Marx to write a systematic exposition of their doctrine for the English proletariat, but Engels had no great faith in the idea. The influence of the two friends was constantly growing on the Continent, but in the country for which they had once hoped so much, they had no footing whatever. In 1881 the trade-unionist Shipton founded a weekly paper, the *Labour Standard,* to advocate the revival of an independent political workers' movement in England; and Engels agreed to contribute regular articles to it. In them he did full justice to the service which the trade unions had performed in defending the standard of living and in lowering the hours of labour. But at the same time he reproached them for ignoring the task of making the working class the owners of the means of production, of abolishing wage-labour, and of waging war against capitalism with political weapons. The English working class had better-organized trade unions than any other in Europe; it was unworthy of it to lag so far behind the Continental movements in political activity. Everywhere the proletariat was fighting for political power — everywhere except in Great Britain, where complete democracy would bring with it the supremacy of the working class. How could the British proletariat take over the government of that great Empire if it did not prepare itself at once and use all the means to power which it could command? Nothing was needed but the will: if the will was there, the potential majority which the proletariat held both locally and nationally would be converted into an effective majority. In an article on the wage-theory of the Anti-Corn-Law League, Engels explained to the workers that the men whom they trusted in the liberal camp were supporting free trade only because they wished to make English industry a stronger competitor in the world market, by reducing the price of English bread. For five months he attempted to influence the British workers in the spirit of Chartism and of the *Communist Manifesto*. But at last he gave up his efforts, for the only response they evoked was that even the editor "got scared by the Continental heresies." He wrote resignedly to Marx: "The British working man will not go forward; he must be shaken up by facts, by the loss of the British industrial monopoly."

After that disappointment Engels was convinced that the British proletariat would never organize itself as a political party based on the class-conflict until the English monopoly of world commerce was broken — and he held that it had already received severe blows. He recurred to the problem in the prefaces which he wrote to English translations of Marx's and his own works, and also in press articles and private letters. He emphasized the fact that the doctrine of free trade was originally based on the idea that England was the industrial centre of a mainly agricultural world, which would always continue to supply her with grain and cotton. But her industrial monopoly was no longer compatible with the development of the other civilized countries in Europe. They needed industrialization if they were not to sink to the level of Ireland. The commercial policy of the U.S.A. also now showed that they meant to shake off the yoke of the English industrial monopoly. At first Engels thought that the American protective tariffs were justified, but later he held that America and Germany would be more certain to outstrip England in the world market if they maintained free trade. He regarded the formation of trusts in the protected industries as a sign that protective tariffs had now fulfilled their function in America. Tariffs were now protecting the producers, not against foreign imports, but against home consumers.

He believed that the U.S.A. would inevitably become the centre of world industry. The English bourgeois would survive the loss of their national monopoly for some time: the Venetians and the Dutch had remained the bankers of the world long after the decline of their commerce. But what was to become of the English proletariat? Engels answered his own question thus: after America had beaten the English iron and textile industries in the world market, she would abolish her protective tariffs, and that would mean the final victory of socialism in England. In Britain the present industrial system could not be maintained without a rapid and constant expansion of production. The moment would come when the unemployed (increasing year by year) would lose patience and take their destiny into their own hands. Marx had prophesied that England would be the only European country where the social revolution could be carried through by peaceful and legal means. Engels called attention to this, in his preface to the first English edition of *Capital,* and said that Marx had always added that he found it hard to believe that the English ruling classes would submit to this peaceful and legal revolution without a violent rising of the oppressed classes. About the time of Marx's death the British proletariat began to realize that the English commercial monopoly was broken. Calls for socialism were now more frequent, and there was a growing movement to form an independent labour party. Engels's relationship with this new movement was much affected by the fact that he refused to meet Henry Hyndman, the English socialist.

Engels did not deny Hyndman's "shrewdness," but he was repelled by his overweening ambition, his "business ability," and his "impatience to play the dictator." He called him a "jingoistic John Bull." Hyndman had been very little affected by the materialist conception of history, but was strongly influenced by *Capital*. He visited Marx frequently during the last years of his life, but Marx, too, disliked him personally. Then and later Engels avoided meeting Hyndman, whom he nicknamed a "miserable caricature of Lassalle." Hyndman was hurt, and nicknamed him the "Teutonic Grand Lama of Regent's Park Road." Later one of Hyndman's political associates (the faddist Belfort Bax) asserted that Mrs. Hyndman sought to turn Frau Marx against Engels and even intrigued with her against him. Hyndman himself declared that Jenny Marx told his wife that Engels was Marx's evil genius. We attach no importance to such gossip. When Engels remarked to Bebel that Hyndman had behaved "pretty filthily" to Marx and that they both had given him the cold shoulder on that account, he meant that the agitator had freely borrowed from the "foreigner" Marx in his *England for All*, without mentioning his name.

When the first socialist groups were formed in England, Engels did not over-estimate their importance. He warned Bebel not to let Liebknecht fool him into believing that a real proletarian movement existed in England. In 1883 he wrote to him that "the elements which are active at the moment, now that they have accepted our theoretical program," might become important if a spontaneous movement arose among the proletariat, and they managed to take command of it. He wanted Hyndman's Social-Democratic Federation to be "finished" before the hour of a serious political labour movement arrived in England. A Socialist League had, as is well known, broken off from the Federation; it contained some people who tried to win Engels's favour. But although he recognized the goodwill of a man like William Morris, he kept away from the League, which later became tainted with anarchist ideas. In the same way he held aloof from the Fabian Society on principle, because it rejected the class-war. Of all its members he had the greatest respect for Annie Besant.[1] He considered that her pamphlets were among the most influential which the society published. When Edward Pease, later secretary of the Fabian Society, invited him in 1886 to write one of these pamphlets answering the question: *What is Socialism?* he refused. He thought, and told others, that an enormous working class was not to be set in motion by "preachers." In the nineties, when Bernstein became friendly with Sidney Webb, Bernard Shaw, and Graham Wallas, Engels grumbled at his "silly Fabianitis."

Hyndman was defeated at the 1885 election. But the economic crisis of 1886 shook the working-class faith in the blessings of free trade, and Hyndman seized the opportunity and organized a great demonstration of the unemployed in Trafalgar Square. A meeting of dock-labourers to demonstrate for protective tariffs had been called for the same place and time, and the two clashed. They were provoked by shouts from club-windows, and there was some looting of the city shops by the unemployed. Engels wrote to Bebel

[1] Annie Besant (1847–1933), in the beginning an active member of the Fabian Society, for which she conducted a number of important socio-political inquiries. In 1889 she joined the theosophist movement and in 1907 was made president of the Theosophical Society. She went to India in 1892, where she worked actively for home rule.

about the affair; its bad result would be, he said, that such childishness would disgust the English proletariat (which was quite unprepared); its good that the liberals must at last recognize the existence of the want and poverty which they had hitherto denied. He blamed Hyndman and his friends for taking such a revolutionary attitude " in the absence of any organized support among the masses." " These socialist gentlemen," he said, " want to conjure up a movement by main force, overnight — a thing which here and elsewhere takes years of work, though I agree that if it once got going and the masses were driven into it by the force of events, things might go far quicker here than on the Continent."

During that year Engels sometimes thought he saw traces at last of " a really socialist labour movement." If the domination of the old trade unions (who were averse to all political action) was to be broken, the poorest sections of the proletariat must first be swept into a socialist movement.

One of Hyndman's keenest opponents was the writer Edward Aveling, who was living with Eleanor Marx. He was a gifted man, but a perverted character. Engels did not see his true nature, and, since he treated Marx's daughters like his own children, he supported Aveling through and through, allowed Aveling to use him politically and financially, and did not notice that, because of this, he was alienating the best of the English working-class leaders. In 1887 he encouraged Eleanor and Aveling to start an energetic campaign in the East End of London. They had some success; and Engels thought it was a definite step forward, that this " enormous slum was shaking off its frozen despair " and producing a new type of trade union suited to the workers who had been neglected by the old trade unions and the " aristocracy of labour." He was filled with pride when the Avelings managed to found new trade unions in the East End for the gas-workers and the unskilled labourers, and considered these new unions responsible for the great dock-strike of 1889, " which stirred the lowest dregs of the East London working class out of the slough of despond."

The first May Day demonstration in London, in 1890, made an enormous impression on him. He watched it from the roof of a large freight-car and described it afterwards in the *Wiener Arbeiterzeitung*. He now lost his last doubts that the real socialist mass movement had begun in England, soon to align itself with the great international army of the Continent. " What would I give if Marx had lived to see this awakening!" he thought as he watched the many thousands who met to support the international proletarian cause. He wrote to Bebel: " I held my head two inches higher when I climbed down from the old freight-car." He felt that after a long sleep the English proletariat had at last arisen. " The grandsons of the old Chartists are taking their place in the battle-line."

Keir Hardie had now started to agitate (at first in Scotland and later in England too) for the foundation of an Independent Labour Party. There are reasons for thinking that Engels knew of the plan — possibly that he helped to start the " conspiracy against the Social-Democratic Federation" (as Hyndman called it). Still, he decided to wait and see what became of the movement before he came out on its side. And he warned the German social democrats not to proclaim it " the only real independent labour party " without further evidence. He had learned from experience " that a great nation cannot be hammered into accepting doctrines and dogmas without some trouble," even if it was presented with a theory which (like Marx's) had " grown out of its own life-history." He took care not to expect that the English would produce the same sort of program as a " nation with a taste for theory, like Germany." At the end of 1889 he assured Sorge that the movement was now at last under way, although it was not yet out-and-out socialist. " It is still styled a trade-union movement, but it is entirely different from the old trade unions of skilled labourers, the aristocracy of the working class." Even its members did not yet know the goal at which they were aiming. They must learn from their own experience, from the results of their own mistakes. But unlike the old trade unions, they received with scornful laughter any suggestion that the interests of capital and labour were identical, and this meant that they would soon get on.

He was certain that the masses of new recruits would soon clear away the cliques and create the unity which was necessary. The " frightful cliquishness " arose " only from the fact that the masses did not trust themselves," and would disappear as soon as a working class which could really move *en masse* appeared. In the year of his death Engels still found " the different little sects running in the same old grooves," but he also saw that the masses were moving with increasing urgency towards socialism. He was not perturbed that " the process of reaching self-consciousness " was slower in England than elsewhere. He declared that this was the right way for Anglo-Saxons, and patience was necessary. The German professors had long been able to say, with an appearance of truth, that the English workers only wanted to "beautify" the wage-system. But now the idea that social peace had really been achieved in England was over and done with. The "practical" English might be far behind the Germans and French, but " as soon as they know what they want, state, land, industry, and everything will belong to them." And Engels died with that faith unimpaired.

As long as the English working classes felt that they shared the blessings of increasing national prosperity, it was difficult to persuade them to give any credence to the idea of the class-conflict. And this was even truer of the Anglo-Saxon workers in the U.S.A. Engels had long been in correspondence with German socialists who had emigrated to America, and had thus been able to follow social developments in the

United States. But he had always seen that at first socialism could only find a home there among the working-class immigrants who had brought socialist ideas with them from Europe — and that it could not spread to the Anglo-Saxon majority until America's economic situation (and therefore its social conditions) had approximated much more nearly to conditions obtaining in Europe.

As early as the fifties he had described it as an illusion to hope that the Anglo-Saxon workers might accept the socialist doctrines brought by the German immigrants. He did full justice to the good work which the Germans had done in spreading socialism in the U.S.A., but he knew that a "real movement" could be created neither by Lassalle's adherents nor by Bebel's. In 1890 he told the German Social Democrat Hermann Schlüter, who had been exiled and gone to America under the Socialist Exception Law: "The American working classes are coming, but they must come their own way, like the English. They won't let theory be shoved down their throats, but they will soon be shoved up against it by their own experience and their own blunders and the results of them . . . and then, all right. Independent nations go their own way, and the English and their kinsfolk are the most independent of all." He viewed the aristocratic attitude of native-born workers towards the immigrants as a special impediment to the development of the working-class movement in the New World. But he told himself that in a young country which had always grown up on bourgeois principles, the working classes must at first share the prejudices of the bourgeoisie.

With unshakable optimism he held to his conviction that in time the set-backs would cease and there would come a period of steady progress towards a nation-wide socialist movement in U.S.A. "America is based on purely bourgeois principles, with none of this pre-bourgeois flummery; it is developing with colossal energy — an energy which is manifested even in the insane exaggerations of their protective tariff system; and one of these days that energy and these principles will produce a change which will astonish the whole world. If the Americans once begin, with all their energy and virulence, we in Europe shall look like children."

Engels could not hope to see that beginning. But he was destined, not only to see, but to help in the rise of the socialist working-class movement in most European countries and to direct them in the path which he thought best.

The little group of Italian socialists, who began to create a modern social-democratic party, looked to the German party as their model. They considered Liebknecht and Bebel to be pupils of Marx and Engels. In the second half of the eighties a few intellectuals in Italy began to translate the works of Marx and Engels, in order to popularize them among the masses. Their devoted work had considerable reward. These translations allowed Engels to influence the movement in Italy, and he increased his influence by contributing to the *Critica Sociale,* started in Milan in 1891, which was the first Marxist organ in Italy; but he had a more immediate effect through the advice which he gave on all important occasions to Filippo Turati, parliamentary leader of the Italian Social Democracy, until it was suppressed by Mussolini. He was also in correspondence with Antonio Labriola, the professor of philosophy in the University of Rome, the chief subject of discussion being the economic conception of history, which Labriola was especially exercised to preach in his native country.

Engels was not in uninterrupted contact with the Austrian working-class movement until the end of 1888, when a social-democratic workers' party was founded in Austria on the German model. By far the most important personality in the party was Victor Adler, who had formerly been a doctor. He visited Engels first in 1883. He repeated his visit in 1889, and Engels wrote in the *Labour Elector* (on which John Burns, Keir Hardie, and Tom Mann, one of the organizers of the great dock-workers strike in 1889, were collaborators) of the " wonderful energy, tact, and tenacity " with which Adler had reorganized the Austrian socialist movement during the previous three years. The old man and his brilliant disciple entered on a friendship which can only be compared with that between Engels and Bebel. Adler honoured him as a master and cared for him as a patient. Engels responded with an unobtrusive willingness to help. When Adler's family troubles made it necessary for him to have financial assistance, Engels pressed it on him; the letters in which he urged its acceptance and those in which Adler accepted it are documents of true dignity and warm-heartedness. Adler in Austria kept a watchful eye on Engels's health, and Engels in London watched over the political health of the movement for which his young friend felt himself responsible. He was admired by Adler as the one man who could teach coming socialist leaders how to apply theory *in corpore vivo*.

Engels also made his ideas felt in Belgium, Holland, Switzerland, Denmark, Sweden, Norway, Poland, Hungary, Spain, Portugal, Roumania, and Bulgaria. But his influence had the greatest historical effect in a country which was then in the background of the European working-class movement.

We have seen how his speculations about the future always centred on the approaching Russian revolution, the revolution which was to clear the way for the proletarian revolution in the West. Of its approach he had no doubt at all after the abortive agrarian reforms of 1861. During the seventies and eighties he was only uncertain when it would break out and what its issue would be. Marx and he constantly discussed these questions between themselves, and Russian revolutionaries too would ask them for their views. Engels knew enough Russian to read the printed matter which they sent him, but he always felt that his knowledge of the economic situation in Russia was too scanty for him to pose as an authority on such problems. His opinion became steadily more in request, however, for a new party had arisen to oppose the ·Narodniki, the first leaders of the Russian movement. This opposition declared that the near future in Russia (but only the *near* future) would be dominated by capitalism; and they began to study the works of Marx and Engels more deeply than the intellectuals of any other nation had ever done.

We can do no more than allude in passing to the important dispute between the Narodniki and their Marxist critics. The former stood out against the assertion that, even in Russia, communism could not be achieved until the long process of industrial development had been completed. They clung to the belief that the mighty peasant nation of Russia would pass at once from its primitive communist system to full-blown modern communism. The thesis that it must first go through a capitalist period was at first put forward mainly by liberal writers. It was not until the terrorist movement which killed Alexander II had been wiped out by his successor that the Russian " Activists " also came to believe this prognosis of their country's future; until then they had feared that they were condemned to a long period of inactivity by the Marxist doctrine — which had after all been based on social conditions in western Europe — and they could not bear to wait until the proletarian revolution had won its victory in England and France.

The chief theoretical question for all Russian socialists was whether the communist institutions of the future could be grafted on to the primitive communism which still prevailed in the village communities of Greater Russia, or whether the collective system must, even in Russia, grow out of a capitalist system of production. Engels avoided answering this question where possible; but where he was forced to give an answer, he realized that he was thereby defining his position not only on a scientific, but on a political problem. Some considered that the peasants, others that a still non-existent industrial proletariat, would carry through the great change; and these two points of view produced totally different ideas of the program and tactics of the future communist revolution.

When Engels first turned his attention to these problems, he was still influenced by his dislike for the muddle of socialism and Pan-Slavism which he had seen in Bakunin and Herzen. These early Russian socialists had claimed that the Russians were the chosen people of the socialist cause, which Engels could not grant. He held that the Russians were not the vanguard but the rearguard of the European proletarian revolution. Communal ownership of land had persisted, it is true, longer in Russia than among any other Indo-Germanic people; but he explained this by pointing out that communism in such a primitive form was compatible only with a low stage of production. He did not assert that the " mir " had no positive significance for the future socialist transformation of Russia, but he held that the relics of that system would not help Russia to skip the bourgeois stage of peasant proprietorship unless the proletarian revolution in western Europe came in good time. This judgment was expressed in the preface which Engels wrote with Marx in 1882 for the second Russian edition of the *Communist Manifesto*.

The dearest wish of Marx and Engels was to see the fall of Czarism. To help to achieve it, they would, if necessary, abandon their scruples about the party program. They had the greatest admiration for the Narodnaja Wolja secret society, which, after the Russo-Turkish War, began the terrorist activity which culminated in the assassination of Alexander II; and they would not argue on points of theory with the men and women who would thus venture their lives for an ideal. As long as the Narodnaja Wolja was operating successfully, Engels fully understood that they could not be in a hurry " for the leap into capitalism."

Warned by their earlier experiences, the two friends maintained an attitude of strict reserve towards most of the political exiles from Russia, until some refugees appeared who could boast of really revolutionary acts. But among

these Engels found people (as he told Becker in 1872) who
" have talents and character equal to the best of our party,
fellows with a marvellous stoicism, strength of character,
and brilliance in matters of theory." These words certainly
referred to Hermann Lopatin. He was far superior in originality and in strength of character to Leo Hartmann, who
was a frequent visitor at Engels's house after his unsuccessful
attempt to wreck the Czar's train. From these two men
Engels got an exaggerated impression of the power of the
Narodnaja Wolja; years later he still retained a wrong idea
of the balance of power between the autocratic Czar and the
little group who defied him.

Engels always took up the cudgels when the Czarist government tried to press for the extradition of Russian revolutionaries from the countries to which they had fled. On the
same day in January 1885 that the English press reported a
Russo-German agreement for the mutual extradition of political criminals, there were several dynamite explosions in
London. Engels asked, in the *Züricher Sozialdemokrat*, who
was benefited by these explosions. And he answered: " The
dynamite may have been laid by Irish hands, but it is more
than probable that they were directed by a Russian brain and
paid for with Russian gold." Since German government organs often chose to confuse anarchist and social-democratic
tactics, he thought it necessary to make a definitive statement
on the attitude of European social democracy to terrorist
action. He said: " The tactics of the Russian revolutionaries
are prescribed by necessity and by the actions of their enemies. They are responsible to their nation and to history for
the means which they employ. But the gentlemen who produce pointless schoolboy parodies of these tactics in western
Europe, who try to make Dick Turpin revolutions, who
use their weapons not against real enemies but against the
general public — these gentlemen are not followers and
comrades of the Russian revolutionaries, but their worst enemies." In Russia, too, Engels hoped that the period of ter-

rorism would soon be replaced by open political warfare in a constitutional state. But he expected that the capitulation of the Czar would be caused more certainly by the rapid development of capitalism than by the acts of the terrorists.

He thought that the coming Russian revolution would be entirely bourgeois, especially at the outset; and that the nihilists would only be the cat's-paws of the constitutionalists. After the continued attacks which disposed of one Czar and condemned his successor to voluntary imprisonment, he believed that the revolution would not be long in breaking out. Shortly after Marx died, he told Lopatin what he thought would be its immediate effects, and added that he was expressing Marx's opinion also. He stressed the fact that it was not, at that time, the task of a Russian revolutionary party to strive to realize a socialist theory whose practical application to Russian conditions had not yet been fully worked out. The real task was to intimidate Alexander III into summoning a national assembly. Speeches to the masses during an election contest would be far more effective than any other form of revolutionary propaganda. In the actual conditions of Russian life there was enough misery to cause a revolution. That revolution would work itself out as soon as the force of inertia was overcome and the people set in motion for a moment. Lopatin sent to the executive committee of the Narodnaja Wolja an account of this important conversation, emphasizing the fact that Engels did not expect that the revolution would lead straight to communism, but to a transformation of society which, once started, could not be stopped. But, alas, the central committee was arrested, the Narodnaja Wolja completely broken up. The Russian revolutionaries at home and abroad had to acknowledge the hideous truth that the forces of reaction again held their ground. Engels never heard, or never believed, this news. For long he hoped that something would soon be heard of the executive committee.

As the Russian socialists lost hope of being able to take a

direct and effective part in politics, they turned their attention to those questions of principle on which they regarded
Engels as *the* authority. The Liberation of Labour group
which was formed in Geneva in 1883 was the first Russian
socialist organization which endorsed the views of Marx and
Engels. The most important personalities in it were Plekhanov, Axelrod, and Vera Zasulich. Engels was delighted to
know that there was at last the nucleus of a party which
accepted his and Marx's doctrines without qualifications or
limitations and broke with all anarchist and Slavophile traditions. But although he approved of the content of Plekhanov's pamphlet, *Our Differences of Opinion,* he disliked his
intolerance of " the only people who are doing anything in
Russia at this moment." At that time he thought that theoretical consistency was less important than the co-operation
of all revolutionary elements (irrespective of programs) for
action.

Some years later these Russian Marxists paid personal
visits to Engels in London. He explained to them, as he had
already done to Zasulich, why he would not interfere in their
disputes with other Russian socialist groups. His inadequate
knowledge of the inner history of the movement and of the
present condition of Russia kept him from expressing any
opinion on the tactics necessary at any particular moment.
He had already, in 1885, told Zasulich how he expected the
Russian revolution would develop. " People," he said, " who
imagined that they had ' made ' a revolution always saw next
day that they did not know what they were doing, and that
the revolution which they had made was nothing like the one
they wanted to make." It was immaterial whether this sect
or that sect or even a court-revolution set the match to the
train. Where practically every condition of a revolution is
present, where the economic situation of the huge mass of
the people becomes more impossible every day, where all the
stages of social development already exist, and where all
opposition is forcibly suppressed by a powerful despotism,

" there, if the year 1789 once comes, the year 1793 will follow." Engels always described the future Russian revolution
in the likeness of the French Revolution, without including
one phenomenon — Napoleon.

But the Russian revolution did not come, and in the later
eighties Engels spoke less of it. Instead, he paid much attention to the Czar's foreign policy (which will be spoken of
later) and to economic developments in Russia. He admired
the talent and keenness with which his Russian followers absorbed Marxism. But he objected that when they dealt with
the all-important agrarian problem they abandoned themselves to their passion for controversy instead of making a
scientific study of the question. He urged them to agree on a
program for the future expropriation of the land, so that the
great estates should not be parcelled out piecemeal among
the peasants, without regard to the economic requirements
of the country. Neither in western and central Europe nor
yet in Russia had he any confidence in the survival of peasant
proprietorship. He was firmly convinced that agriculture of
the future, like industry, would be rationalized and run in
large-scale units by machinery. He did not neglect the fact
that capitalist development would find in Russia a country
which had a far larger peasant population than any other.
He wrote in 1893 to the Petersburg political economist
Nikolai Danielson that the process of replacing about five
hundred thousand proprietors and some eighty million peasants by a new class of bourgeois landowners would cause
frightful agony and convulsions. " But history is the cruellest
of all goddesses, and she drives her triumphal car over heaps
of corpses, not only in war, but also in ' peaceful ' economic
development."

In the spring of 1892 a meeting was arranged in Engels's
home between the leaders of the two parties among the Russian socialist refugees, in order to unite the parties. Engels
feared that hasty attempts at unification would only cause

more violent quarrels, and he can hardly have grieved when the plan fell through. He disapproved of the Russian Marxists for relegating the Narodniki to the lake of fire and brimstone " with the other reactionaries " — although the Narodniki were far superior to them in realizing the importance of the agrarian problem. He wanted the Narodniki to have time to convince themselves that their political fairy-tale could not stand up to economic facts. And he thought that many Russian Marxists were far too ready to make controversial use of his and Marx's sayings without having grasped the theory behind them. In 1893 the Russian agrarian writer Isaak A. Hourwich [1] wrote from Chicago to ask him, in the interests of unity, to make a pronouncement on the role of the peasantry in the coming revolution. But he refused. He was certain, he answered, that anything he as an outsider could say would at best have no more than a temporary effect. It was inevitable for political refugees to split up into small opposing parties as long as things were quiet in their own country. " If you have followed the writings of the Russian exiles during the last ten years, you will know yourself how the various groups among them interpret passages from Marx's writings and letters in the most contradictory ways, just as if they were texts from the classics or the New Testament. And anything I could say on the question you propounded to me would probably be used in a similar way, if any attention was paid to it at all." Excessive controversy should be avoided, he said; and in order to avoid it it was necessary that the Russian Social-Democratic Party should soon find energetic leaders in Russia itself.

Engels held it to be impossible to control a revolutionary

---

[1] Isaak A. Hourwich (1860–1924) escaped from Siberia, where he was a political prisoner, and fled to the United States in 1891. In the New World he was one of the first economists to support publicly the Marxian theory. He wrote, among other works, *Economics of the Russian Village* (1892) and *Immigration and Labor* (1922). He was, besides, one of the most distinguished Jewish publicists in America.

movement from a foreign country. He did not live to see the rise of a serious movement in Russia. And he never imagined that his ideas might triumph, in that Empire lying on the very edge of European civilization, before capitalism was overthrown in western Europe.

CHAPTER XXII

EUROPEAN POLITICS TO THE FALL OF BISMARCK

✍

Engels condemned the annexation of Alsace-Lorraine partly because he believed that the frontiers existing in western Europe in 1871 were ultimate and immutable. But he well knew that between the Slavonic and the Germanic world, and especially within the Slavonic world, there were as yet no fixed frontiers. And he reflected that it would be almost impossible to find a peaceful political settlement here which would reconcile the various national demands with the varying stages which economic development had reached in the different countries. He abhorred every increase in the power of the Czar; and the only justification he could see for the existence of the Habsburg monarchy was as a check on Russia's desire to incorporate the western and southern Slavs. After the fall of Czarism he hoped that the separate nationalities of Austro-Hungary, the Little Russians, and the Jugo-Slavs would all be masters of their own political destinies. Engels embodied these thoughts in an article when (in 1876) the Balkan Slavs rose against the Turkish dominion and next year Russia took up arms for " the Slavonic cause."

As early as 1848 Engels had opposed the bourgeois democrats' dogma of national self-determination. He did not wish the Serbs to gain their independence at the cost of a European war; they should wait in patience until the proletarian revolution in western Europe liberated them. " It is our task to work for the liberation of the proletariat of western Europe and to subordinate everything else to that."

So he told the editor of the *Sozialdemokrat* in 1882, adding that, as far as he was concerned, the Balkan Slavs could " go to blazes " if ever their struggle for freedom collided with the interests of the proletariat. This conflict of interests became obvious when these " interesting little nations " came to hope that they would be freed by the irreconcilable enemy of democracy and socialism; " they remain directly opposed to us, as much our enemy as their comrade and protector the Czar."

Engels did not consider that a Turkish Empire in Europe had any chance of survival, but in the war of 1877–8 he was driven to take the Turkish side both strategically and politically, because Russia was supporting the Balkan peoples. The Turks won some victories at first, but later their resistance collapsed. In a letter to Liebknecht in February 1878, Engels blamed the maladministration of the government and the diplomatic intrigues of the " Russian agent, the Marquis of Salisbury." If Russia managed to extort acceptance of her exorbitant peace-terms (as he thought she would), the result would be the break-up of Austria, with the consent of Germany.

After the set-back which Russian nationalism received from Disraeli's victory at the Congress of Berlin, Pan-Slavism became the guiding principle of the government of Alexander III. Engels was convinced that Russia was preparing a Pan-Slavist war as a last attempt to bolster up Czarism and reaction; and he more than ever regarded Pan-Slavism as the most dangerous enemy of the European working-class movement.

Now that the German social democracy had entered on its great advance, he ceased to wish (as he had wished in 1848) for a victory of the revolution in Russia and western Europe resulting from a great European war. He even feared that such a war might postpone the rule of the proletariat. In describing the results of a future world war he sometimes emphasized the factors which were favourable to the victory

of communism, and sometimes those which were not, according as his attention was fixed on the immediate or the more
distant sequel of the war. He had no doubt that in the end a
world war would lead to the triumph of communism. But
there are countless remarks of his which show how eager he
was to avoid paying the price of a world war for the general
revolution. For instance, in December 1882 he wrote to
Bebel: " I should consider a European war to be a misfortune. This time it would be terribly serious; it would set
jingoism going everywhere for years, because every nation
would be fighting for its own existence. All the work of the
revolutionaries in Russia who are now nearing success would
be rendered useless; our party in Germany would be temporarily swamped and ruined by the flood of jingoism, and it
would be the same in France." He even told his friends that
he feared a war would push the movement into the background for years, so that, just as after 1850, they would
" have to begin all over again, late in the day."

But if the great war came, he had no doubt that it would
be the last. " Such a war means the complete collapse of the
class state, politically, militarily, economically (financially
too), and morally. It may lead to a revolt of the war-
machine, for the armies may refuse to shoot one another
down for the sake of the lousy Balkan peoples." He closed
his letter to Bebel with the assurance that the butchery was
unnecessary. " But if it must come, I shall only hope that my
old fracture doesn't keep me from mounting my horse again
at the right time." It was because Engels considered a world
war unnecessary and shrank from the idea that in the last
years of his life he was drawn to take a very active part in
politics.

In November 1886 he was afraid that Balkan troubles
would lead to the outbreak of a general European war; and
in the *Socialiste* (the organ of his comrades in Paris) he
asked what France would do in such a case. There was as yet
no Franco-Russian agreement, and Bismarck was using all his

guile to prevent its conclusion. But the Russian alliance was getting an alarming amount of support in France. Since the rise of General Boulanger the spirit of jingoism had become increasingly rife, even among the working class in Paris. When Wilhelm II became his own Chancellor, and the alliance between the Third Republic and the Czarist despotism was concluded, Engels strove with all his might to open the eyes of the French socialists to the immense consequences which the alliance might have for the future of the whole European working-class movement. It was vitally necessary for the European proletariat, he said, that Czarism should be repelled, by peaceful or warlike means. It was best for it to be overthrown by a revolution in Russia : if it were, Russia's policy of conquest would come to an end, and internal problems would occupy all her attention. But the probability of such an event was much diminished by the military alliance between Russia and France.

Was it possible to foretell the victor in a world war? In March 1886 Engels explained to Bebel that the German army was without question the best and the best-led, but it was only one army among many. The Austrians had always good soldiers, but always managed to be beaten. The Russians were exceptionally weak in offensive, and strong in defending their own country. Turkey had the best soldiers, but their generals were wretched. The Italian army was sure to be beaten by any army of equal size. It was impossible to foresee how the powers would group themselves in a world war. " The importance of England will grow as the war lasts (both because of her fleet and because of her enormous resources) ; though she may keep her soldiers in reserve at the beginning, an English army corps of sixty thousand men could very well give the finishing blow in the war. All this presupposes that nothing happens within the various countries. But in France a war could very well put the revolutionary elements in charge of the government, and in Germany a defeat or the death of the old man could transform the whole system; and that could in its turn cause a regrouping of the belligerent powers. Briefly, there'll be chaos, with only one certain result: mass butchery on an unparalleled scale, the exhaustion of all Europe to an unparalleled degree, and finally the complete collapse of the old system."

At the outbreak of a general war Germany would be the strongest power, from a military point of view. It was good that this should be so. Bismarck should not be overthrown owing to a military defeat, until the Russian revolution was in progress. So Engels wrote, in pretty much the same terms, to Sorge and to Liebknecht in February 1888. His military knowledge told him that the German generals would have no easy task in a war with France. " The new French fortifications — the lines on the Meuse and Moselle, the two groups of fortresses in the north and south-east, and finally the beautiful new forts round Paris — will be a hard nut to crack. As things stand now, Germany cannot beat France, nor France Germany. Excellent! If the worst comes to the worst, there will probably be a static war on the frontiers, with varying luck, which will impress both armies with respect for their enemy and make a passable peace easy to arrange. But the Russians may get a fearful drubbing, and that would be best of all." But we read on a page of notes dating to the same period: " Tragicomic conflict: the state must wage political wars, which never arouse national enthusiasm; and for them it needs a national army, which is only reliable for national defence and for the offensives directly following on it (1814 and 1870). In this conflict the Prussian state and the Prussian army go smash — probably in a war with Russia, which may last four years, and in which there's nothing to be gained but diseases and broken bones."

Engels never ceased to fear that after the death of Wilhelm I and Friedrich III, Wilhelm II might throw open the way to Constantinople for the Russians and in return get their permission to deal with French chauvinism. In that case Germany would have allied herself with Russia against the whole world, and then she must certainly be defeated in the end. " I hope this danger will pass," he wrote to Liebknecht in April 1888; for Engels, the Chief of Staff of the European working-class movement, felt the "millstone of alliances" which weighed so heavily on Bismarck too. Both Engels and Bismarck knew that any world war was a leap in the dark, and that it might sweep away with it many things which seemed to their contemporaries stable and secure. And a protracted European war might threaten the whole economic future of the Continent. "In that case American industry would be victorious all along the line and would thrust this choice upon us — either a relapse into pure agriculture on a subsistence basis (American grain would prevent it from being any more than that) or . . . a transformation of society." That note was found among his papers, and probably dates from 1887. On another page of notes we read: "A war? Easy enough to begin it, but it defies conjecture to say what will happen when it has begun." And on another: "Peace continues only because the technique of armaments is constantly developing, and consequently no one is prepared, and so they all tremble at the thought of a *world* war (which is the only possibility), with its absolutely incalculable prospects."

Engels thought it to be the last of his tasks to lead the campaign, within the European working-class movement, against the danger of a war. The task became easier when, after the International Socialist Congress of 1889, a new Socialist International began to take shape.

In dealing with a man who always kept his own personality in the background, a biographer is tempted to pay too little attention to his private life. After the death of Lizzy her niece, Mary Ellen (who had grown up in Engels's house), tried to take charge of the household. But an empty-headed city merchant called Percy Rosher seduced the foolish girl, and in 1882 Engels compelled him to marry her. We must know all the attendant circumstances before we can accuse Engels of conduct inconsistent with his attack on bourgeois marriage in *The Origin of the Family.* When Rosher failed in business, he and his family came to live with Engels. Later they went to Canada, but did no better there. The affair cost Engels much sorrow and much expense. And finally the Roshers made trouble about Engels's will, although Mary Ellen was one of his chief heirs. So far as she returned the lasting affection Engels showed her, she had love for his purse rather than his personality. It was therefore a great stroke of fortune for him when the faithful Helene Demuth, who had shared the struggles of Karl and Jenny Marx for many years, became his housekeeper after Marx's death. She was a kind and clever woman, who embodied the whole history of the Marx household, so closely linked with his own life. He welcomed her as an old and trusted friend.

During the week Engels lived a simple quiet life. But on Sunday he liked to entertain guests. Most of them were party comrades from various countries who were visiting London or had settled in it. He generally presided at table in high spirits and sometimes sang an old German student song or his favourite English air, the *Vicar of Bray.* Eleanor Marx and Aveling were almost always present. From 1885 till 1890 Karl Kautsky and his young wife, a vivacious girl from Vienna, joined the circle; Engels had a special affection for her and was deeply grieved when the marriage broke up in 1888. In that year the staff of the *Sozialdemokrat* (which had been deported from Switzerland) came to London — Bernstein, Richard Fischer, and Julius Motteler. Bernstein won Engels's trust and affection, thereby benefiting his paper also. The commonest French visitors were Marx's sons-in-law, Paul Lafargue and Charles Longuet; also Charles Bonnier, who was a lecturer in languages at St. John's College, Oxford. Bonnier was a zealous Marxist and a not less enthusiastic Wagnerite; Engels, who detested the " music of the future," had many a tussle with him. From Germany came Liebknecht, Bebel, and Paul Singer, publisher of *Vorwärts,* to talk with Engels at length. Among the Russian Marxists, Vera Zasulich often visited the house, and among the Poles Stanislaw Mendelssohn.

Engels had few close friends among the English. The chief was John Burns, whose proletarian instincts Engels trusted and whom he described as an upright man, although he knew of his sympathy for the liberals. Will Thorne, too, came in frequently; Eleanor Marx had taught him to read and write. There were many visits from Belfort Bax, with whom Engels would argue for hours about the philosophy of history. Cunninghame Graham came less often, and still less William Morris, whose passion for the Middle Ages Engels bore with humorous tolerance. Keir Hardie (whom he did not altogether trust) and Harry Quelch, the editor of *Justice,* came only on rare occasions. Most of the English socialists and trade-unionists avoided a house where Aveling was a frequent visitor. Later Aveling revealed himself as a criminal, but at this period the English saw deeper into his character than Engels himself. Sidney Webb once told Bernstein: " When we run down Marxism, we mean Aveling." Engels was hurt that his house (which Continental admirers called " the Mecca of socialism ") did not attract the Englishmen.

Engels was at bottom a child of the north and had long been under the spell of the North Sea. He never went back to the south after settling in England. He usually spent his annual holiday on the English coast, by preference at Eastbourne. But even at an advanced age he travelled farther than that. In 1888 he went on a " little jaunt " to the United States and Canada, with his close friend Schorlemmer, the distinguished chemist, and the Avelings. And in 1890 he toured Scandinavia right up to the North Cape with Schorlemmer.

He spent only a month in America, and there was nothing official about his visit. He wanted only to have a little diversion and recreation before starting his work once more, and to visit old friends like Sorge and Harney. He saw what an attentive tourist might see, sometimes grasping the truth and sometimes generalizing too hastily. The Americans he met on the *City of Berlin* were not at all inclined, as he had feared, to despise the " sleepy, antediluvian Europeans "; he found them " more approachable than the English, and often rather blunt." He made a few notes of his impressions of America, no doubt with the intention of making them into an article. New York seemed to him to be bent on becoming the future " metropolis of capitalist production." In the streets he was struck by " the overworked appearance of the people, including the women." Wherever he looked, he saw " advertising, puffing, and croupier-faces "; everywhere he heard " hideous sounds on water and on land." All æsthetic considerations were dropped if there was a chance of a quick profit. The *nouveau riche,* he thought, had become a national type, and he found it very queer that " the Americans have no faculty of enjoyment." He thought about the men as he did about the horses, that there were the elements of a good breed, but the breeding process was not complete. He did not believe that the Americans had become a nation; he distinguished five or six national types, but he recognized that they were given coherence " by the Civil War, which proved that it was necessary to combine, and by the feeling that America had it in her to become the greatest nation of the twentieth century." In Canada Engels at first thought he was back in Europe, but later that he had entered a decaying and retrogressive country. But he felt that sleepy Canada would one day be ripe for annexation by the United States, and then John Bull would not dare to say no.

Engels was still tied to his desk by the work of editing *Capital,* by the development of political conflicts throughout the world, and by the growth of working-class parties in an increasing number of countries, when his seventieth birthday approached. After a short illness Helene Demuth died on the 4th of November 1890 — the last " of the old guard of the days before 1848." On the day after she died, he wrote to Sorge: " Now I am alone again. It was really due to her that Marx had peace to work for many years, and I myself for the last seven. I don't know what will become of me now. And I shall sadly miss her wonderfully tactful advice in party affairs." When Helene was buried, beside Karl and Jenny Marx, Engels exclaimed with tears in his eyes: " There has been sunlight in my house until now, and now there is darkness! " But happily the emptiness in the old man's home and heart was filled: Luise Kautsky received a delicately worded invitation from him and consented to come to stay with him. When the new year began, he could write to Sorge: " I have once more got peace and can work better than ever, because she acts as secretary as well." She still held this position in 1894 after she married the Austrian doctor Freyberger; the three lived together in a larger house in the same street.

Luise Kautsky was already living in Engels's house on his seventieth birthday, when good wishes poured in on him from all over the civilized world. He had a deep-rooted dislike for any demonstrations which honoured him personally, and actually said so when the choral society of the Communist Working Men's Educational Association in London wanted to sing a serenade in his honour on his next birthday. He answered the " absolute shower " of good wishes which poured in on him with the same " brazen modesty " for which his friends often reproached him, but which was really quite genuine. " No one knows better than I," he said, " that most of this homage is not due to me and my services. It is my destiny to reap the fame and honour which was sown by a greater than I, Karl Marx. And I can only promise to spend the rest of my life in the active service of the proletariat, so that if possible I may come to be worthy of that honour."

CHAPTER XXIII

THE LAST FIVE YEARS.
DANGER OF WORLD WAR

✍

As early as 1890 Engels had pointed out the dangers which threatened Germany from the character of Wilhelm II. And after the fall of Bismarck, Bernstein published leading articles in the *Sozialdemokrat* (prompted by Engels) which showed how little he was blinded by the Kaiser's temporary infatuation for social measures and his pretensions of winning over the working classes. Engels's prognosis was different from Wilhelm's. He foretold that social democracy would soon be driven to take over the supreme power in Germany. In June 1890 he wrote to Schlüter in America : " Willie is threatening to abolish universal suffrage — nothing better could happen for us! Even as it is, we are pressing on fast enough either to the world war or to the world revolution or to both."

As long as the Antisocialist Law was in force, Engels had hoped that the proletarian elements in the party would shake off the petty bourgeois the moment free speech was legalized once more. But the rapid rise of social democracy made him alter his views. "The greatest party in Germany," he now declared, "cannot exist without allowing full play to all different shades of feeling in it." He received from Eleanor Marx accounts of the first party congress to be held in Germany after the repeal of the law. (It took place in October 1890 at Halle.) She praised Bebel, on whose shoulders almost all the work rested. But she said that the party in the Reichstag had grown rather bourgeois, and she thought the German party had a more narrow-minded outlook than the French. On the back of her letter Engels noted: " Meanwhile, as long as the gang submits to Bebel, I don't care." He had complete confidence in Bebel's dependability and sureness of instinct. Nevertheless, soon after this he abandoned his usual practice and tried to influence the German party on an important occasion without consulting Bebel. He had good reason for doing this, for Bebel would have tried to dissuade him, and his mind was made up.

Engels had never forgiven Liebknecht for the fact that the criticisms which Marx and he had directed against the Gotha compromise in 1875 had been disregarded. Under the Antisocialist Law there had of course been no opportunity to revise the party program, but after its repeal Engels awaited a revision with great impatience. At Halle it was agreed to undertake it at the next party congress. Engels determined to do his utmost to ensure the elimination of all formulas which proceeded from Lassalle or from the petty-bourgeois People's Party. The new official program was to be Marxist in the strictest sense; but would it be, if he did not interfere personally? Liebknecht fancied that the program could be created by the " collective labour of the whole party "! But Engels did not believe in such creations. He was determined to keep the new program from " half-measures and phrasemongering "; and to do so, he decided to publish Marx's *Marginal Comments* (still very little known) in Kautsky's *Neue Zeit* without asking for the sanction of a party official.

The party executive had no grounds for taking action against him, but it declared that the publication had taken place without its knowledge or that of the parliamentary faction and was not approved as it stood by these two bodies. At first Engels was afraid that Kautsky might be made the scapegoat. He wrote to Bebel: " What is the difference between you people and Puttkamer,[1] if you pass antisocialist

---

[1] Robert von Puttkamer (1828–1900), Prussian Minister of Police from 1881 to 1888, bitter enemy of Social Democracy, was dismissed from office when Frederick III ascended the throne.

law against your own comrades? It does not matter to me
personally. No party in the world can condemn me to be
silent when I am determined to speak. But I think you should
reflect whether you would not be wise to be a little less sensitive and a little less Prussian in your behaviour. You — the
party — need socialist science, and such science cannot exist
unless there is freedom in the party."

He knew that it was dangerous to lift the veil which had
always hidden Marx's real opinion of Lassalle and to make
that opinion known to the German working-class party. For
years he had wished to explode the " legend of Lassalle," and
now he felt the right time had come. Later Bebel declared
that he would never have objected to the publication in itself.
But Engels doubted that, and with justice. Liebknecht, he
replied, would have done anything to prevent the publication
of the *Comments,* which he had " deliberately hidden " from
Bebel in 1875.

The next congress was held at Erfurt in October 1891 and
adopted the new program. Engels's influence had been felt
before the debate began, since he had seen to it that the draft
program " paid fitting respect " to Marx's criticisms of the
Gotha compromise. (" Fitting respect " was Liebknecht's
bitter-sweet phrase.) As soon as the draft came to Engels, he
abandoned all his other work to study it. He agreed that " the
main survivals of an outworn tradition " had really disappeared from it. Still, there was much to be criticized. He
raised a successful objection to the statement that the number and the misery of the proletariat were constantly increasing. He could not allow such an unconditional assertion of the
" theory of increasing misery." " The organization of the
working class," he remarked, " and their steadily growing resistance will possibly act as a check on the growth of their
misery. It is the uncertainty of life which *is* certainly increasing." In criticizing the political demands embodied in the
draft, he delivered a special attack on the delusion that the
existing legal system would allow all the party's demands to

be satisfied peacefully and legally. He said that it was out of
the question for Germany to develop peacefully into a socialist society so long as she was semi-absolutist and so long as
the states retained their independent existence. Such a change
was possible in France, America, or England, where the constitution allowed a legislator to do what he liked provided he
was backed by a majority of the nation; but not in Germany.
And he added that if a program refused to discuss the concrete problems which would put themselves on the order
paper at the first great crisis, the party would have no policy
at the decisive moment. The future of the movement should
not be sacrificed to the present.

Kautsky also found much to criticize in the official draft;
accordingly he proposed a new draft for discussion — he had
worked out its theoretical side, and Bernstein its practical.
This attempt found full approval from Engels, who had
borne a share in the work through detailed discussions with
Bernstein. But he could have wished even this new draft to
be altered here and there. One of his proposed changes was
especially characteristic of him. Kautsky proposed the sentence, which was eventually embodied in the official program:
" This transformation of society means the liberation not
only of the proletariat but of the whole human race, which
is suffering under the existing conditions." Engels thought
this was " quite colourless " and amended it to the assertion
that because of the class-conflict the ruling classes are intellectually and morally crippled, even more than the oppressed
classes. Bebel wrote from Erfurt to Engels on the 18th of
October: " The draft proposed by the *Neue Zeit* has been
taken as the basis of discussion, much to Liebknecht's annoyance, for he held fast to our own draft." After everything was arranged to his taste, Engels told Bebel he was
delighted, and wrote to Sorge: " We have this satisfaction:
that the Marxist criticisms have won all along the line."

At that time the right wing of the party, led by Georg von
Vollmar, held that it was possible to acquire power by a

WILHELM LIEBKNECHT

gradual process, on the strength of a " policy of prudent negotiation." But this was a point of view which Engels always opposed. He held that any negotiations with Wilhelm II would lead into the same blind alley in which Lassalle's manœuvres with Bismarck had ended. Nothing could reconcile the socialism of the *Communist Manifesto* with a democratic state-socialism which refused to force its way towards the classless society by a social revolution. If possible, Engels's belief was even strengthened by the disappearance of the Kaiser's " social-reformer mood " after he saw that " the masses could not be won over by a mess of pottage." Engels was not surprised that Wilhelm II now meditated a forcible suppression of the social-democratic movement, which he saw he could not otherwise master.

As we have seen, Engels hoped that the movement would not come to blows with the rulers of Germany until the " crack regiments " contained a majority of social democrats. " This official love of the working class has as its complement a hankering after military dictatorship (you see how all modern governments become Bonapartist willy-nilly) and therefore we must take care that they don't get a chance of anything of the sort "; so he wrote to Sorge in April 1890. At that time he hoped that the still undecided struggle between the monarchy and capitalist society would be the next item on the program. But he saw that it was possible that " chance — that is, the Unintended, the Unreckonable — " might bring about the open clash between the army and social democracy before the other struggle had taken place: or at least that the propertied classes might join the ruling classes in acting against the proletariat. He therefore watched with grave distrust the growing influence of the representatives of heavy industry upon Wilhelm II. But he did not believe that the government could stop the progress of social democracy even by a move to the Right.

At that time there were many rumours that universal suffrage might be forcibly abolished. They were not groundless. We now know that when the Kaiser declared war on revolutionary activities after the murder of President Carnot by an anarchist, he was very near a *coup d'état*. If such a coup had taken place, the social-democratic party would have been forced to take momentous decisions. Engels seized the opportunity in his preface to the new edition of Marx's *Class-Conflicts in France* to explain the tactics which the party should adopt in such a crisis. Speaking from long experience, he said that he considered barricades out of date, in view of the improved equipment and training and the better organization and discipline of the modern army. He showed why the prospects of street-fighting had completely changed since 1849 and were now all in favour of the army. Improved rail-transport allowed the government to bring up reliable troops much quicker than before; the small-bored breech-loading magazine rifle shot four times as far and ten times as quickly as the smooth-bored muzzle-loading percussion rifle of former times. Bombs and dynamite cartridges could nowadays destroy the best barricade without delay, and modern streets were so wide and straight that they were perfectly adapted for new rifles and heavy guns to have their greatest effect. " If a revolutionary deliberately chooses to fight behind barricades in the modern working-class districts of Berlin, he must be out of his head."

A new bill to suppress subversive activities was at that moment under discussion. In view of this the party executive thought it necessary to be prudent. They suppressed the passages in which Engels added that street-fighting could still take place in a great revolution, but that if it did, it would be wiser to take the offensive with superior forces than to maintain a passive defence of barricades. He had gone on to say that the reactionary forces knew why they were challenging the proletariat to open warfare and taunting it with cowardice for refusing to expose itself to certain defeat. But " these gentlemen are wasting their petitions and their challenges. We are not so stupid as all that. They might just as well ask their enemy in the next war to adopt the line-formation of the Great old Fritz or to form in column of division *à la* Wagram and Waterloo, and to carry flint-locks in their hands!" The conditions of the class-war, like those of national wars, had completely changed. Outside Germany, also, there was far less wild hitting without preparation; there also the proletariat had determined to use its voting power to get hold of all the posts which the party could reach. Nevertheless, the right of revolution had not been relinquished. German social democracy, he went on, was the most compact force in the international proletarian army, so that it had (at least to begin with) a special mission. Its growth was as spontaneous, as irresistible, and as quiet as one of the processes of nature. It was important to maintain that growth uninterrupted until it overtopped the existing governmental system. The party must not waste its energies in vanguard skirmishes before the day of battle. True, its development could only be temporarily arrested by a massacre like that which followed the Commune, for the victor could not shoot down a whole party which numbered millions. But a defeat would hinder the normal course of development and make the decisive struggle later, longer, and more costly.

Engels was obviously emphasizing the fact that in contemporary Germany the revolution could be better served by keeping the party within legal bounds than by an attempt at armed revolt. But the Prussian generals knew that as well as he did; and he recognized the possibility of a *coup d'état*. However, his short remarks on the position of social democracy in such a situation were omitted by the executive. Since he was not allowed to speak plainly about future developments, he closed this, his final exhortation to the German working classes, by telling them the same truths in a historical disguise. The " dangerous revolutionary party " in the Roman Empire, he said, "undermined religion and all the foundations of the state; it even denied that the will of Cæsar was the highest law; it was international, it had no fatherland; it spread throughout the Empire from Gaul to Asia and even over the frontiers of the Empire." It entered the army too, and whole legions were converted to Christianity. The authorities produced no effect by the usual drill-sergeant methods, and even *the special decree,* which the Emperor Diocletian passed, was useless. Indeed, seventeen years after the great persecution of 303, the Roman army was chiefly composed of Christians, and the autocrat who succeeded Diocletian proclaimed Christianity the state religion.

In these terms Engels repeated for the last time, five months before his death, his unshaken confidence in the victory of social democracy. But he solemnly warned his party not to allow their enemy to lure them on to a battle-field where they must lose the fight.

In view of the bill against subversive activities, he consented to certain omissions in this work. But he was very indignant when he received the printed version of his introduction and saw that it presented him " as a pacific champion of legality *quand même."* He wrote about this with much heat, to Lafargue, Kautsky, and Richard Fischer. He said he had wanted the French especially to realize that he had recommended peaceful tactics " only for contemporary Germany, and that, too, with many reservations. In France, Belgium, Italy, and Austria these tactics, taken as a whole, cannot be followed, and even in Germany they may prove useless tomorrow." This quotation is enough to dispose of the theory that towards the end of his life Engels was opposed to all employment of force. On the contrary, until his death he was always clear that the proletariat could not, except in very exceptional circumstances, manage to seize power without desperate battles.

During the long economic crisis of the seventies and eighties all European countries were faced by severe unemployment. The proletariat began to feel that an economic order which was powerless to deal with unemployment could not exist for ever. As Engels was among the first to point out, political anxieties increased the effect of the economic slump and aroused the working classes of the various European countries to co-operate with one another. For the first time, in the age of widespread capitalism, the shadow of a world war fell over Europe. If it broke out, it must needs be fought by enormous armies drawn chiefly from the proletariat. But the industrial proletariat, whose hands fashioned the instruments of destruction, refused to see in the impending terror the hand of Fate. They did not all see equally far into the facts, but they all believed that the working classes could avert the danger of war by co-operative action, if they held together as national and international movements. Engels took no active part in the official negotiations of the various socialist parties, but his superior knowledge of the problems, his exceptional insight, and the peculiar authority he had acquired allowed him to disseminate his explanation of the crisis far and wide. He was anxious to illuminate all the facts of which a sober and objective understanding was required, so that the leaders of the various working-class parties would not pass resolutions at their congresses which were foredoomed to failure. Meanwhile the Second International was taking shape; and within it all turned to Engels as teacher and arbitrator on all important problems, especially when disputes broke out.

In 1889 the International Congress in Paris had resolved that the proletariat of the world should demonstrate once a year on behalf of the eight-hour day. But it had not been unanimous on the form these demonstrations should take. The French and Austrians wished them to take place on the 1st of May, while the English and Germans said they would be content with the first Sunday in May—and raised the objection that the May Day demonstrations would be used by some members as propaganda for the general strike. At the next International Congress, in Brussels in 1891, the

German delegates were in the minority; they agreed, though unwillingly, to a compromise which fixed the demonstration for the 1st of May " so far as that is not made impossible by the conditions obtaining in individual countries." But the German employers' associations (favoured by the economic crisis) threatened to lock out their hands *en masse* if work was stopped on the 1st of May 1893. Both the parliamentary faction and the party congress of November 1892 refused to enter on a trial of strength which, in the strained political situation, might have consequences no one could foresee. It was declared impossible to order a general stoppage, and the festival was postponed till the evening. This decision caused a great hubbub in the French party.

Bonnier took it on himself to explain the French feeling to Engels. Already in February Guesde had informed him — via Bonnier — that the French would not change their attitude even if the Germans chose to retreat. He now added that at the next International Congress, at Zürich in 1893, the French intended to propose either to revoke the compromise resolution passed at Brussels or to discontinue the demonstrations altogether. In France people would only laugh at a postponement to the first Sunday in May. Engels was aggrieved that the German party had promised more than they could perform in Brussels; but he approved of their decision not to undertake a difficult struggle with the employers' associations, perhaps with the whole authority of the state, simply for the sake of the May Day festival. He therefore replied to Bonnier's " threatening letter " by taking up Bebel's cause. He made mock of the French logic which allowed the English but not the Germans to snap their fingers at the Brussels resolution, and wrote to Bebel: " It is a priceless idea to direct the European working-class movement from Oxford, the only bit of the Middle Ages that survives in Europe. I shall make a firm protest in Paris against this go-between Bonnier." Shortly after this Bonnier visited him, and Engels explained, forcibly enough, that his " ultimatum manner " was scarcely calculated to produce mutual understanding. Then he wrote to Bebel that Bonnier was the only man in the Parti Ouvrier who knew German, which made it impossible to dispense with him as mediator. But his terrific thirst for action and the enthusiasm which was bottled up in him by the loneliness of Oxford made him more likely to produce rows than reconciliation. That was unfortunate, because the dangerous state of Europe made it of primary importance for the Germans and French to co-operate harmoniously.

Another example of Engels's mediation between the German and the French parties is the answer he gave to Lafargue at the end of January 1887. Lafargue accused the German policy of being responsible for the warlike tone adopted by the press of Paris; Engels said this vengeance motif was the result of Russian bribes. Bismarck did not wish for a war which must involve all Europe, but if France and Germany once came to blows, a war between Russia and Austria was inevitable. " From that moment Bismarck would be faced with a situation of incalculable possibilities, and I do not consider him sufficiently stupid to create a situation like that in cold blood. It is Russia's interest to involve France and Germany in a war — after that she has only Austria, and at worst England, to deal with. But the Russian jingoes despise Austria and England alike, and they would take this to mean a free hand for Russia in the East. There lies the danger. The French and Germans will be at each other's throats — entirely for the profit of the Czar and the continuance of despotism in Russia."

In February 1890 he wrote an essay of some length for a Russian paper published in Zürich by Plekhanov and Axelrod. In it he emphasized the fact that the final decision in a general European war would rest with England, since she could cut off imports of grain into either France or Germany and so starve one country or the other into submission. He pointed out that the foreign policy of the Russian government was shaped by the " gigantic progress " of the social revolution in Russia. The press was wildly enthusiastic for the Emperor's imperialist policy: but it expressed only the thoughts of the newly created town bourgeoisie. As soon as the vast peasant majority of the population was allowed to speak in a national assembly, things would change. Then Russia would turn to her internal problems and leave dreams of world dominion alone. A Russian revolution would immediately do away with the danger of a world war. At the fall of the greatest stronghold of reaction, every government in Europe would lose the last spark of self-confidence it possessed. And then at last the West would turn, unhindered by foreign interference, to take up the tasks prescribed to it by history — " the conflict between proletariat and bourgeoisie and the shift from capitalist to socialist society." But if the change in Russia was long delayed, Europe would slip down with ever increasing speed into the abyss of a world war of unexampled violence and universality.

This essay appeared also in French, in the *Idée nouvelle,* and in English, in the socialist paper *Time.* Bismarck's conservative opponent Rudolf Meyer (with whom Engels had discussed the blockade which threatened Germany in the event of a war with England) sent a copy to Lord Lansdowne, then Viceroy of India. Engels told Vera Zasulich that he hoped the English reprint of his article would have some effect; " At this moment the reports from Siberia, Kennan's book, and the latest disturbances in the Russian universities have shaken the liberal faith in the Czar as a great liberator. That is why I hurried my article through the press, so as to strike while the iron was hot. The diplomats in Petersburg think their campaign of ' rapprochement with the West ' will be helped by the rise of the Czarophile Gladstone, who calls Alexander III the ' divine figure of the North.'" France was truckling to the Czar, and England was extremely friendly; so that Russia thought she could occupy Constantinople without interference from Germany.

In the light of subsequent history it is especially interesting to recall the deliberations of the International Socialist Congress in Brussels upon the danger of a world war, and the means which the European proletariat possessed to avert it or nip it in the bud. In the name of the commission (which had sat behind closed doors), Liebknecht and his French colleague Vaillant tried to persuade the congress to adopt without dissent the following resolution: That the only method of averting a catastrophe was the continuous protests of the working class of all countries against the war-spirit and against all the alliances which encourage it, and the completion of the international organization of the proletariat for the triumph of socialism. But there was one delegate who ventured to ask if that was all the European proletariat could do to prevent a world war.

This was Domela Nieuwenhuis, an ex-clergyman and a brilliant orator, who was at the head of the little Dutch socialist party. Victor Adler once nicknamed him the " Don Quixote of socialism." He had occasionally corresponded with Engels and had adopted many of Marx's and Engels's doctrines. Later, however, he became an anarchist and an anti-parliamentarian. He despised the pusillanimous moderation of the German social democrats and prophesied for them the fate of the Chartists. At this congress he demanded that when war broke out, the socialist party in every country should stop the masses from marching out at the word of command to butcher one another. He said that the distinction between a defensive and an offensive war was worthless, because diplomacy could make any war appear either defensive or offensive. He demanded that at the outbreak of war the proletarians of all countries should refuse to serve in the army, and call a general strike. They would of course risk imprisonment, but was not prison better than death? That phrase made it easy for Liebknecht to answer him. He said that at the outbreak of war martial law would be declared, and anyone who refused to serve would be im-

mediately court-martialled and shot. Still, a minority of the
congress (including some of the English and French delegates) endorsed Nieuwenhuis's demand for a general strike
at the outbreak of war. He repeated his proposal at Zürich
in 1893, but there the Russian Plekhanov replied that a strike
of that kind would only disarm the civilized countries and
give western Europe up to the mercy of the Cossacks.

Bebel, Adler, and Guesde agreed with Liebknecht and
Plekhanov; and Engels merely shrugged his shoulders over
the simplicity of the Dutch crank. He wrote to Lafargue
after the congress at Brussels that the episode had shown
that the European working class had passed through the
age of high-sounding phrases and now realized their re-
sponsibilities. He was very proud that the socialists had
formed themselves into a " fighting party " in Brussels — a
party which had its eyes open to all the facts and their
promise of imminent revolution. He believed that since the
end of the eighties the murmur of approaching revolution
could be heard once more; and he was confident that they
could anticipate, or at least overtake, the world war before
it became a reality. That is the only explanation for the fact
that Engels — although he usually saw so far into the future
— never asked himself whether the European proletariat
would ever find itself in the situation described by Nieuwenhuis. A famine had just broken out in Russia; Engels hoped
that it would endanger the Czarist system and at least postpone Russia's attack to a later date. But, for all that, he
did not believe that a world war was no longer a danger to
be reckoned with; he tried, indeed, to explain the danger as
clearly as possible in all those circles where his words carried
some weight.

The Franco-Russian alliance had now been concluded;
Engels might have doubts of its permanence, but not of its
existence. He welcomed, therefore, an invitation to contribute to an *Almanac* published by the Parti Ouvrier. The
Almanac was to be widely distributed, and Engels prepared

his article with a good deal of care. He sent his manuscript for a preliminary opinion to Laura Lafargue and was obviously relieved when she, with Lafargue and Guesde, approved it whole-heartedly. It was an attempt to describe to the French the origin and growth of socialism in Germany. He gave Bebel a preliminary sketch of his intentions: " People must realize that if France, in alliance with Russia, declared war on Germany, she would be fighting against the strongest social-democratic party in Europe; and that we should have no choice but to oppose with all our strength any aggressor who was on the side of Russia. For if we are defeated, the social-democratic movement in Europe is smashed for twenty years; if not, we shall come to power ourselves. The present system in Germany," he added, " cannot possibly survive a war."

In his introduction he told his French readers that the position he had earned by fifty years of work prevented him from representing the socialist party of one nation against that of another, although it did not prevent him from remembering that he was a German by birth. It was probable that Wilhelm II would not long remain inactive before the rising tide of socialism. There might be a struggle, and the superior forces of the counter-revolution might conquer for a time. But such a conquest would not hinder the ultimate victory of socialism, but rather make its triumph more complete. Naturally, that favourable outcome depended on there being no war; but war might break out at any moment.

Engels had now reached the really important point. He assured the French working classes that German social democracy did not identify itself with the existing German Empire and condemned the forcible annexation of Alsace-Lorraine. He conceded that the Third Republic represented the revolution (only the bourgeois revolution, however) in contrast to the German Empire — but only as long as it was not allied with Czarist Russia. In an alliance with the Czar the French would be denying the whole of their revolutionary history and would allow the German monarchy to pose as the representative of Western progress against Eastern barbarism.

He next showed how behind Imperial Germany stood the power of socialist Germany, soon to decide German foreign policy by encouraging the rehabilitation of Poland and allowing North Schleswig and Alsace-Lorraine to determine their own futures, and reproached the impatience of the French " patriots " who were unwilling to wait for that moment and wished to attain their immediate goal by plunging the whole continent into devastation and enslaving it to the Czar's knout. He described the coming world war, kindled by Russia, in which France and Germany would suffer most. In the existing situation it was ten to one that a French army would march on the Rhine as soon as the first gun was fired on the Vistula. " And then," he said, " Germany will be fighting for her very existence." If she conquered, she would have nothing to annex, for she already had too many non-German provinces. But if she were crushed between the French hammer and the Russian anvil, she would lose East Prussia and the Polish provinces to Russia, Schleswig to Denmark, and the whole left bank of the Rhine to France. Germany so mangled could not play her proper part in the development of Europe; in order to keep herself alive, she must wage another war to re-establish herself as a nation. If so, the doom of German social democracy was sealed; the Czar and the ministers of France and Germany would embrace over the corpse of German socialism.

In the present international working-class movement, he went on, German socialism held the most responsible post; and it was its duty to defend it to the last man and to capitulate neither to domestic nor to foreign enemies. " If the French Republic were to enter the service of His Majesty the Czar, Autocrat of all the Russias, the German socialists would fight them — regretfully, of course, but they would fight them." As against the French Republic in the Czar's service, he said, German socialism would be the real representative of the proletarian revolution. And if the French soldiers entered German territory, they would be greeted with the words of the *Marseillaise*: "*Quoi, ces cohortes étrangères feraient la loi dans nos foyers?*" If peace continued, social democracy would rule Germany before ten years were past. If war broke out, it would either be victorious in two or three years or be totally ruined for at least fifteen or twenty. War was bound to bring either the immediate victory of socialism or a total upheaval in the old order of society, leaving behind such a heap of ruins that capitalist society would become more impossible than ever. Then the social revolution would be postponed for ten or fifteen years, but after that it was bound to develop more rapidly and ruthlessly than ever.

Bebel and the other leaders of the German party agreed with Engels. But the response from France was not friendly. The deputy Protot (whom Engels considered to be a Russian police agent) wrote a lampoon calling Engels a poisonous reptile who had been creating mistrust between France and Russia for twenty years and whose aim was German supremacy. Engels paid no attention to this. But the leaders of the Parti Ouvrier were embarrassed when Protot asserted that the German social democrats and their chief adviser, Engels, were more nationalistic than the French socialists. Until then the Parti Ouvrier had held that the German social democrats would always oppose a war. The Parti Ouvrier had to combat a rigid national spirit in France and therefore adopted a radical internationalism. This internationalism was in fact not far from Nieuwenhuis's outlook (with its belief in the general strike) : it pretended to itself that it could really practise what it preached, and closed its eyes to the dangers which Engels now suddenly pointed out. That is why Engels was condemned for publicly asserting the possibility of a German war of defence in which the German social-democratic party would have to play a part.

Vaillant and Bonnier were furious with him for giving
such unconditional recognition to the duty of national defence. Guesde, however (who was a Minister in the Cabinet
of National Defence in the World War), declared that the
French workers were also bound to join the colours as soon
as another state " betrayed the peace of Europe." Bonnier
wrote to Engels that if the social democrats were strong
enough to prevent a war no matter where it arose, they
need not discuss the question of " marching to the frontier,"
and if they were not "(which is infinitely more probable), it
is not urgent to reveal our weaknesses." To this objection
Engels replied: " If the French socialists do not expressly
state that in a defensive war they would be willing to repulse
an attack by Kaiser Wilhelm, it is because this is something
which is so glaringly obvious, so self-evident, that it is not
worth mentioning. There is not a single socialist in Germany
who does not think that in such an event the French socialists
would simply do their duty in defending their national independence. Everybody would agree with them and in fact
approve of their action." That, he said, was the point of
view from which he had written his article. It would be a
ridiculous article if it were not based on the supposition that
the French socialists would take up arms as soon as their
native land was attacked. All he asked was that the German
socialists should be given the same right in the case of a
Russian attack, even if it were backed by the French government. " People in France who reproach us are like those who
say *quod licet Ioui gallico non licet boui germanico*. I consider it the duty of the French socialists to bring them to
reason." Engels said he did not hanker after a Russian or
French victory any more than after another Sedan. If the
class-conscious proletariat was to achieve its end, both Germany and France must remain masters of their own destinies.
And he declared himself a convinced western European, who
fully endorsed Saint-Simon's proposal for an alliance be-

tween England, France, and Germany: "*Voilà la vraie triple alliance.*"

The French socialist attacks on Engels's statements were opportunist in purpose; but Domela Nieuwenhuis produced a more fundamental criticism of them. Writing as a consistent pacifist, he pointed out the contradictions of Engels's and Bebel's attitude in abandoning the class-war and considering bourgeoisie and proletariat as a united body in the event of a Russian attack. In a pamphlet called *Currents in German Social Democracy* he wrote: "French socialist workers will march shoulder to shoulder against German socialist workers; they, on their side, will be marshalled in their regiments to murder their French brothers. That must be avoided at all costs. Whether we are applauded or not, whether we are called anarchists or what you will, we declare that those who agree with Bebel are fostering jingo sentiments and are far from the principle of internationalism."

Nieuwenhuis did not know that Engels, true to his thesis, had come to the conclusion that the social democrats in the Reichstag should not refuse to approve war-credits to resist a Russian attack. "If we are convinced," wrote Engels to Bebel on the 13th of October 1891, "that the thing will start next spring, we could hardly be opposed to the credits on principle, and then we should be in a pretty desperate position. The lick-spittle parties would boast that they had been right, and that we had to eat our own words. Also, such an unexpected change of front would cause appalling friction within the party — and internationally as well." In view of all these facts, Engels advised that the party should not agree to any credits being used for altering existing equipment and forming new cadres, since that would not be in time for a war in the spring; but that they should vote credits for measures "which will bring the present army nearer to a people's militia, which will simply strengthen our defences, which will train and arm all men who have not yet enlisted, from seventeen to sixty, and which will dispose them in fixed cadres, without increasing all that ' control.' " He added : " We cannot demand that the existing military organization should be completely altered while the danger of war persists. But if there is an attempt to take the great mass of men who are fit for service but have not been trained and train them as well as possible and dispose them in cadres — for real fighting, not for parading and all that nonsense — then that is an approach to our idea of the people's militia, which we can accept. If the danger of war increases, we can tell the government that we should be ready, if they made it possible for us by decent treatment, to give our support against the foreign enemy — on the presupposition that they will fight relentlessly and use every means, even revolutionary means. If Germany is attacked from east and west, all means of self-defence are good. The existence of the nation is then at stake, and we, too, have a position to maintain and a future which we have won by hard fighting."

These, then, were the concessions which the great German international socialist was prepared to make to the Imperial German government if Germany were forced to defend her life against the Russian Empire and its ally, the French Republic. He considered that the national life of the great civilized nations was a real value which could never be disputed. But next year he spoke no more of such concessions, when the controversy flared up about the army estimates in which it was proposed to increase the size not only of the army but also of the corps of officers, a well-known stronghold of reaction.

The armament race between the great military states threatened world peace more and more. Engels therefore published a series of articles in *Vorwärts*, called *Can Europe Disarm?* It appeared in February and March 1893, while the Reichstag was discussing the army estimates. He would have liked to call it *Social-Democratic Estimates*, but if he had tried to, the social democrats in the Reichstag would have had to endorse it *en bloc* before publication, which he rightly held to be improbable. Since he wished to do all in his power to prevent the " general war of annihilation," he limited his proposals deliberately. " It is my intention to show," he wrote in the preface to the offprint which appeared at the same time, " that these changes are possible at this moment. They can be made by the existing government and in the existing political situation. That is the basis of my position: I limit myself to such proposals as any existing government can accept without endangering the security of its country. I am only endeavouring to show that from the purely military point of view there is nothing to prevent the gradual abolition of the regular army; and that if the regular army *is* still maintained, it is maintained not for military, but for political reasons — in a word, that the army is meant for defence, not against a foreign enemy, but against a domestic one." He signalized " the gradual diminution of the term of military service by international agreement " as the " kernel " of his proposals. This, he said, was the simplest and shortest way to adjust the general transition from the regular army to a popular militia. It was impossible to confuse the militia system which he proposed with any existing system, because he considered that the gymnastic and military training of the entire male youth of the country was an essential condition of the transition to his system.

He also pointed out the " peculiar contrast " between the " frightfully conservative " mentality of the higher officers in the German army and the increasingly rapid technical transformation of the whole of military science. Such a contrast, he said, benefited neither the army nor the nation. " We need fresher, keener brains: and I must be gravely mistaken if there are not enough of them among our ablest officers, longing for liberation from the routine and red-tape which have become so rampant in twenty years of peace. But until they have the courage and the opportunity to drive home their beliefs, we outsiders must step into the breach and do what we can to show that we also have learned a little soldiering." At an earlier date Engels had told Marx that a rational military organization was something between the Prussian and the Swiss systems; and that only a communist society could get really near the full militia system, " and even that approach would only be asymptotic." Even then he had affirmed that good cadres must exist before large masses of men could be trained in a short time, and he held to that belief when the armament race began. Then he even came to fear that if peace was almost more costly than war, a war would come not as a terrible scourge, but as a saving crisis which might end an impossible situation. Until the end he hoped that the Prussian system, which all Europe had adopted, might be replaced by a militia in which every fit man would have to serve a period sufficient for military training. Those who had been trained would form reserve cadres so organized that every geographical unit would furnish its own battalions to an army which would be as useful for defence as it would be useless for conquest. Then every citizen would have his gun at home. But did not von Moltke tell the social democrats, when they made that demand in 1874: " Guns are easy to distribute, but hard to get back "? And now Engels did not expect the German government to behave any differently; he foresaw that his own proposal and " the whole militia business " were bound to fail " because of Alsace-Lorraine " as well as the internal situation in Germany. But his purpose in putting forward these proposals was by no means purely propagandist: he also wished to raise a serious discussion among military experts.

With his eye always on the danger that Germany might have to fight on two fronts, he began his exposition with the remark that Germany could not alter the term of service on the principle that all fit men must serve with the colours. He even declared that only a social-democratic government could carry out that requirement in full. But he pointed out that the period of service was the point on which the leverage for disarmament must be based. He proposed that the great Continental powers should hold a disarmament conference, at which they should frame an agreement on the maximum period of active service in all branches of the army — the time at first to be two years, perhaps, " but with the aim of further decreases in the period as soon as possible, and with the militia system as the final goal." If an attempt was made to carry out this proposal, it would show that military training depends for its efficiency on instruction received in youth. Prussia had begun the armament race, and therefore (in this Engels agreed with previous declarations of the leaders of the social-democratic party) it would be best that the initiative in disarmament should proceed from Germany. If France accepted the proposal, the danger of war was over, and Germany had earned the glory of introducing disarmament. If she did not, France would be worse off in case of war; for there was little to hope from Russia as yet, and England could not refuse benevolent neutrality towards a Germany resolved on disarmament. In a war between the Dual and the Triple Alliance, the decision would lie with England, for " when she puts her fleet at the disposal of one side, the other will be simply starved out and its imports of grain will be cut off. It is the blockade of Paris again on a colossal scale, and the blockaded side must capitulate, as sure as two and two are four."

If Engels had hoped that the social democrats in the Reichstag would adopt his point of view, he was disappointed. Liebknecht, Karl Grillenberger, Bavarian Social-Democrat, and many other party comrades agreed with the main proposals. But Bebel considered that in the circumstances any plan for disarmament was utopian. He wrote to Engels to explain in detail why a storm would sweep away the parliamentary faction if they adopted his plan. He concluded thus: " As a matter of fact, there is no need for us to rack our brains to help the gentlemen up above. They are concerned solely with revolutions in military technique, but in every other sphere they are clogged to the teeth with conservatism. And the more they see themselves forced to democratize the army by increasing the numbers and shortening the term of service, the more firmly they will stick to everything else which the conservative tradition can keep unchanged. On one side is absolutely clear insight into the truth, on the other a narrow-minded pre-Jena spirit which will probably ruin the whole system when things become serious. All we can do is to explain how things stand, and leave things to go their way." Engels soon saw that he, too, must resign himself, despite the vocation he felt to guide Europe away from the abyss for which it was heading.

Another International Congress was called for August 1893 in Zürich and was at first faced by the same difficulties as previous congresses. Engels helped to remove them. The British trade unions had received their invitation to Zürich in good time, but had called an international congress on the eight-hour day for the same month in London. In this Engels saw a trial of strength between the class-conscious proletariat of the Continent and the conservative English trade unions — who, as he complained to Bebel, considered the "wage-system an eternally immutable law of nature." He addressed Bebel, Adler, and Lafargue and managed to get the German, Austrian, and French trade unions to pass resolutions which ended in the cancellation of the English congress. The English came to Zürich instead.

At this congress, also, the chief point of discussion was the attitude to be adopted by social democracy in case of war. Once more Domela Nieuwenhuis spoke with all his eloquence for a general refusal to serve. But it was in vain for him to deny that he was a utopian and to call it real utopianism to hope that paper protests could answer shells and rifle bullets; it was in vain for him to laugh at the " Russian bogy " which would drive the German social democrats to approving any military expenditure whatever; it was in vain for him to say he would rather have a civil war against capitalism than a national war. He was told by Adler, Plekhanov, and Turati, by Liebknecht and Aveling, that his proposal could not be realized in any country with a working-class movement of any importance, and that any attempt to realize it would give militarism a chance to strike social democracy to the ground. " If the military strike and the general strike were anything more than a pious wish, if the social-democratic parties in Europe and in the whole world had the power to carry these strikes through, then there would be conditions in Europe which would make any war impossible." That was Liebknecht's reply to him. And Aveling said: " If we are strong enough to carry through this military strike, we can do something quite different: then our job is to send capitalism to heaven or to hell." Nieuwenhuis's resolution was defeated, and one put forward by the German party was carried; it recommended the working class to use all their forces in the struggle against nationalism and declared that only the fall of capitalism would mean the end of war. Engels had previously given his approval to this resolution. We know his hopeful view of the course of events in Europe. He repeatedly prophesied that the end of the century would bring the victory of social democracy in Germany, and expressed the hope that he would live to see it.

During this congress Engels spent some time in Zürich. Ever since the repeal of the Antisocialist law his friends in Germany had given him no peace until he consented to come and see with his own eyes how his homeland looked, now that it had become a leading industrial country and the stronghold of social democracy in Europe. He went to Cologne with Luise Kautsky and Freyberger. As the train sped through the Rhineland where he had been born, memories of his youth crowded upon him; and when he saw the towers of the cathedral he said, with rising tears: " A lovely land, if only one could live in it! " From Cologne Bebel went with him up the Rhine past Mainz and Strasbourg to Switzerland. There he " stole away " for a fortnight to Graubünden, where his brother Hermann was waiting to see him; he did not appear in Zürich till near the end of the congress.

We need not describe the universal homage which was paid to the Nestor of European social democracy. Among the delegates were Labriola, Turati, and other notable men who had corresponded with Engels without having met him. He was not attracted by the lengthy discussions and conferences, but he attended the social gatherings in high spirits. He sailed to Bendlikon with Eleanor Marx, Bebel, Kautsky, Labriola, and others. The professor would have liked to monopolize him completely, but Engels drew a distinction between the hours he gave to serious discussion and those in which he enjoyed a fresh breeze or " drank a modest glass " with good friends. At Axelrod's house he had to give audience to a group of Russian girls who admired him; and at it not only three or four young things " with marvellous eyes," but also Vera Zasulich — who was more of a propagandist than a beauty — were honoured with a kiss from his lips. " But my real darling," he told his brother, " was a delicious little factory girl from Vienna, with the sort of delightful face and enchanting manners that are really rare." This was Adelheid Dvorak, who later became Adelheid Popp; she came to be the leader of the socialist women's movement in Austria.

As honorary president of the congress, Engels could not refuse to deliver the closing address. When he entered the hall of the Tonhalle, there was universal applause; he was a legendary figure to most of the delegates, and they were overjoyed to see him in person. In his speech he declined to take their homage to himself; it was due in the first place, he said, to " the great man " with whom he had published the first socialist articles, exactly fifty years before, in the *Deutsch-Französische Jahrbücher.* " From the little sects of those days," he cried, " socialism has now developed into a powerful party before which the whole world of officialdom trembles. Marx is dead; but if he were still alive, there would be no man in Europe or America who could look back on his lifework with better reason for pride."

Some weeks later he went to Vienna with Bebel. There he told his party comrades that if he as Marx's comrade-in-arms had done anything for the movement in the fifty years he had been in it, he asked for no reward. He added: "We are a great power now; we are to be feared; more depends on us than on the other great powers. That is my real pride! We have not lived in vain." He travelled on to Berlin, which he had not seen since his days in the army, when he had been one of the most revolutionary in the daring group of "the Free." There he addressed a mass meeting in the Concordiasaal and reminded it that in his youth the Prussian capital had consisted of the court, the garrison, the nobility, and the officials. Now it was the capital of the strongest workers' party in the world, a party which moved from victory to victory.

But despite the interest with which he saw these new scenes, he was glad to return to his study in London. "People were all very nice," he wrote to Sorge in Hoboken, "but I don't care for all that, I am glad it is over." He said that the next time he went over, he would write beforehand to make sure that he "did not have to parade before the public." He was astonished at the reception they gave him, but he would rather leave that to parliamentarians and orators: "that sort of thing is more in their line, it really doesn't fit my own work."

On his return he at once took up his work. The first task was nearly finished: the third volume of *Capital*. After that there was another volume to do, and then he meant to revise his *German Peasant War,* so that it embraced his whole conception of German history. At seventy-three he was planning even greater works. He felt that no one else should write the life of his great friend, and the history of the International Workingmen's Association. At the same time he constantly reflected on the problems which current history presented to the social-democratic movement. The age of imperialism was approaching: for the first time an Asiatic state took the initiative in a great political change. " Once more the magnificent irony of history," he wrote to Kautsky on September 24th, 1894: " only China is still to be conquered by capitalist production, and while the conquest is being completed, capitalist production is making itself impossible in its own home."

CHAPTER XXIV

THE END

On Engels's seventieth birthday the General Council of the Parti Ouvrier conveyed to him the wish that he might live to see the proletariat enter the promised land of communism; and he himself had a great fancy " to get just a peep into the new century." The old fighter tried hard to complete his life-work — but he over-estimated his remaining strength. Down to the end strangers who came to visit him spoke much of his lively humour, his caustic remarks, his tall, erect figure, and his brisk and impetuous thought and speech. But his intimates could not fail to see the traces of age. He did not care to speak of his own health, but he was bound to give some information to his close friend Adler, who was a doctor. On his last birthday Adler advised him to take more care of himself, and he replied that he was letting his doctor bully him thoroughly, " just as an old broken man should do."

On New Year's Day 1895 he thanked Adelheid Popp for her congratulations on his " latest, but — it is to be hoped — not last, birthday." On the 8th of February he could still say that his health was better than it had been for a long time, and that he was enjoying his work. But in March Freyberger had to inform Adler that he had diagnosed cancer of the œsophagus. Engels never knew that he was marked for death. He wrote Danielson at the beginning of June that he felt poorly for the moment, but it was nothing serious. At the end of June he wrote to Richard Fischer that he was not yet fit to do any work and did not know

how much longer he would be held up by this illness — natural
enough at his age, but devilish slow to run its course. When
Adler heard that the disease was making rapid strides, he
got leave of absence from prison and came to see his old
friend once more. He found that Engels was bearing his
pain " with stoicism, even with humour," which could be
seen from the remarks he wrote on his slate when he was
unable to speak. During Adler's visit the disease took a
decisive turn for the worse. When he had to leave on the
3rd of August, Engels had lost consciousness. On the evening
of the 5th of August, in his house in London, Engels passed
peacefully away.

He had not been told that his disease was incurable, but
he had known that he was going downhill. True to his philosophical view of death, he had quietly set his affairs in order.
He left a considerable sum, of which twenty thousand marks
went to Bebel and Singer " for election purposes," with the
note that, by English law, he could not leave the money to
the German party in any other way. " So take special care,"
he wrote in November 1894, " that you get it and, when
you get it, that it does not fall into the hands of the Prussians. And when you feel sure on that score, drink a bottle
of good wine on it. That will be a fine memorial to me."
This sum was only a small part of his property; the rest was
divided between Marx's daughters, Luise Freyberger, and
Mrs. Rosher. His executors were Samuel Moore, Luise
Freyberger, and Bernstein. He made over his library to the
party in Germany and entrusted Bebel and Bernstein with
the disposal of his unpublished literary work.

He had said that it was his " positive wish " that his body
should be cremated and the ashes thrown into the sea. Perhaps he made this decision because he knew he was leaving
behind no one who would be deeply attached to him after
death; or it may have been due to his abhorrence of hero-
worship in any form; and perhaps also to the love and kin-
ship he felt for the changing, restless sea. He had directed

that the funeral ceremony should be strictly private, and that no mere political associates should attend, but only personal friends. His wishes were followed. When Eleanor Marx invited John Burns, she expressly asked him to tell no one the place and time of the ceremony. It was held at the West-minster Bridge station of the South-Western Railway, be-fore the body was taken to the crematorium at Woking, and only about eighty persons attended. Liebknecht, Bebel, Singer, and Bernstein came from the German party, La-fargue from the French, Edouard Anseele from the Bel-gians, Van der Goes from Holland; the Russians were represented by Vera Zasulich, Volchovski, and Stepniak. Besides these there came a Pole and an Italian. The Ave-lings, Will Thorne, Quelch, and a deputation from the Socialist League represented the working-class movement of England. There were also Kautsky and Frederick Lessner (the tailor, who had been a friend of Engels since the days of the Communist League) and some members of the Engels family. One of Engels's nephews spoke beside his coffin, extolling the unselfishness and amiability with which he had always treated his family, despite their political dif-ferences. Samuel Moore, deeply moved, made a short speech for his personal friends. Liebknecht, in the name of the German party, Bebel for the Austrians, and Lafargue for the French expressed their gratitude to "the international confidant of the class-conscious proletariat throughout the world." The German Workers' Education Association of London, which Engels considered to be the oldest inter-national society, held a memorial ceremony on the 10th of August, at which Bebel spoke. Only the Avelings, Lessner, and Bernstein journeyed to Eastbourne, and, as Engels had asked, dropped his urn into the sea about five sea-miles from Beachy Head. It was a stormy autumn day.

As soon as the European working-class movement was deprived of the services of Engels, it was compelled to set up an international bureau in order to keep up regular correspondence between the parties of the various European countries. Engels had been the first to recognize the necessity of encouraging such correspondence, and, half a century before, he had taken over the duty and fulfilled it alone. Through it he was enabled to have a wider conspectus of the movement than was possible for the national party leaders and to ensure that its progress was always in the direction which Marx and he had pointed out in the *Communist Manifesto*. Victor Adler, in his obituary in the *Wiener Arbeiterzeitung,* described Marx as the " greatest theorist of international socialist democracy " and ranked Engels beside him as its "greatest tactician." And it was Engels in fact who had — from the seventies to the nineties — schooled the leaders of the new and growing European working-class parties and shown them how to apply theory to political practice. Bebel and Adler, Guesde and Lafargue, Plekhanov and Axelrod, Turati and Anseele, when they came to ask him for advice, were constantly astonished to find how acutely he had followed the developments in their countries, and how to the end of his life he endeavoured to do justice to individual historical factors in each country as well as to the great main lines of development which were common to all.

He had an unshakable faith in the final victory of communism. Sometimes he would under-estimate the importance of political impediments, but his eagerness was never foolhardiness, and from it sprang the confidence with which the leaders accepted his judgments and the masses took up his war-cries. He often expected that the forces of conservatism would yield while they were still strong. But many of the greatest revolutionaries in history have done the same, and many great generals, after their enemy was forced on to the defensive, have unjustly despised the weight of his reserves. Engels's sanguine temperament laid him open to many grave errors, but he was saved from the gravest of them by his strong sense of actuality and his honourable anxiety to see all sides of a question, even those which were unfavourable to him.

Nature was kind to him. The seeds which were in him she brought to fruition, as she does for few men. By the highest standards, he was fertile and fertilizing rather than truly creative. It will often be asked what historical importance he would have had if Marx had not met him. The first chapters of this biography have attempted to show how far he had gone alone along the path which he and his friend pursued together after they met. Lafargue once told of a conversation in which Engels said: "Doubtless one would have managed to understand and analyse the mechanism of capitalist production and to discover the laws of its development — only it would have taken a long time, and all the work would have been patchwork and pieced together. Only Marx was able to follow all economic categories through their dialectical movement, to connect their successive phases with the causes which determined them, and to reconstruct the whole framework of economics in a comprehensive theory whose individual parts mutually control and support one another." In these words Engels indicated what he himself had been unable to do. He saw in himself a certain "indolence *en fait de théorie*," which proved to him that he was not qualified to work out an economic or philosophical system and to grapple it together with hooks of steel. It is true that he had a natural talent for observing theoretical connexions, but he was content to grasp them by intuition, to understand the direction in which they pointed, and especially to draw inferences from them to action — for action was for him the crown of life. These were the qualities which made Engels the Chief of Staff of the proletarian-class movement in Europe during the period of its brilliant rise to power.

He could give himself up with passionate interest to scientific study. But the faculties of research and of logical analysis were less developed in him than the talent for stimulating, disseminating, and popularizing, in the noblest sense of the word. Accordingly his thoughts were better embodied in a brilliant sketch than a slowly ripened treatise. He wrote in a crystal-clear style, full of suggestive force; and he could express highly complicated theories in a language which the simple layman understood.

Engels and Marx had the highest opinion of each other, and each valued his friend's criticism of his work far above all others. They considered their lifework to be a unity, in which there was a division of labour, but not private property. They shared their pleasure in their individual literary successes as well as in the common conquests which were made by their political ideas. The crushing attack on the Young Hegelians in *German Ideology,* the elaboration of the theory of surplus value, the propagandist effect made by the critique of Dühring, the completion of the first volume of *Capital,* and the respect which Engels won as a military specialist — all these achievements were for them merely battles fought together in the same campaign. Through the whole of history there is not another example of such devoted partnership between two great and gifted men.

It is not an accident that Engels was a keen amateur strategist, and that Marx's economic works contain many military metaphors. Neither of them ever commanded large bodies of men, as their great pupil Lenin did; but throughout their lives they felt that they were a belligerent power, they two alone, in alliance with the future. They were resolved not to accept peace until all the great political and social powers of their time laid down their arms before them. And their most determined enemies knew that they were dangerous men to face. We can see this from the article printed after Engels's death by the *Post,* which was owned by Freiherr von Stumm, the well-known Saar industrialist and Wilhelm II's adviser on social legislation. " The

nation," says the *Post*, "is in far less danger when its se-
ducer thinks that anarchy is an end in itself (as Bakunin
did) than when he is slowly undermining the existing order
under the pretext of creating something new and better.
If there was ever a man whose life-work was to wage this
war of annihilation against all existing order, discipline,
and morals, that man was the socialist Friedrich Engels."

The socialist parties of the whole world felt his death
deeply. The young Belgian party leader Vandervelde,
wrote of the impression Engels made when he entered the
assembly hall in Zürich. "We wanted to close the meeting;
the last votes were taken in feverish haste. One name was
on every lip. Friedrich Engels entered the hall; among
storms of cheering he came to the platform. And after he
had spoken (in the three official languages of the congress)
of the battles of the past, the successes of the present, and
the unlimited hopes of the future — it was as if the sunshine had suddenly dispersed the mists. The spiritual unity
of socialism shone out bright as day from among the peculiarities of individual nations; and the whole assembly re-
echoed the words with which Engels closed the congress,
as he had once ended the *Communist Manifesto:* 'Workers
of the world, unite!'"

Engels enlisted in a movement of vast historical importance when it was in its earliest stage; and he helped to form
the conception of history which believes that this movement will carry humanity one stage further on its upward
path. Therefore it was not only possible but obligatory for
him to help to inspire that movement with the faith which
filled him. His long life allowed him to watch and help its
rise and development and to guide it in accordance with his
dialectical interpretation of how the new era in the history
of the world would come. The character of that interpretation, and his own self-confident straightforward nature, prevented him from having doubts. He remained unshakably
confident that the proletariat in its struggle for emancipa-

tion must necessarily move along that path, and that no other would lead so directly to that millennial time when modern man's curse, the division into classes, would be lifted from him. And it was fortunate for Engels that during the later period of his life both his conception of history, and the social and political movement which (as he believed) the "world-spirit" had destined to realize it, had after hard and successful struggles entered upon a period of expansion and conquest. That was his justification for holding that the ultimate victory was close at hand.

But among all the gifts which fortune gave him, perhaps the greatest was this: his life ended before the great disappointment, before the goal which had been so near receded into the far distance, before it became clear that his opponent, Domela Nieuwenhuis, had judged more truly than he those events which Engels himself had felt to be dark and threatening, but had always explained away. For he had hoped that the proletariat of Europe would never be sundered by that tragic situation which would have seemed to him the cruellest mockery of the appeal with which he and Marx had closed the *Communist Manifesto* — "Workers of the world — *unite!*"

He had not wished for a world war. But he had prophesied that if it came, a flood of nationalism might swamp Europe, and the victory of socialism might be delayed for some decades. If he could live again today, he would believe that we are now passing through that period. Yet he would hold fast, as he always did, to the conviction that it was only a postponement, not a cessation, of the march of world history, which in the end must lead to the attainment of the classless society and the complete development of human nature.

INDEX